A Hard Trip

MERCER
UNIVERSITY PRESS

Endowed by
TOM WATSON BROWN
and
THE WATSON-BROWN FOUNDATION, INC.

A Hard Trip

A History of the
15th Mississippi Infantry, CSA

Ben Wynne

Mercer University Press

Macon, Georgia

MUP/P406

Original publication in Hardback, ©2003 Mercer University Press.

∞The paper used in this publication meets the minimum requirements of American National Standard for Information Sciences—Permanence of Paper for Printed Library Materials, ANSI Z39.48-1992.

Library of Congress Cataloging-in-Publication Data

Wynne, Ben, 1961-
  A hard trip : a history of the 15th Mississippi Infantry, CSA / Ben Wynne.— 1st ed.
     p. cm.
  Includes bibliographical references (p.) and index.
  ISBN 978-0-88146-179-4 (paperback : alk. paper)
  1. Confederate States of America. Army. Mississippi Infantry Regiment, 15th. 2. Mississippi--History—Civil War, 1861-1865—Regimental histories. 3. United States--History—Civil War, 1861-1865—Regimental histories. 4. Mississippi— History—Civil War, 1861-1865—Social aspects. 5. United States—History—Civil War, 1861-1865—Social aspects. I. Title.
  E568.515th .W96 2003
  973.7'462—dc21

                                                          2003006565

To Patricia Wynne and Noelle Wynne

Table of Contents

Acknowledgments

This book could not have been completed without the assistance and support of a number of people to whom I am indebted. Ron Howard of Mississippi College in Clinton, Mississippi, directed the Master's thesis that evolved into this book, and his constant encouragement helped the project take shape. Kirk Ford and Keith Harper of the Mississippi College history department were also instrumental in making my stay at the school a rewarding experience. I owe a great intellectual debt to several members of the history faculty at the University of Mississippi. Robert Haws, Ted Ownby, Nancy Bercaw, Charles Reagan Wilson, Sheila Skemp, and Michael Namorato all allowed me to benefit from their example, as did Charles Sallis of Millsaps College. James C. Cobb of the University of Georgia also contributed to this effort through his encouragement of my writing. As I revised the manuscript I was fortunate to have two readers who are also good friends. Scott Poole of the College of Charleston and Brant Helvenston of Live Oak, Florida, were both kind enough to take time out of their schedules to review the manuscript and provide valuable input.

In doing research for the book I benefited from the assistance of the staffs of a number of libraries and archives, including the Mississippi Department of Archives and History, the Tennessee State Library and Archives, the Alabama Department of Archives and History, the Georgia Department of Archives and History, the Robert W. Woodruff Library at Emory University, the Special Collections Department in the J. D. Williams Library at the University of Mississippi, the Southern Historical Collection at the University of North Carolina, the Memphis Public Library, the Old Capital Museum in Jackson, Mississippi, the Old Court House Museum in Vicksburg, Mississippi, and the Library of Congress and National Archives in Washington, DC. Penny Rice and Jack Wright in the Faculty Technology Development Center at the University of Mississippi were especially helpful as I produced the maps for this book. The task of collecting photographs was made much easier by the generous contributions of H. Grady Howell Jr., Gay E. Carter, Jim Eckerman, Bill Gore, Jeff Giambrone, Phil McCoy, Hal Fleming, and Mary Arick Self. Last but certainly not least, my greatest debt of thanks is to my family for their unwavering support in all my undertakings.

List of Maps

Brothers (left to right) Thomas, James, and Lewis Alexander served in Company I. James succumbed to disease in 1863 while in the Confederate army (photo courtesy of Jim Eckerman).

Charles C. Frierson of Company F was wounded while bearing the 15th Mississippi's colors during the Confederate attack at Franklin (photo courtesy of Gay Carter).

Edward Cary Walthall began his military career in 1861 as a lieutenant in the 15th Mississippi Infantry's Company E. He ended his service to the Confederacy in 1865 as a major general and after Reconstruction became one of Mississippi's most influential politicians (photo courtesy of the Mississippi Department of Archives and History).

John Thomas Parker of Company E was wounded and captured during the Battle of Mill Springs. He was later released and left the army as a result of his wounds (photo courtesy of Henry McCabe and H. Grady Howell, Jr.).

Brothers (left to right) James and Thomas Shuler of Company A. Thomas was killed during the Battle of Mill Springs while James survived the war (photo courtesy of H. Grady Howell, Jr.).

Laurence Synnott of Company D was killed during the Atlanta Campaign (photo courtesy of James D. Synnott, Jr. and H. Grady Howell, Jr.).

Henry Augustus Moore of Company F died from a wound sustained during the Vicksburg Campaign (photo courtesy of Roger Synnott and H. Grady Howell, Jr.)

Brothers Elias G. Gore (left) and Thomas M. Gore of Company D. Elias died at Mill Springs in 1862. Captured at Nashville, Thomas was paroled from Camp Chase, Ohio, in 1865 (photo courtesy of Bill Gore).

Attorney William F. Brantley began his military career as a captain in the 15th Mississippi's Company G and later became a brigadier general. He was murdered in 1870 (author's collection).

John B. Love of Company A (from F. M. Glass, *History of the Long Creek Rifles*).

Asa E. O'Neal of Company E died in 1864 (photo courtesy of Hal Fleming).

Wartime photo of Corinth, Mississippi, occupied by Federal troops (photo courtesy of the Mississippi Department of Archives and History).

Vicksburg, Mississippi, circa 1860. The men of the 15th Mississippi were stationed in Vicksburg during 1862 and the following year took part in the unsuccessful effort to save the city from Grant (photo courtesy of Old Court House Museum, Vicksburg, Mississippi).

From the heights at Port Hudson on 14 March 1863 the men of the 15th Mississippi watched the Confederate bombardment of the Federal fleet, shown here in an artist's depiction (photo courtesy of the Library of Congress).

Jackson, Mississippi. In July of 1863, after a short siege, the men of the 15th Mississippi and the rest of Joseph Johnston's Confederate force abandoned the state capital (photo courtesy of the Mississippi Department of Archives and History).

Confederate works around Atlanta in 1864 (photo courtesy of the Library of Congress).

Post-war photograph of the John McGavock home, Carnton Mansion at Franklin, Tennessee. The home became a makeshift field hospital after the Confederate debacle at Franklin. The 15th Mississippi's leader Michael Farrell died there (photo courtesy of the Tennessee State Library and Archives).

The state capitol building at Nashville in 1864. John Bell Hood's dream of capturing the city would never be realized (photo courtesy of the National Archives).

Bennett House, near Durham, North Carolina. In these inauspicious surroundings Joseph Johnston surrendered his army, including the remnants of the 15th Mississippi Infantry, to William T. Sherman on 26 April 1865 (photo courtesy of the Library of Congress).

In 1905 local residents gathered on the courthouse square in Carrollton, Mississippi, to dedicate a monument to Carroll County's Confederate veterans, including former members of the 15th Mississippi Infantry (photo courtesy of the Mississippi Department of Archives and History).

The surviving Confederate veterans of Montgomery County (formerly part of Carroll County), Mississippi, home of Company B and Company E of the 15th Mississippi Infantry, in a photo taken around 1920 (photo courtesy of Mary Arick Self).

A 1915 Confederate veterans reunion in Water Valley, Mississippi (photo courtesy of Phil McCoy).

In 1861 the Eureka Masonic College building in Holmes County, Mississippi, housed members of the Quitman Rifles before they left for Corinth to become Company C of the 15th Mississippi Infantry (author's collection).

Monument in the Water Valley, Mississippi, cemetery dedicated to the dead of the 15th Mississippi's Company F (author's collection).

Monument dedicated to the 15th Mississippi Infantry in Duck Hill, Mississippi (author's collection).

CHAPTER 1

PRELUDE

> Our position is thoroughly identified with slavery—the
> greatest material institution in the world.[1]
> *Declaration of Immediate Causes of Secession, Mississippi*
> *Secession Convention, January 1861*

In the late afternoon on Memorial Day 2000, dozens of small American flags fluttered gently in the breeze at the 160-year-old North Union Cemetery in Bellefontaine, Mississippi. Local residents had carefully planted the flags on the graves of the small town's military veterans as a time-honored patriotic gesture. More than an acknowledgement of wartime sacrifice, the banners were a symbol of community, involving the memory of men who had gone to war to protect the future of their country's most basic social components. For a nation to mobilize for war, individual communities within that nation must mobilize for war. Citizens must feel a tangible threat in a way that makes them willing to send their sons, usually with great fanfare, into harm's way. The veterans buried in North Union Cemetery entered the military as extensions of their community and as defenders of the family and friends with whom they lived. By celebrating the soldiers' service, local residents of the new century reaffirmed their own commitment to community, a commitment

---

[1] Mississippi Commission on the War Between the States, *Journal of the State Convention and Ordinances and Resolutions Adopted in 1861* (Jackson: Mississippi Commission on the War Between the States, 1962) 86.

that had been personified on battlefields by Bellefontaine citizen-soldiers for generations.[2]

A flat granite marker in front of which one of the American flags fluttered at Bellefontaine is dedicated to the memory of infantryman Elias Gore. Upon close examination, however, Gore's stone stands out from the other soldiers'. It is conspicuous not because of its size or shape, but because of the words etched into its facing. Gore's monument pays tribute to a soldier who did not fight for the United States and who, at the time he enlisted in the army, would have found the notion of fighting for the United States abhorrent. Gore was killed in battle as a member of the 15th Mississippi Infantry, CSA. In 1861 he actually turned his back on the country of his birth, but in the year 2000 the American flag that paid tribute to his service was appropriate. The flag celebrated community, and while Gore had fought against the United States and lost, he and the rest of the men in the 15th Mississippi Infantry had not let their communities down.

The 15th Mississippi Infantry, like many other Confederate regiments, came into being in the spring of 1861. Farmers' sons filled its ranks. Like all young men destined for battle, the soldiers of the 15th Mississippi were victims of their times. They were born a generation after the Missouri Compromise and were children as debates over the Compromise of 1850 raged in Congress. They were teenagers during the decade of Dred Scott, *Uncle Tom's Cabin*, and John Brown. Left undisturbed, these farmers' sons would have rarely set foot outside their county, much less their state, with principle concerns ever revolving around the annual growing season. Even before they were born, however, fate intervened. Most of their families did not own slaves, but the institution doomed them. The young men of the 15th Mississippi did not belong in the Confederate army, but that is exactly where they found themselves in 1861. Like their contemporaries throughout the South, they were ill prepared for war.

As they left home in the spring of 1861, the men of the 15th Mississippi did not know their ultimate destination. They did not know precisely when they would engage the hated Yankees and had no way to assess the potential dangers of their service to the Confederacy. The regiment drew its membership from five north-central Mississippi

---

[2] The author visited the Bellefontaine cemetery and personally surveyed the markers there.

counties—Attala, Carroll, Choctaw, Holmes, and Yalobusha. The men had no military training and only limited knowledge of military affairs, most of which lay grounded in vague, romantic tales of bravery exhibited by previous generations of Southerners in distant conflicts. Politicians sold secession to the people of the Southern states as a noble, patriotic effort to uphold the republican tradition of the founding fathers, which generally centered upon personal independence based on property ownership and the notion that all men had the right to advance themselves, free of outside encumbrances, as far as their talents might take them. Secessionists evoked the names of George Washington, Thomas Jefferson, and James Madison in their discourse, claiming that it was the North rather than the South that had drifted from its constitutional moorings. In reality, withdrawal from the Union established the men of the 15th Mississippi Infantry, along with thousands of other Confederate soldiers, as standard-bearers for a cause destined to fail before it was ever defended.

Ironically, most of the men of the regiment were newcomers to the "native soil of Mississippi" that they went to war to defend. When the Civil War began, most of their families had resided in the state for less than thirty years. Mississippi entered the Union in 1817 with most of its population concentrated in the southwest, around the old Natchez district. At the time, and for most of the next two decades, most of central and north Mississippi remained the domain of the Choctaw and Chickasaw Indians. The tribes had lived in the region for centuries, but like their brethren throughout North America, they would inevitably succumb to the white man's concept of property rights. In 1830 the U.S. government forced the Choctaws to give up what remained of their homeland. The Chickasaws ceded their holdings two years later, and both tribes relocated west of the Mississippi River. While some scattered whites previously lived in the area, the removal of the Indians officially opened more than twelve million acres of Mississippi for settlement. In 1833 the government surveyed the old Choctaw lands and organized sixteen new counties, collectively called the Choctaw Cession Counties. Among them were the five counties that would produce the men of the 15th Mississippi Infantry.[3]

---

[3] John Edmond Gonzales, "Flush Times, Depression, War and Compromise," vol. 1 of *A History of Mississippi*, ed. Richard A. McLemore (Hattiesburg: University and College Press of Mississippi, 1973) 284.

The peopling of north-central Mississippi over the course of the next quarter century followed traditional patterns of American westward expansion. The call of new land and the quest for prosperity drew thousands of dissatisfied residents of the Southern states on the Atlantic seaboard to a new life in a ruggedly landscaped wilderness. Some established homes in the region even before the government officially organized the old Indian holdings. "This country was just settling up," one observer of the period wrote. "Emigrants came flocking from all quarters.... The new country seemed to be a reservoir, and every road leading to it a vagrant stream of enterprise and adventure." For many, the move west seemed to be a generational right of passage. The family histories of many settlers included a father and mother born in Virginia, the Carolinas, or Georgia, older children born in Alabama or Tennessee, and younger children born as true first-generation Mississippians. Although no one knew it at the time, many of the small sons that these immigrants brought with them, or those born in Mississippi soon after their family's arrival, would serve in the Confederate army. Unlike their parents, the legacy of these children as pioneer settlers ultimately gave way to a collective legacy of defeat that branded them as casualties of a unique regional identity.[4]

Within a remarkably short time after their initial settlement, the 15th Mississippi counties produced dozens of small communities with families trying to recreate some semblance of the social environment that they had known in the East. In some cases groups of families had traveled to Mississippi together, in a sense making the trip as a community, and many would not have gambled their futures at all without the mutual support of others that they knew or to whom they were related. Once relocated, it was easier for them to establish the tenets of cooperative neighborhood. Other families had made the trip in smaller groups, or alone, but still felt the necessity, once they had established their individual homes, to become part of a larger social unit.

Establishing themselves as part of a community was important to the immigrants because the process also established their identities in the new land. In the East they had been able to draw comfort from the socio-cultural interaction within their communities. The familiarity of

---

[4] Frank E. Smith, *The Yazoo River* (Jackson: University Press of Mississippi, 1988) 42; Joseph G. Baldwin, *The Flush Times of Alabama and Mississippi, A Series of Sketches* (San Francisco: Bancroft-Whitney, 1887) 82–83.

neighborhood bred a sense of security, and a community hierarchy fostered order and stability. By immigrating to the frontier, settlers in the 15th Mississippi counties had broken old community ties and cast themselves socially adrift. As a result they tried to transplant, or create, a sense of community in their new home as quickly as possible. They sought to bring order to their new, usually isolated, social universe. Without order there could be no community discipline and subsequently no feeling of the security that is so vital for community prosperity and expansion. From a practical standpoint, the burden of taming the Mississippi wilderness would be lightened in a cooperative effort. To civilize their new home, roads would have to be carved through forests, public buildings were needed, as were churches and some type of local network of commerce. Settlers knew that, once established, both their identities within their community and the social and physical infrastructure of their community should be defended at all costs.

The state created all of the 15th Mississippi counties in 1833, and county residents immediately went to the polls and elected representatives to the state legislature. They also elected county sheriffs, circuit clerks, and boards of police. The legal establishment of the 15th Mississippi counties and the election of public officials gave county residents a broad political identity. However, while these were important milestones, the true foundation of community identity for the immigrants took shape in more intimate settings. Individual settlements that would soon turn into towns had begun to take shape, in many cases before the state drew county lines. Bellefontaine and Greensboro in Choctaw County, Bluff Springs in Attala County, Water Valley and Coffeeville in Yalobusha County, Duck Hill in Carroll County, and Richland in Holmes County—all of which would produce volunteer companies for the 15th Mississippi Infantry—were beginning to thrive by the late 1830s. The first homes in what would become Coffeeville were built as early as 1821, while the first settlers built homes in Water Valley and Duck Hill in 1834. By 1839 Greensboro, the county seat of Choctaw County, boasted a new brick courthouse. As the 1840s began, citizens of the 15th Mississippi counties could optimistically report that "the sound of the hammer is forever ringing in our ears, and our vision is bounded on every side by new houses. Our streets are thronged from day to day, and our taverns are overflowing night after night." The settlers were building towns, but they were also constructing their identity in both the physical and emotional sense. They were now Mississippians, but the foundation of their self-definition came from being members of individual communities and, in a broader sense, individual counties.[5]

As communities developed in the 15th Mississippi counties, social hierarchies evolved. Some settlers had come to the region with more goods than their new neighbors, making them more prosperous. Others initially had little but arrived early and acquired prime land on which they could work their way up in a relatively short time. Through means that they already possessed, hard work, or the right combination of ambition and luck, some citizens prospered more than others and established themselves as community leaders. Those around them were willing to follow their lead in various civic matters, either by calling on them for advice or by electing them to public office. A crude class system developed that would soon be better defined through intermarriage among the more prominent families. Although the class system of the Mississippi frontier was fluid, within a generation sharper distinctions would develop between the few "haves" and the many "have nots" in the 15th Mississippi counties. In 1861 these community hierarchies would help provide the chain of command for the 15th Mississippi Infantry.

John A. Binford was typical of the immigrants who established themselves among their community's elite. In 1834 he left North Carolina as a moderately prosperous farmer and moved to Carroll County, Mississippi, near a place that would soon become the town of Duck Hill. Binford built the first home in the area after acquiring several hundred acres. Because he had the funds he was able to periodically add to his holdings. Binford made the most out of the new land and soon became one of the region's most successful slaveholding planters. He owned thirty-nine slaves in 1840, and would own ninety-six by the eve of the Civil War, both significant numbers when compared to most of his Carroll County neighbors. He was elected to the state legislature, where he established ties with other prosperous Mississippians and continued adding to his fortune. Where John Binford had been only a middling

---

[5] James P. Coleman, *Choctaw County Chronicles* (Ackerman MS: James P. Coleman, 1974) 9, 33; Yalobusha County Historical Society, *Yalobusha County History* (Dallas TX: National Share Graphics, 1982) C-18; James F. Brieger, *Hometown, Mississippi* (Mississippi: Privately printed, 1980) 190, 546; *Brandon Republican*, 18 June 1844.

farmer in North Carolina, in Mississippi he was among the elite of his region and state. His Duck Hill neighbors looked to him for counsel and, rather than being outwardly jealous of his material worth, were proud that their young frontier community could produce such a prominent man to represent their interests in the legislature.[6]

Binford's children grew up with all the advantages of their father's wealth. His sons left the state for their education and returned to take their place at their father's side. As they entered their twenties two of the sons, James R. Binford and John A. Binford Jr. established themselves as heirs to the mantle of community leadership for Duck Hill and the surrounding area. Naturally, when Duck Hill raised a volunteer company in 1861 that would become part of the 15th Mississippi Infantry, the men of the company elected the Binford brothers as officers. James Binford would eventually command the entire regiment.[7] Just as their neighbors were willing to follow the Binfords in civic matters, they were willing to let them lead during wartime.

For every man like John Binford that came to the 15th Mississippi counties, there were scores of men like John Mecklin. The son of an Irish immigrant, Mecklin was a South Carolina native who left his home state in the late 1830s after struggling for several years on a small farm. Mecklin settled first in Alabama with his wife and five children. His struggles continued, and in 1845 he decided to move again. Loading his family and all of their possessions into "a two horse wagon and a one horse carry-all," Mecklin moved west into Mississippi with $12 in his pocket. He settled in Choctaw County near a tiny community called Poplar Creek, where, like most other settlers in the region, he built a small log cabin. According to one of Mecklin's sons, the one room home was sturdy, but simple: "The cracks between the logs were closed by wedging in a piece of wood and plastering clay on the outside.... The roof was held by heavy poles. There was no ceiling. The fire place

---

[6] "John A. Binford" and "James R. Binford," Subject Files, Mississippi Department of Archives and History Library, Jackson, Mississippi; United States Census 1840, Mississippi (slave schedule).

[7] Compiled Service Records of Confederate Soldiers who served in Organizations from the State of Mississippi: 15th Mississippi Infantry, Mississippi Department of Archives and History Library, Jackson, Mississippi, microfilm. Cited afterwards as Compiled Service Records: 15th Mississippi Infantry.

occupied one half the end and was made of wood and mortar. It was an airy room about 16 by 14 [feet]."[8]

Making minor improvements to the cabin from time to time, the Mecklins lived in the home for years. John Mecklin established a tanyard, although admittedly "there were few to buy leather" in the area. By 1860 he was working on 60 acres, which provided enough food for the family but few luxuries. At one time the Mecklins acquired a small family of slaves but were forced to sell them. With the outbreak of the Civil War, three of the Mecklin sons, Augustus, James, and George, volunteered for service as privates in the 15th Mississippi Infantry. George would die while in the army. The Mecklins had no illusions of becoming officers and were typical of the hundreds of 15th Mississippi footsoldiers who came from struggling farm families. They belonged at home, but they felt an obligation to the Confederate cause and were willing to be led into battle by a handful of their more prosperous neighbors.[9] In short, they were honor-bound to their duty.

Along with the development of communities in the 15th Mississippi counties came the development of a concept of personal honor peculiar to the South that bonded white Southern males together regardless of their social standing. In the antebellum South, honor was a loosely defined system of beliefs that transcended social divisions and placed the worth of the individual in the context of how others perceived him. Communities in the 15th Mississippi counties were small, close-knit settlements, isolated and containing a relatively small number of social relationships. At the local level the rule of law was tenuous at best. Communities policed themselves and established order by pressing a particular code of behavior, "one standard of social merit," on their citizens. As a result, an individual's standing in the community was not completely based on his material wealth, but on his reputation. Such an environment bred confrontation in that even the simplest dispute between two individuals could bring their personal honor into question. As heads of their respective households, white males were particularly sensitive to

---

[8] Augustus Hervey Mecklin Papers, Mississippi Department of Archives and History Library, Jackson, Mississippi. This collection consists of a diary kept during the year 1862 by Augustus Hervey Mecklin of Company H, 15th Mississippi Infantry, CSA; a short, undated autobiography written by Mecklin circa 1900; and other miscellaneous items.

[9] Ibid.

their "good name" in that it reflected their status and the status of their family. Individuals went to great lengths to protect their reputations, and neighborhoods were uncompromising in a collective defense of community honor in the face of outside calumny. Younger white males in particular realized that to advance themselves within their communities, they must establish their reputations as honorable men.[10]

Military service was the traditional vehicle for many young men to publicly display their honor. Tales of the wartime bravery of Southerners during the American Revolution, the War of 1812, and in various conflicts against Indians were part of the Southern existence. Such stories, either factual or embellished, transformed common men into heroes, and many Southern families drew a positive sense of self-worth from the fact that their lineage included soldiers who would "leap at the first blast of the trumpet" without hesitation.[11]

For the first generation of young adult males in the 15th Mississippi counties, the first opportunity to "take a bold and manly stand" on the battlefield came in 1846 with the outbreak of the Mexican War. Like the rest of Mississippi, the 15th Mississippi counties displayed unbridled enthusiasm for the war effort. "Mexico will soon learn," one local editor proclaimed at the war's outset, "that with American citizens and soldiers there never has been, and we trust in God there never will be, such a word as fail." All of the counties contributed men, and each county produced at least one volunteer company. In Carroll County, John Binford chaired a citizens' committee that enrolled volunteers and raised money for the war effort. A Carroll County newspaper lauded the volunteers, stating, "Actuated by no other feeling than devotion to their country, they leave their family, friends and pursuits at the first intimation that their service is needed." At Greensboro in Choctaw County "a full company of the right sort" enrolled for service as the Choctaw Volunteers. As the company left home its commander said that he and his men were departing for battle, "obliged to bring Mexico to our terms," as if they alone were capable of defeating the entire Mexican army. An area newspaper captured the mood of the day when it reported

---

[10] Bertram Wyatt-Brown, *Honor and Violence in the Old South* (New York: Oxford University Press, 1986) 25–39; Kenneth H. Greenberg, *Masters and Statesmen: The Political Culture of American Slavery* (Baltimore: The Johns Hopkins University Press, 1985) 141.

[11] *Carrollton Democrat*, 6 January 1847.

on several local companies: "They go, impelled by a noble patriotism, to serve the country and win the honors of war. The character of our state for chivalry and deeds of daring, may be safely entrusted to their keeping." Fifteen years later similar language would send volunteers off to war against their own countrymen.[12]

Despite the fact that the United States was fighting with questionable motives against an overmatched foe, and regardless of the fact that more soldiers died from disease than battle wounds during the conflict, the Mexican War was a triumph for the South. The war produced nationally acclaimed Mississippi war heroes, including Jefferson Davis, but more importantly it produced community heroes as well. In the 15th Mississippi counties veterans returned to Greensboro, Richland, Water Valley, Bellefontaine, and other small towns with reputations as honorable men who "stood first among those who so gloriously conquered at Monterey." Those who died during the struggle were installed as community martyrs. The participation of community sons had localized the war and given individual communities a stake in its outcome. The men had represented their communities well, and through the soldiers' service the war's end was celebrated as a community victory.[13]

In addition to bolstering community pride, the Mexican War localized subsequent national issues that the war's outcome created. Paramount among these would be the issue of the spread of slavery into the newly acquired western territories. For residents of the 15th Mississippi communities, proposals to halt slavery's expansion in the years following the war became more than distant maneuverings of Northern politicians at the national level. They represented an effort to deny the South the spoils of war that community sons had helped win and, as such, were an affront to the communities' support for the war effort. As sectional tensions increased, local politicians, as well as those at the state and national level, reminded their constituents again and again that all Mississippians, "in common with the citizens of all the slaveholding states, have been virtually excluded from their just rights in the greater portion, if not all, of the vast and rich territories acquired from Mexico in the late war; and thus, by unjust and insulting

---

[12] *Carrollton Democrat*, 10 June 1846, 6 January 1847; *Yazoo City Whig*, 15 May 1846; *Yazoo City Democrat*, 13 May 1846.

[13] *Carrollton Democrat*, 16 December 1846.

discrimination, the advantages and benefits of the Union have been denied them."[14] In addition, the war established the standard of personal and community honor through military service for the next generation of males. As war clouds gathered in 1861, young men in the 15th Mississippi communities did not have to look far for examples of how to behave.

Through the late 1840s and the 1850s the collective population of the 15th Mississippi counties increased dramatically, from 42,183 in 1840 to 86,674 in 1860.[15] By 1860 local communities were well established. A network of dirt roads linked towns with one another and with the state's developing markets. Through improvements in communication and transportation, the counties were also increasingly affected by events taking place outside their immediate vicinity. In 1840 residents of the 15th Mississippi counties had busied themselves creating a social sanctuary in the Mississippi wilderness. Twenty years later they had created their communities, but a new threat seemed to loom on the horizon. Most of the individual communities that would produce the 15th Mississippi had access to a local newspaper that kept readers apprised of state and national politics, usually with a partisan slant. Some of their community leaders had become county leaders, and several of those men had become influential politicians at the state level.[16] The outside world was encroaching on even the most isolated settlements, making it difficult for anyone in the 15th Mississippi counties to ignore the most significant issue of the day.

By 1860 Mississippi was deeply entrenched in the socioeconomic quagmire of slavery. From the time the state entered the Union through the end of the antebellum period, its economic, political, and social foundations rested squarely on agriculture and increasingly on a slave-based cotton culture. During the 1850s Mississippi established itself as the nation's top cotton producer. In 1859 the state produced a record 1,202,507 ginned bales of cotton. For the well-to-do planters of the era, the 1850s were a time of great prosperity, evidenced by the fact that during that ten-year period the value of farm lands in Mississippi increased by 176 percent—more than any other state, with the exception

---

[14] *Mississippian*, 1 November 1850.

[15] United States Census 1840, Mississippi; United States Census 1860, Mississippi.

[16] Robert Lowry and William McCardle, *A History of Mississippi* (Jackson MS: R. H. Henry and Company, 1891) 443–611.

of recently settled California and Oregon. Of course, Mississippi's cotton kingdom was built by slave labor, and by 1860 slaves represented 55 percent of the state's total population.[17]

From the end of the Mexican War the slavery issue drove Mississippi politics. It helped destroy the Whig Party and ultimately allowed the states' rights wing of the Democratic Party to emerge unchallenged. A fledgling states' rights movement had developed in Mississippi in response to the Nullification Crisis of the early 1830s, but once that crisis passed its leaders were unable to influence significant numbers of voters. Following the Mexican War, however, states' rights advocates pointed to the Wilmot Proviso and speeches by Northern politicians as tangible evidence that an "abolitionist conspiracy" existed in the North. They used fear to draw voters to their cause through exhaustive rhetoric that centered around the demise of slavery and the subsequent breakdown of Southern communities, and white culture in general, once emancipation had taken place. This argument was increasingly potent in a state where the white population was in the minority. After extensive debate the Mississippi legislature voted to accept the Compromise of 1850, and in 1851 the state narrowly elected a governor who had run on a pro-Union platform. After the Kansas agitation of 1854, however, states' rights politicians had enough rhetorical ammunition to make the abolitionist threat real in the minds of many Mississippians. For the rest of the decade Mississippi Democrats consolidated their strength around a strict states' rights platform, which was complex but had at its foundation the protection of slavery at all costs. Their position left no room for compromise and at the end of the 1850s lit the fuse that would ignite civil war.[18]

After 1855 Democratic candidates carried the 15th Mississippi counties and most of Mississippi in state and national elections, and all factions vying for local leadership positions knew that they could not

---

[17] William A. Scarborough, "Heartland of the Cotton Kingdom," vol.1 of *A History of Mississippi*, ed. Richard A. McLemore (Hattiesburg: University and College Press of Mississippi, 1973) 310, 322–25; William L. Barney, *The Secessionist Impulse* (Princeton NJ: Princeton University Press, 1974) 4; United States Census 1860, Mississippi.

[18] Cleo Hearon, "Nullification in Mississippi," vol. 12 of *Publications of the Mississippi Historical Society* (University MS: For the Society, 1912) 37–71; Glover Moore, "Separation from the Union, 1854–1861," vol. 1 of *A History of Mississippi*, ed. Richard A. McLemore (Hattiesburg: University and College Press of Mississippi, 1973) 420–45.

achieve their goals without embracing the states' rights philosophy. Political leaders at the county level used states' rights rhetoric in speeches that made sectional tensions a part of local discourse. One local politician from the 15th Mississippi region warned that if abolitionism were allowed to triumph, "the rich man's property [will be] ruinously depreciated, the poor man will be robbed of the reward of his daily labor—his all.... The whole framework of society will be disorganized. The laws will be suspended and disregarded, and lawless violence and anarchy [will] take the place of law and order." He appealed to the fears of citizens who had worked to build communities and to establish the security that their communities provided.[19]

More and more in the 15th Mississippi counties, citizens held meetings to discuss current political issues, all of which had become tied to the slavery debate. These meetings did not necessarily advocate secession as a singular course of action, but most recognized secession as a possible solution to sectional tensions. They also brought the slavery question into the individual counties. One typical resolution of Holmes County Democrats denounced any interference with the institution of slavery and insisted that any compromise on the issue "would be a dishonorable solution on our part, would invite and encourage further aggressions from [the North], lead either to a speedy dissolution of the Union, or the total destruction of the institution of slavery, or to a result still more appalling—a servile war of extermination of the white or black race throughout the South."[20]

The message was clear. A threat to slavery was not simply a threat to the property of slaveholders. The demise of the institution would quickly lead to societal degeneration, chaos, and violence, exposing all whites to "the butchery of African assassins." Democratic leaders took advantage of the fears that their state and national party had helped create by constantly reminding the masses that "the Southern Rights party, then, is emphatically the Democratic Party. It is composed of all who oppose the legislation of Congress against the institution of slavery in the States, and who are determined to resist the legislation whether they are for resistance in the Union or out of it." By inciting fear among their

---

[19] Moore, "Separation from the Union, 1854–1861," 420–45; *Mississippian*, 2 December 1855, 28 November 1859; John W. Wood, *Union and Secession in Mississippi* (Memphis: Saunders, Farrish and Whitmore Printers, 1863) 12.

[20] *Attala Democrat*, as reported in the *Mississippian*, 13 September 1850.

constituents, states' rights Democrats continued their rhetorical onslaught through the 1850s until most voices of reason in their party had been either converted or silenced. According to one local politician from the 15th Mississippi region, many average citizens eventually accepted states' rights rhetoric as fact simply because "it had been so often sounded in their ears that they had become somewhat accustomed to it." In 1859 John Jones Pettus, the fire-eating Democratic candidate for governor, carried the 15th Mississippi counties with 78 percent of the total vote, winning with 77 percent of the vote statewide.[21]

Like politics, religion played a major role in the Southern existence. The actively religious among the white population in the 15th Mississippi counties were almost exclusively Protestant. Evangelical Protestants populated most of the South, with Baptists, Methodists, and Presbyterians representing the major denominations. Baptist and Methodist congregations were the most numerous, with the requirement for an educated clergy and a theology more intellectual than emotional in character hampering Presbyterian growth in the South. At the turn of the nineteenth century, approximately 10 percent of whites in the South belonged to a church, but within a short time a great spiritual awakening would take hold through much of the region.

Sparked by revivals in south-central Kentucky during the summer of 1800, evangelical religion swept though the Southern states, and thousands of converts swelled church memberships. By 1860 at least 40 percent of white Southerners actively participated in organized churches, and of those about 80 percent were Baptists or Methodists. Even in areas where a majority of the population did not regularly attend meetings, churches exerted varying degrees of influence. They became the social center of many communities, a place where locals gathered to both worship and take part in secular fellowship. Ministers, usually recognized as the definitive moral arbiter in individual communities, often held sway over public opinion on a variety of issues not necessarily religious in nature.[22]

---

[21] *Mississippian*, 7 March 1851, 24 December 1856; Wood, *Union and Secession in Mississippi*, 13; *Mississippian*, 24 November 1859.

[22] William J. Cooper Jr. and Thomas E. Terrill, *The American South: A History* (New York: McGraw-Hill, 1991) 263–68; Gardiner H. Shattuck Jr., *A Shield and Hiding Place: The Religious Life of the Civil War Armies* (Macon GA: Mercer University Press,

Because religion occupied such a conspicuous place in Southern society, it could not help becoming intertwined with the slavery debate of the antebellum period. In New England much of the religious activity and rhetoric traditionally centered upon the betterment of American society. The Puritans who had founded the New England towns bound themselves by covenants that served as constant reminders of the responsibilities of collective citizenship. As the Northern population spread west the Puritan ideal was diluted, but the undercurrent of social responsibility as part of religious life remained. The influx of significant numbers of foreign immigrants into the North during the first half of the nineteenth century eventually forced native Christians there to accommodate social change. Despite harsh resistance in certain quarters, ethnic, cultural, and religious pluralism at least became accepted facts of life in the North.[23]

The South's population during the antebellum period was scattered. There were few large cities in the Atlantic seaboard states, and most residents of the Southern interior lived a relatively isolated, primitive existence. Evangelicalism spread with the shifting population through Alabama and Mississippi during the 1820s. The traditional elements of civilization were not yet present in many parts of the South; therefore, the betterment of general society was of little religious relevance. Southern religion emphasized the individual, concerning itself with the welfare of the individual soul. Hence, Southern religion was passed on from one generation to the next as a personal concern, rather than as a vehicle to assert a positive moral influence on the whole of society.[24]

Fundamental differences in the general nature of religion in the North and South manifested themselves in the slavery debate. As sectional tensions escalated, the religious schism between the regions widened. Many Northerners came to view the South as a barbaric land where the institution of slavery prohibited the practice of true religion. In return, many Southern evangelicals claimed that Northern clergy had abandoned biblical teachings and that dangerous and irresponsible movements for social reform, particularly abolitionism, had poisoned Northern society. As the South consolidated its position around slavery,

---

1987) 1–12; Sidney J. Romero, *Religion in the Rebel Ranks* (Lanham MD: University Press of America, Inc., 1983) 1–7.

[23] Ibid.

[24] Ibid.

Southern ministers of the major denominations became some of the chief defenders of the institution. They used selected passages from the Bible to justify slavery just as Southern politicians pointed to the rhetoric of selected Northern leaders when trying to convince the masses that their "way of life" was in danger. By the late 1830s most of the South's religious community was united in promoting the idea that bondage was actually beneficial to the slaves' spiritual welfare. They argued that slavery had rescued "the wild African, in a state of idolatry," and that through the institution slaves had "become civilized and Christianized, and in a short time, pious and contented." Throughout the South evangelicals condemned "Northern politicians and religious fanatics" as conspirators in a misguided plot "to detract from the social, civil, and religious privileges of the slave population." In the mid-1840s Southern Baptists and Methodists officially split from their Northern counterparts over the slavery issue, foreshadowing the political division among the states that would take place less than twenty years later. While individual ministers generally counseled caution with regard to secession, support for slavery from Southern pulpits ultimately lent religious credence to the secession movement in the minds of many Southerners. In 1861 it also promoted the notion that Confederate soldiers were undertaking both a military effort and a religious crusade.[25]

Baptists, Methodists, and Presbyterians had all penetrated the Mississippi Territory by the turn of the nineteenth century, and over the next several decades each denomination in the state would follow the Southern pattern and take a pro-slavery stand. By 1860 most church members in Mississippi were either Baptists or Methodists, with the Presbyterians exerting significant influence despite their relatively small numbers. Of Mississippi's 1,441 churches on the eve of the Civil War, 83 percent were either Baptist or Methodists, while 10 percent were Presbyterian. The 15th Mississippi counties were typical of the rest of the state with regard to both the distribution of churches and the disposition of church membership on the slavery issue [see fig. 1]. Baptists, Methodists, and Presbyterians were the principle denominations in the area, and local leaders in all three churches actively sought to "elevate

---

[25] Ibid.; Edward R. Crowther, "Mississippi Baptists, Slavery, and Secession, 1806–1861," *Journal of Mississippi History* 56/2 (May 1994): 139–44.

slavery up to the Gospel standard" by promoting the practice as "the patriarchal institution that is recognized by the Bible." [26]

Church Denominations
15th Mississippi Counties, 1860

County	Denomination					
	Baptist	Methodist	Presbyterian	Cumberland Pres	Other*	Total
Attala	31	17	4	1	3	6
Carroll	5	6	8	2	2	23
Choctaw	36	27	4	4	2	73
Holmes	2	8	3	0	1	14
Yalobusha	15	13	5	3	0	36
5 County Total (%)	89 (44%)	71 (35%)	24 (12%)	10 (5%)	8 (4%)	202
Mississippi	529 (41%)	606 (42%)	148 (10%)	60 (4%)	98 (7%)	1,441[27]

*denotes four Christian churches, three Lutheran churches, and one Episcopal church in the 15th Mississippi counties and a number of denominations statewide.

[figure 1]

Although they were aligned politically and religiously, by 1860 the 15th Mississippi counties had developed their own individual socio-economic characters. Most area households made their living in agriculture, primarily on small farms, but there were disparities of wealth in the region, as well as differences in the racial composition of each county. To the west the Yazoo and Big Black Rivers framed the richer soil of Carroll County and Holmes County, giving them an advantage in cotton production, a formidable plantation economy, and more total wealth. To the north, Yalobusha County also produced a significant amount of cotton. While large planters still comprised a distinct minority of the population in these counties, some families had considerable

---

[26] James J. Pillar, "Religious and Cultural Life, 1817–1860," vol. 1 of *A History of Mississippi*, ed. Richard A. McLemore (Hattiesburg: University and College Press of Mississippi, 1973) 378–410; United States Census, 1860; Crowther, "Mississippi Baptists, Slavery, and Secession, 1806–1861," 139–44.

[27] Unites States Census 1860, Mississippi.

holdings. Farther east, the yeomen of Attala County and Choctaw County on average worked smaller plots, sustaining themselves on weaker soil and producing a smaller cotton yield. The 15th Mississippi counties also produced a significant amount of food crops, primarily corn, peas, beans, and sweet potatoes. Because they devoted less acres to cotton, farmers in Attala County and Choctaw County fared marginally better in terms of total production of major food crops when compared to the three wealthier counties. Carroll County ranked first in the total production of both cotton and food crops in the five-county region and seventh in cotton production among the state's sixty counties. Since the average farm in the three wealthier 15th Mississippi counties included more acres on superior soil, its average cash value was far greater than the average cash value of a farm in the two poorer counties [see fig. 2].[28]

15th Mississippi Counties
Crop Production and Farm Size (1860)

Cotton Production

Rank	County	Total bales	Bales per farm	Rank among state's 60 counties
1	Carroll	42,880	45	7
2	Holmes	41,840	65	8
3	Yalobusha	24,760	34	17
4	Attala	14,587	12	30
5	Choctaw	13,558	9	32

Selected Food Crops Production

Rank	County (Corn in bushel)	County (Peas/Beans in bushels)	County (sweet potatoes in bushels)
1	Carroll (1,140,174)	Carroll (158,282)	Carroll (159,158)
2	Holmes (845,724)	Yalobusha (57,284)	Choctaw (110,265)
3	Choctaw (599,995)	Attala (39,843)	Holmes (104,217)
4	Attala (567,159)	Holmes (12,119)	Yalobusha (76,536)
5	Yalobusha (553,656)	Choctaw (9,226)	Attala (64,025)

---

[28] United States Census 1860, Mississippi (population and agricultural); Scarborough, "Heartland of the Cotton Kingdom," 325.

Number of Farms, Farm Size

County	# of farms	1-99 acres (%)	100-499 acres (%)	500+ acres (%)	avg. cash value per farm
Holmes	630	229 (36.3)	327 (51.9)	74 (11.7)	$9,642
Yalobusha	712	371 (52.1)	288 (40.4)	53 (7.4)	$8,712
Carroll	950	472 (49.7)	400 (42.1)	78 (8.2)	$4,544
Attala	1,149	861 (74.9)	275 (23.9)	13 (1.1)	$2,119
Choctaw	1,387	1,144 (82.4)	234 (16.9)	9 (0.6)	$1,714
5 county total	1,813	3,077 (63.8)	1,524 (31.6)	227 (4.7)	$4,651
Mississippi	37,007	23,250 (62.9)	11,480 (30.8)	2,349 (6.3)	$5,115[29]

[figure 2]

As in the rest of the Deep South, the slave populations of the various regions of Mississippi were in direct proportion to the amount of cotton that each region produced. Affluent planters who owned large numbers of slaves usually acquired rich lands along the state's major rivers. The highest concentration of slaves in Mississippi during the 1850s was in the western half of the state in those counties along the Mississippi River and its major tributaries. Farmers of lesser means, who were in the majority, generally settled east of this region on poorer soil. They produced less cotton and, therefore, their slave populations were not as great. As was the case in the rest of the state, varying levels of cotton production affected the racial composition of the 15th Mississippi counties. In the five-county region, Choctaw County had the lowest percentage of white households owning slaves, followed by Attala County and Yalobusha County. In Carroll County and Holmes County around two-thirds of the white households owned slaves. However, while a significant number of white households in the region held slaves, the majority of slaveholders owned less than ten and almost half owned fewer than five [see fig. 3].[30]

---

[29] United States Census 1860 Mississippi (population and agricultural).

[30] United States Census 1860, Mississippi (population and slave schedules).

15th Mississippi Counties
Population and Slave Distribution (1860)

Population

County	White pop. (%)	Slave pop. (%)	Total pop.
Holmes	5,816 (32.7)	11,975 (67.3)	17,791
Carroll	8,227 (37.3)	13,808 (62.7)	22,035
Yalobusha	7,421 (43.8)	9,531 (56.2)	16,952
Attala	9,159 (64.8)	5,015 (35.2)	14,174
Choctaw	11,525 (73.3)	4,197 (26.7)	15,722
5 County Total	42,148 (48.7)	44,526 (51.3)	86,674
Mississippi	353,901 (44.8)	436,631 (55.2)	790,532

Slave Distribution

	Carroll	Holmes	Yalobusha	Attala	Choctaw
% of total households owning slaves	66.6	65.4	51.3	40.2	29.9
% slaveholding households owning:					
1 slave	12.4	9.7	15.3	21.3	23.7
2–4 slaves	23.8	21.8	23.3	30.2	29.1
5–9 slaves	24.6	24.6	21.2	22.2	24.7
10–19 slaves	17.5	19.8	18.7	17.5	15.4
20–49 slaves	16.2	18.1	16.9	6.6	6.8
50–99 slaves	4.7	5.1	4.0	1.6	0.3
100+ slaves	0.9	0.8	0.6	X	X[31]

X – no slaveholding households owning 100 or more slaves

[figure 3]

Despite variances in each county's socioeconomic makeup, the perceived threat to the institution of slavery united most white residents of the region, just as it united most white Mississippians, and most white Southerners. Throughout the South racism left most whites in a dilemma

---

[31] Ibid.

that would not reconcile itself. Slavery defined the self-perception of every white Southerner. For the planter elite, slavery signified power, status, and paternalistic control of not only their slaves but also, as fellow dependants in the household, of their wives and children. The ability of white males to hold property established the social order in the South and included claims over their dependants based in both custom and law. For the large planter, a disruption of the slave system meant a disruption of his societal authority and the so-called natural relations between the male head of the family and his charges. One jurist of the period reflected the social environment of the slaveholding South when he explained in court that violence was justified in any case where one man could prove that another had "traduced his character, had insulted his wife or daughter, or [been found] within his enclosure attempting to steal his goods or to excite his negroes to insurrection."[32]

The impact was similar on poorer, non-slaveholding white males. Though not directly involved as slaveholders, they recognized the social impact that the demise of slavery would have on their world. Regardless of their economic condition, they drew strength and self-esteem simply from the fact that they were white males and heads of their own households. Their white skin bonded them to their more affluent planter neighbors, with whom they periodically interacted. They recognized the importance of property as the traditional barometer of independence and feared a future in which they might compete with free blacks for land or in the labor market. Many small farmers also aspired to one day become prominent, slaveholding planters. The South's slave-based society allowed poorer white males the comfort of viewing themselves as free men in a society where most of the population was subordinate. They defined their own independence through the bondage of others and believed that the demise of slavery represented a negative impact on their status in the community. "With us the two great divisions of society are not rich and poor," one politician of the era explained, "but white and black; and all the former, the poor as well as the rich, belong to the upper class, and are respected and treated as equals, if honest and industrious." The small farmers' race-based status was illusionary, but their fears were

---

[32] Stephanie McCurry, *Masters of Small Worlds: Yeomen Households, Gender Relations, and Political Culture of the Antebellum South Carolina Low Country* (New York: Oxford University Press, 1995) 12–27; Barney, *The Secessionist Impulse*, 105.

ripe for exploitation by secessionist politicians as sectional tensions increased. [33]

Although concerns over the protection of slavery united white residents of the 15th Mississippi counties, social, political, and economic factors caused differences of opinion in the region with regard to the secession issue. As the 1850s drew to a close, much of the political leadership of Holmes County, Carroll County, and Yalobusha County enjoyed heady financial prosperity as players in Mississippi's cotton-based economy. From their wealth they gained confidence, which gave way to political arrogance. They had the most to lose in the shadow of the abolitionist threat that fire-eating Democrats used repeatedly to rally the state's white population. They also had enough financial resources to create a belief in their own political invincibility, even if secession became a reality. According to one observer, in the wealthier 15th Mississippi counties "loud expressions were heard of the great value that would attach to land and negroes in the event of secession, and some were heard to say that they would sell their land and negroes at half price if Mississippi did not secede."[34] Conversely, political leaders in Attala County and Choctaw County were more cautious. They appreciated the potential threat of Northern abolitionism but were not as prone to radical action because they were not as financially secure as the elite of the other counties. Meanwhile, the average voter in all of the 15th Mississippi counties remained ambivalent with regard to the secession issue. The mass of yeomen farmers that populated the region would have likely opposed disunion had they known the full extent of its consequences, but many were under the impression that Southern independence would not lead to bloodshed. Still others believed that disunion would bring concessions from the North, resulting in a peaceful reconciliation.[35]

In Carroll County, where the slave population far outnumbered the white population, the political community made considerable efforts to ensure white solidarity between the slaveholding and non-slaveholding public. Though they dominated state politics through a disparity of wealth, Mississippi planters, like their wealthy brethren throughout the South, knew that their power depended on the loyalty to slavery of the

---

[33] McCurry, *Masters of Small Worlds*, 12–27; Barney, *The Secessionist Impulse*, 105; Cooper and Terrill, *The American South: A History*, 277.

[34] Wood, *Union and Secession in Mississippi*, 19.

[35] Moore, "Separation from the Union, 1854–1861," 445.

non-slaveholding majority. As a result, non-slaveholders constantly heard the message that the abolition of slavery would have dire consequences. Freedom for slaves, it was said, would destroy the South's labor system and, more importantly, lead to the social equality of blacks and whites on every level.[36]

In the autumn of 1860 a committee of leading citizens of Carroll County drafted a letter to Albert Gallatin Brown, a fire-eating United States senator from Mississippi, which posed this question: "What interest have non-slaveholders in the South in the question of slavery?" Copies of Brown's written response circulated widely through the 15th Mississippi region. The purely political manifesto played to the fear of poorer white males that the end of slavery would directly threaten their place in the social order:

> It is easy to see the course things will take after we have passed the point of emancipation. The large slaveholder, and thousands of smaller ones, will abandon the country.... Then the non-slaveholder will begin to see what his real fate is. The negro will intrude into his presence—insist on being treated as an equal—that he shall go to the white man's table, and the white man to his—that he shall share the white man's bed, and the white man his—that his son shall marry the white man's daughter, and the white man's daughter his son. In short, that they will live on terms of perfect social equality.... It is his [the non-slaveholder] duty to move, move vigorously, actively and energetically. An active blow now is worth more than a life of active service will be when the day is lost.[37]

In Attala County sentiments were cooler. The slave population was not as great, and there was a sincere belief in many circles that, regarding the slavery issue, "the best course for the South to pursue [is] first to attempt measures of pacification and, this failing, to fight for our constitutional rights within the Union and under the national flag." As secessionist rhetoric increased, the *Kosciusko Chronicle* warned Attala County residents that withdrawal from the Union would "involve

---

[36] Barney, *The Secessionist Impulse*, 4.

[37] Percy Lee Rainwater, *Mississippi: Storm Center of Secession 1856–1861* (Baton Rouge LA: Otto Claitor, 1938) 145–48.

consequences which no eye could fully see, and no mind fully comprehend." Some residents agreed with Joel Harvey, who soon after the war began, angrily announced to the congregation of the Pilgrim's Rest Church, "I don't owe allegiance to Jeff Davis or Abe Lincoln." One county politician foreshadowed the realities of secession when he published his own short treatise on the sectional crisis that counseled, "There can be no such thing as peaceable secession. Peaceable secession is utterly impossible." While they were generally less enthusiastic about secession, Attala County residents were far from avowed Unionists. Once withdrawal from the Union became a reality, most residents dutifully "placed patriotism and loyalty to their state above all considerations" and united behind the Southern cause.[38]

During the spring of 1860 the slavery issue split the national Democratic Party, thus ensuring a Republican victory in the presidential election the following fall. The Democratic National Convention met in Charleston, South Carolina, in April. There, Northern Democrats passed resolutions endorsing the concept of popular sovereignty as a solution to the slavery problem, while Southern Democrats insisted on federal protection of the institution. The convention endorsed popular sovereignty, and in response delegates from Mississippi and other Southern states walked out of the proceedings. Eventually the two wings of the party met separately to nominate candidates for president. Northern Democrats nominated Stephen Douglas of Illinois, while the Southern states' rights advocates chose Kentuckian John C. Breckinridge. John Bell of Tennessee rounded out the field that would oppose Republican Abraham Lincoln. Bell was the candidate of the recently formed Constitutional Union Party. Members of the new party hoped to create an alternative organization based on an allegiance to the Constitution and the Union that would appeal to both sections. They accused Southern Democratic leaders of abandoning the protection of Southern liberties in favor of personal political gain through the

---

[38] Leon Edmund Basile, "Attala County Mississippi 1850–1860, A Social History" (master's thesis, University of Massachusetts, 1977) 103; John K. Bettersworth, "The Home Front, 1861–1865," vol. 1 of *A History of Mississippi*, ed. Richard A. McLemore (Hattiesburg: University and College Press of Mississippi, 1973) 520–21; Wood, *Union and Secession in Mississippi*, 13; James Wallace, "History and Reminiscences of Attala County," 1916, Mississippi Department of Archives and History Library, Jackson, Mississippi, photocopy.

secession movement. They argued that Southerners should fight for their rights within the Union, and they did their best to avoid any inflammatory political discussions of slavery. The strategy would have only limited effect in Southern states still haunted by the ghost of John Brown.[39]

In November, Lincoln, who was not on Mississippi's ballots and whose countenance one Mississippi Democratic editor described as being "strongly marked with the blood of his negro ancestry," was elected President of the United States. Breckinridge carried Mississippi over Bell by a vote of 39,962 to 24,693 with Douglas garnering 3,597 votes. Bell's support came primarily from old Whig strongholds along the Mississippi River. Breckinridge carried all of the 15th Mississippi counties with approximately 65 percent of the total vote. [40]

As the year 1860 drew to a close, emotion outweighed reason in the sectional conflict. Lincoln's election polarized sectional sentiment and ripped the United States apart. The expansion of slavery into the western territories had been the primary issue of the campaign, and the victory of Lincoln's "Black Republican" Party seemed to find the South on the verge of realizing its greatest fear: The Republicans insisted on halting the western expansion of slavery, and it was only a matter of time until they pressed for complete abolition. Southern Democratic leaders, whose unyielding stand on the slavery issue had split their national party, began taking steps to use the Republican victory to inspire Southern secession. These men emphasized their own interpretation of the Constitution. The United States, they claimed, was a collection of sovereign, independent states. Under this theory each state had entered the Union voluntarily and, therefore, was free to leave the Union if its citizens felt politically, socially, or morally abused.[41]

Even before Lincoln's inauguration, fissures in the Union widened. South Carolina voted to secede on 20 December 1860. On 6 January 1861 Florida troops seized the U.S. arsenal at Apalachicola, and the next day the state seized Federal forts in Marion and St. Augustine. Within a

---

[39] Carl Degler, *The Other South: Southern Dissenters in the Nineteenth Century* (New York: Harper & Row, 1974) 158–69; Cooper and Terrill, *The American South*, 334–36; Rainwater, *Mississippi: Storm Center of Secession 1856–1861*, 177–97.

[40] Rainwater, *Mississippi: Storm Center of Secession 1856–1861*, 158–60, 198–99.

[41] Allen Nevins, vol. 1 of *The War for the Union* (New York: Charles Scribner's Sons, 1959) 10.

few weeks several other Southern states followed South Carolina out of the Union. After the surrender of Fort Sumter on 13 April, Lincoln put out the call for 75,000 Northern volunteer troops, and suddenly the United States was at war with itself.[42]

In Mississippi events moved quickly following Lincoln's election. A number of state political leaders encouraged Governor John Jones Pettus, a firm believer in the right to secede, to act. In the state capital the *Jackson Mississippian* reflected the dominant mood in an editorial titled "The Deed Is Done, Disunion the Remedy," published soon after Lincoln's victory. After consulting Mississippi's congressional delegation, Pettus advised the state legislature that withdrawal from the Union was the only alternative to "Black Republican rule." Believing that such a withdrawal from the Union would be only temporary and filled with a certain degree of misguided missionary zeal, he told the assembly that it was time for Mississippi to "go down into Egypt while Herod rules in Judea." The legislature responded by passing resolutions sanctioning secession and by calling for a state convention to consider Mississippi's withdrawal from the Union.[43]

In December of 1860 Mississippians elected delegates to the state secession convention on a county basis. Candidates for these positions were not necessarily nominated on a particular platform, although their public positions on the secession question were well known to their neighbors. In general, county conventions that nominated candidates did not establish strict guidelines for delegates with regard to their vote, choosing instead to let the delegates exercise their best judgment during deliberations. The procedures used were not uniform, but in most counties elections involved candidates who either favored separate state secession or leaned toward Southern cooperation. Cooperationists generally took the stand that Lincoln's election alone was not a reason to disrupt the Union. Only after all options within the Union had been exhausted, they argued, should Mississippi consider secession, and then only in concert with the other Southern states. Within this presumably more moderate group, the exact options that individual candidates were willing to explore varied, but only a few candidates labeled cooperationists were firmly against secession. According to one of the

---

[42] Page Smith, *Trial By Fire: A People's History of the Civil War and Reconstruction* (New York: McGraw-Hill, 1982) 32.

[43] Moore, "Separation from the Union," 442–43.

small group of pro-Union delegates at the convention, the cooperationists' ultimate strategy was not as much about cooperating with other states as it was about "cooperating among themselves in getting high offices in the new government." The position of separate state secessionist candidates was more concise. They united in support of Mississippi's immediate withdrawal from the Union and cooperation with the other Southern states after secession had taken place.[44]

The 15th Mississippi counties sent eleven delegates to the secession convention. These included cooperationists Elijah H. Sanders and John W. Wood from Attala County, separate state secessionist James Z. George and cooperationist William Booth of Carroll County, separate state secessionists W. H. Witty, J. H. Edwards, and William F. Brantley of Choctaw County, separate state secessionists J. M. Dyer and W. L. Keirn of Holmes County, and separate state secessionists Francis M. Aldridge and William R. Barksdale of Yalobusha County. As would be the case with the state as a whole, the 15th Mississippi counties sent primarily pro-secession delegates to the convention. George and Booth (who was a cooperationist in name only) ran unopposed in Carroll County, as did Dyer and Keirn in Holmes County. In Choctaw County the Witty, Edwards, and Brantley ticket defeated their more moderate opponents by a vote of 934 to 597. Returns from Yalobusha County were incomplete, although separate state secessionists carried the day. Only in Attala County did two candidates opposed to secession triumph, as Sanders and Wood defeated a ticket of separate state secessionists by a narrow vote of 651 to 614.[45]

A number of factors led to the election of pro-secession delegates from the 15th Mississippi counties and from much of the rest of the state. During the canvas the radicals held a distinct advantage. Most of the state's prominent political voices backed secession, and the radical organization that had helped John C. Breckinridge carry the state by a wide margin in the presidential contest remained in place. Each county elected men who were established in local political circles, which meant that most were established within the state Democratic Party network. As

---

[44] Rainwater, *Mississippi: Storm Center of Secession 1856–1861*, 177–97; Wood, *Union and Secession in Mississippi*, 41–43.

[45] Mississippi Commission of the War Between the States, *Journal of the State Convention*, 5–6; *Vicksburg Whig*, 2 January 1861; Rainwater, *Mississippi: Storm Center of Secession 1856–1861*, 190–213.

such, they were schooled in the states' rights philosophy of the 1850s and had won their political status with the help of states' rights rhetoric. Although returns were close in a number of counties statewide, few counties ran a strictly pro-Union ticket and most candidates throughout the state were at least open to the legality and legitimacy of secession. In addition, voter turnout was significantly lower for the election of convention delegates than for the previous presidential election. Approximately 68,000 voters statewide took part in the presidential contest while only about 38,000 cast ballots for convention delegates. In the 15th Mississippi counties voter turnout was down almost 40 percent for the second election. The lighter turnout favored the secessionists and was possibly a concession by more cautious moderates that Lincoln's election had decided the issue. In general, many voters who had supported Bell were willing to support more radical action with a Republican poised to occupy the White House. After Lincoln's election much of the public was more agitated with regard to the slavery issue, and secessionists became more likely to use various forms of intimidation to accomplish their object. While this could take the form of physical confrontations, it usually meant that the offending party was simply pressured by radical elements within the community. Such was the case with John H. Aughey, who later claimed that he cast his vote for an anti-secession candidate in Choctaw County "amidst the frowns, murmurs, and threats of the judges and bystanders."[46]

Delegates from the 15th Mississippi counties held considerably more wealth than their neighbors in a region where small farmers traditionally looked to the more affluent for political leadership. In the 15th Mississippi counties the average farmer made a living on less than 100 acres of improved land while the delegates owned an average of almost 400 improved acres. Similarly, most households in the region owned few or no slaves while the delegates that they sent to the convention owned an average of 44 slaves. With regard to occupations of the delegates, three were listed in the 1860 census as farmers, three as lawyers, two as lawyer/farmers, two as doctor/planters, and one as planter. Physician W. L. Keirn of Holmes County was the wealthiest delegate, owning a total of 2,650 acres of land and 211 slaves. Lawyer

---

[46] Rainwater, *Mississippi: Storm Center of Secession 1856–1861*, 177–213; Donald Rawson, "Party Politics in Mississippi, 1850–1860" (Ph.D. diss., Vanderbilt University, 1964) 291–303.

John W. Wood of Attala County was the least wealthy of the delegates. Wood owned personal and real property valued at $5,100, but he did not farm and owned only a single acre of land and one slave. While the delegates from the 15th Mississippi counties as a group were not representative of the average white male in the region with regard to wealth and status, they were representative of other Democrats who had been elected to the convention from counties throughout the state.[47] Their election also upheld the community hierarchy that had developed in the 15th Mississippi counties over the last quarter century, a hierarchy in which an affluent minority governed a majority with lesser means.

The Mississippi Secession Convention met in Jackson on 7 January 1861. Although a number of delegates voiced opposition to disunion, conciliatory rhetoric quickly faded in the face of a decidedly pro-secession majority. Before the final vote to withdraw from the Union, three amendments to fend off immediate secession came before the convention and were handily defeated. The amendment making the best showing provided that a secession ordinance should not go into effect until ratified by the state's voters. This proposal lost by a vote of 70 to 29. Finally, on 9 January, an ordinance of secession passed by a vote of 84 to 15. Afterward, one observer heard a number of confident convention delegates claim that secession was "but a demonstration inviting concessions [from the North], which concessions will promptly be made and the disrupted Union fully restored within the next twelve months." Of the delegates from the 15th Mississippi counties, only Sanders of Attala County voted against the ordinance. Wood of Attala County was absent during the final vote but later stated that he would have voted against secession had he been present. Wood was also one of only two delegates who failed to sign the ordinance following passage.[48]

Three delegates who voted for the secession ordinance would have direct connections to the 15th Mississippi Infantry. William F. Brantley of Choctaw County served as an officer in the regiment as did the son of

---

[47] Mississippi Commission of the War Between the States, *Journal of the State Convention*, 5–6; *Vicksburg Whig*, 2 January 1861; United States Census 1860, Mississippi (population, agricultural, and slave schedules).

[48] Rainwater, *Mississippi: Storm Center of Secession*, 211–12; Moore, "Separation from the Union," 442–43; Reuben Davis, *Recollections of Mississippi and Mississippians*, rev. ed. (Hattiesburg: University and College Press of Mississippi, 1972) 403. In addition to Wood, J. J. Thornton of Rankin County did not sign the secession ordinance.

William Booth of Carroll County. By voting to take the state out of the Union, Francis M. Aldridge of Yalobusha County helped seal his own fate. Aldridge served as a captain in the 15th Mississippi Infantry's Company H. Less than a year and a half after casting his ballot for secession he would die at Shiloh.[49]

The convention published both the ordinance and *A Declaration of the Immediate Causes of Secession*. The declaration left little doubt concerning the primary reason for Mississippi leaving the Union:

> Our position is thoroughly identified with slavery—the greatest material institution in the world. Its labor supplies the products which constitutes by far the largest and most important portions of the commerce of the earth. These products are peculiar to the climate verging on the tropical regions, and by an imperious law of nature, none but the black race can bear exposure to the tropical sun. These products have become necessities to the world, and a blow at slavery is a blow at commerce and civilization.... There was no choice left to us but submission to the mandates of abolition, or a dissolution of the Union, whose principles had been subverted to work out our ruin.[50]

After severing Mississippi's ties with the United States, the secession convention remained in session for the purpose of revising the government of the "Republic of Mississippi." Among other business, the convention modified the existing state constitution, appointed a major general and four brigadiers, adopted an official flag, and elected delegates to a convention to meet in Montgomery, Alabama, for the purpose of creating a Southern confederacy. The convention adjourned on 26 January and reconvened two months later to ratify the constitution of the Confederate States of America.[51]

While the Mississippi Secession Convention officially took the state out of the Union, the fight for Southern independence had not yet begun.

---

[49] Dunbar Rowland, *Military History of Mississippi 1803–1898* (Spartenburg SC: The Reprint Company, 1988) 230.

[50] Mississippi Commission on the War Between the States, *Journal of the State Convention*, 86.

[51] Moore, "Separation from the Union," 446.

A violent struggle of unmatched proportion was close at hand as decades of alarmist rhetoric evolved into actions. Rather than a second American Revolution, as many Southerners claimed, secession proved to be a lethal fit of temper. Like those in other parts of the state, the residents of the 15th Mississippi counties would soon feel the full impact of Mississippi's decision to leave the Union. A Choctaw County diarist summarized the events of the day simply but effectively in a single journal entry dated January 1861. "Much excitement in the South over secession," it read. "Look out for war."[52]

---

[52] John W. Brannon, *The John F. Johnson Journal of 1902* (Eupora MS: Privately printed, 1984) 69.

Chapter 2

Organization, 1861

> I was carried away like the rest by the spirit of the times.... This was 1861. The whole country was in a tumult of excitement.[1]
>
> *Augustus H. Mecklin, Company I,*
> *15th Mississippi Infantry*

The soldiers of the 15th Mississippi Infantry came of age at a time when the sectional dispute over slavery was escalating. They were the sons of first-generation Mississippians who had come to the state in search of prosperity, which translated into title to their own property and the potential to improve themselves through hard work. The families of the men had acquired land and established communities with a degree of comfort and security that they hoped would aid them in their quest to advance their station in life.

Through the 1850s it seemed that these communities were in increasing danger. Had they remained isolated, the national slavery debate may not have had a great effect on them as most of their residents owned few or no slaves. But the communities had become part of a larger community that included all Mississippi whites and ultimately all Southern whites who were concerned about the slavery issue. By the eve of the Civil War the slavery debate had trickled down from the national level to the residents of the 15th Mississippi communities. Secessionist politicians had successfully cloaked the slavery question as a states' rights issue, underscored by easily exploitable national events. Northern

---

[1] Augustus Hervey Mecklin Papers, Mississippi Department of Archives and History Library, Jackson, Mississippi.

leaders, they argued, had challenged the admission of Missouri into the Union as a slave state, supported a variety of national tariffs that the South strongly opposed, and given safe harbor to the likes of William Lloyd Garrison and John Brown.[2] The North, it seemed, was determined to deprive Southern citizens of their property and of their independence and rights.

The secessionist rhetoric of national politicians had been parroted by state politicians and, in turn, at the local level. Three of the 15th Mississippi counties had majority slave populations, and even the counties with white majorities had significant numbers of slaves within their borders. None of the white population supported emancipation. For the wealthy few, slaves provided the labor with which fortunes and status were achieved; for the poorer whites, slaves provided a buffer against the bottom rungs of the social ladder. By the time they went to the polls to elect delegates to the secession convention, the simple yeomen of the region had been told over and over again that "unless secession succeeded the negroes would be emancipated and the poor would have to do the menial service of slaves."[3] This was an entirely unacceptable proposition to even the poorest white male whose skin color gave him positive self-definition and who equated any type of property ownership with the potential for rising status. The demise of slavery struck at the heart of community stability and required a community defense. Residents of the 15th Mississippi counties enlisted in the Confederate army to support the Confederate cause and to defend their communities, and their communities responded in kind with enthusiastic support. In the words of one private from the regiment, "Inflammatory speeches and stirring martial music was the order of the day."[4]

A number of other factors drew volunteers from the 15th Mississippi counties into the war. Many men saw service in the Confederate army as a vehicle to display their personal honor. Their communities also viewed military service as a traditional right of passage. For years states' rights orators had made a concerted effort to "assimilate the revolution they were about to inaugurate to the revolution

---

[2] Bell Irvin Wiley, *The Life of Johnny Reb* (Baton Rouge: Louisiana State University Press, 1978) 15.

[3] John W. Wood, *Union and Secession in Mississippi* (Memphis: Saunders, Farrish and Whitmore Printers, 1863) 20.

[4] Augustus Hervey Mecklin Papers.

of our ancestors, which established American independence." According to one observer from the region, "An impression was made upon our young men that unless they took part in the revolution, they would be regarded as Tories of the Revolutionary War. This had a powerful effect on the brave and impetuous youth of our country."[5]

The men also held only a limited view of the dangers that they would encounter in battle. Their immediate frame of reference for combat was the Mexican War, in which the army, packed with Southerners, had crushed the enemy with relative ease. Few doubted that a new Southern army could repeat this feat, and two of the 15th Mississippi volunteer companies would be named for Mississippi Mexican War heroes. Conventional wisdom in the South also held that any fight with the North would be a limited struggle and that most Northerners would not fight if pressed. According to an Attala County resident, "A great delusion disseminated among our people was the great superiority of our Southern soldiers to Northern men. It was often said that 'one Southern man could whip half a dozen Yankees.'" While there were inherent dangers in military service, mortality was only an abstract consideration to men in the 15th Mississippi counties as they volunteered. A general feeling existed that they would fight the Yankees, defeat them handily, and be back home within a few months armed with tales of heroism and adventure. One 15th Mississippi veteran later reflected, "War to us was a novelty and nobody dreaded it. To the boys especially it was to be a romantic frolic."[6]

Against a backdrop of general confusion and uncertainty, Mississippi prepared itself for war during early 1861. After secession, Governor Pettus sent out the call for volunteer troops to be organized into 4, 12-month regiments, but he woefully underestimated the response to his order. Enlistment overwhelmed the initial demand for soldiers, and soon more than eighty volunteer companies clamored to serve. Pettus ordered many of these companies to rendezvous points along the railroad

---

[5] Wood, *Union and Secession in Mississippi*, 17–18.

[6] Wood, *Union and Secession in Mississippi*, 17–18; Unknown Author, "History of the Water Valley Rifles, Company F, Fifteenth Mississippi Infantry," Supplement to the WPA Historical Research Project, Yalobusha County, 16 February 1937, Special Collections, J. D. Williams Library, University of Mississippi, Oxford, Mississippi. Afterwards cited as "History of the Water Valley Rifles."

at Corinth, Enterprise, Grenada, and Iuka.[7] There, the companies were organized into regiments, mustered briefly into state service, and then transferred to the Confederate army. Throughout the South the organization of most Confederate infantry regiments followed the same pattern. A 1,000-man regiment contained ten, 100-man volunteer companies from the same general geographic area. Upon muster into Confederate service, a single letter replaced the homespun company names that the volunteers brought with them from home.[8] For instance, the Long Creek Rifles, a volunteer company organized in Attala County, Mississippi, eventually entered Confederate service as Company A, 15th Mississippi Infantry, CSA.

The ten volunteer companies that would make up the 15th Mississippi Infantry came from various communities in Attala, Carroll, Choctaw, Holmes, and Yalobusha Counties:

Original Company Name	County	Date Organized	Official Designation
Long Creek Rifles	Attala	27 April 1861	Company A
Winona Stars	Carroll	22 March 1861	Company B
Quitman Rifles	Holmes	20 April 1861	Company C
Wigfall Rifles	Choctaw	20 April 1861	Company D
McClung Rifles	Carroll	20 April 1861	Company E
Water Valley Rifles	Yalobusha	23 April 1861	Company F
Grenada Rifles	Yalobusha	19 April 1861	Company G
Yalobusha Rifles	Yalobusha	27 April 1861	Company H
Choctaw Guards	Choctaw	23 March 1861	Company I
Choctaw Grays	Choctaw	4 May 1861	Company K[9]

Named for a stream that ran through the region, the Long Creek Rifles came from Bluff Springs, in Attala County. The company elected thirty-three-year-old Lampkin S. Terry as its captain. The leader of the Long Creek Rifles was a respected member of the community, but more importantly he was a rarity in that he had actual military experience. In

---

[7] Robert W. Dubay, *John Jones Pettus* (Jackson: University Press of Mississippi, 1975) 99–100.

[8] James I. Robertson Jr., *Soldiers Blue and Gray* (Columbia: University of South Carolina Press, 1988) 12–13.

[9] Dunbar Rowland, *Military History of Mississippi 1803–1898* (Spartenburg SC: The Reprint Company, 1988) 228–32.

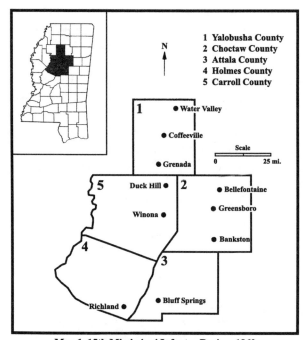

Map 1 15th Mississippi Infantry Region, 1860

1847 Terry served as a private and eventually a sergeant with the 2nd Mississippi during the Mexican War. Other elected officers of the Long Creek Rifles were Lieutenants John B. Love, Elijah Y. Fleming, Thomas J. Clark, and Robert Sallis.[10]

The town of Winona, in Carroll County (later, Montgomery County), produced the Winona Stars. The men of this company elected twenty-three-year-old Thomas Booth as their captain. Booth's father, William Booth, was a delegate to the Mississippi Secession Convention, sheriff of Carroll County, and a primary contributor of funds to finance the company. The elder Booth was a native New Yorker whose status as a transplanted Yankee undoubtedly did not affect his or his son's

---

[10] Rowland, *Military History of Mississippi*, 229; James Wallace, "History and Reminiscences of Attala County," 1916, Mississippi Department of Archives and History Library, Jackson, Mississippi, photocopy; Compiled Service Records of Soldiers from Mississippi Serving in the Mexican War, Mississippi Department of Archives and History Library, Jackson, Mississippi, microfilm.

standing in the eyes of their neighbors. Other elected officers of this company were Lieutenants Napoleon B. Burton, Hugh O. Freeman, and William L. Tyson.[11]

The Quitman Rifles, named in honor of Mississippi Mexican War hero, former governor, and ardent fire-eater John A. Quitman, came from Richland, in Holmes County. James W. Wade, a successful farmer who owned thirty-four slaves, served as captain of this company. At age fifty-seven, Wade was the oldest of the original company captains that served in the 15th Mississippi, and within a few months he would resign his commission due to ill health. Other officers were Lieutenants A. J. Knapp, William Collins, William B. Harrington, and Patrick H. Norton.[12]

Greensboro, in Choctaw County (later, Webster County), produced the Wigfall Rifles, named for the prominent Texas secessionist Louis T. Wigfall. This company elected William F. Brantley, a thirty-year-old attorney and delegate to the Mississippi Secession Convention, as its captain. Brantley would later rise to the rank of brigadier general in the Confederate army. Other elected officers in the Wigfall Rifles were Lieutenants Josiah B. Dunn, Elijah B. Cochran, Andrew Middleton, and L. W. Tribble.[13]

The McClung Rifles, named for Mississippi Mexican War hero Alexander Keith McClung, came from Duck Hill, in Carroll County (later, Montgomery County). Twenty-six-year-old Edgar O. Sykes, son of a prosperous Carroll County family, was the original captain of this company, although he would eventually leave. Other elected officers in the McClung Rifles were Lieutenants John A. Binford, Robert A. Shelton, and Thomas Allen.[14]

Water Valley, in Yalobusha County, produced the Water Valley Rifles under the command of Captain Burrell H. Collins. Collins was the mayor of Water Valley and owned a hotel in the town. At fifty-three, he also was a man of advanced years, considering the rigors of the task that

---

[11] Rowland, *Military History of Mississippi*, 229; W. F. Hamilton, *Military Annals of Carroll County* (Carrollton MS: W. F. Hamilton, 1906) 94.

[12] Rowland, *Military History of Mississippi*, 229.

[13] Rowland, *Military History of Mississippi*, 230; James P. Coleman, *Choctaw County Chronicles* (Ackerman MS: James P. Coleman, 1974) 454; William T. Blain, "William Felix Brantley, 1830–1870," *Journal of Mississippi History* 37/4 (November 1975): 359–65.

[14] Rowland, *Military History of Mississippi*, 230; Hamilton, *Military Annals of Carroll County*, 94.

he and his company faced. Like James Wade of the Quitman Rifles, Collins would resign his commission for health reasons within the first year of the war. Other officers in the Water Valley Rifles were Lieutenants Robert A. Bankhead, Pinckney D. Woods, and B. F. Mitchell.[15]

The town of Grenada, in Yalobusha County (later, Grenada County), was home to the men of the Grenada Rifles. Walter Scott Statham, a twenty-nine-year-old attorney, was elected captain of this company. Born in Georgia, Statham's family moved to Yalobusha County when he was a young boy. He would eventually become the commanding officer of the 15th Mississippi, although his command credentials were based solely on his social standing and the fact that he had established a successful law practice in Grenada. Other elected officers in the Grenada Rifles were Lieutenants E. R. Armistead, Isaac Ayers, Jonah Drummond, and William L. Greer.[16]

The Yalobusha Rifles came from the town of Coffeeville, in Yalobusha County. The men of this company elected thirty-one-year-old attorney Francis Marion Aldridge as their captain. Aldridge, who served as a pro-secession delegate to the Mississippi Secession Convention, would not survive the war's first year. Elected as Aldridge's lieutenants were Edward C. Walthall, Whitfield Morgan, George O. Martin, and William A. Riddick.[17]

The town of Bankston, in Choctaw County, produced the Choctaw Guards. J. W. Hemphill, a twenty-eight-year-old physician who practiced in the nearby community of French Camp, was elected captain of this company, although he would serve only briefly. Elected as his

---

[15] Rowland, *Military History of Mississippi*, 229; WPA History of Yalobusha County, Mississippi Department of Archives and History Library, Jackson, Mississippi, microfilm; Yalobusha County Historical Society, *Yalobusha County History* (Dallas TX: National Share Graphics, 1982) 32.

[16] J. C. Hathorn, *A History of Grenada County* (Grenada MS: J. C. Hathorn, 1972) 32; Rowland, *Military History of Mississippi*, 230; "Gen. W. S. Statham," *Confederate Veteran* 8/1 (January 1900): 176. Walter Scott Statham's name has been mistakenly recorded in some sources as "Winfield Scott Statham." Other sources have the name correct, and "Walter S. Statham" appears on his tombstone in Grenada.

[17] Rowland, *Military History of Mississippi*, 230; Yalobusha County Historical Society, *Yalobusha County History*, 25.

lieutenants were Robert C. Love, Russell Prewitt, Isaac Vinzant, and James C. Taylor.[18]

The Choctaw Grays came from Bellefontaine, in Choctaw County (later, Webster County). Forty-one-year-old Thomas B. Foard, a successful farmer and local political leader, was the original captain of this company, and his lieutenants were John E. Gore, Andrew J. Stearns, and William E. Dumas. Another company, the Oktibbeha Plowboys, was originally part of the 15th Mississippi, but a measles epidemic in the ranks led to a group discharge of its membership. The Choctaw Grays replaced them.[19]

The ten volunteer companies of the 15th Mississippi Infantry were community enterprises in every sense. Because they were recruited locally, they contained many relatives and friends. Company A of the 15th Mississippi included eleven members of the Harmon family, all brothers or cousins. The Johnson family contributed seven members to Company E, and there were five Campbells in Company H.[20] Most of the men who volunteered for service in the companies of the 15th Mississippi had grown up together. Their grand adventure in the Confederate army represented an appealing extension of their neighborhoods, a community undertaking fortified by kinship and friendship ties. While officially they may have gone to war to defend the Confederacy, the men's willingness to fight sprang from the notion that they were protecting their communities. They were also motivated to give a good account of themselves because they knew that those same friends and relatives would be observing their every move.

In the 15th Mississippi Infantry the average enlisted man was twenty-three years old. The majority of the soldiers were single and therefore better able to leave home for extended periods of time. The single men also owned little personal property, and because most came from large families that worked small holdings, they could expect only a minimal inheritance. Two-thirds of the unmarried group worked on

[18] Rowland, *Military History of Mississippi*, 230; Coleman, *Choctaw County Chronicles*, 454.

[19] Ibid.

[20] United States Census, 1860, Mississippi; Compiled Service Records of Confederate Soldiers who served in Organizations from the State of Mississippi: 15th Mississippi Infantry, Mississippi Department of Archives and History Library, Jackson, Mississippi, microfilm. Cited afterwards as Compiled Service Records: 15th Mississippi Infantry.

farms, either as members of their parents' household or as hired labor. Others busied themselves as blacksmiths, carpenters, clerks, teachers, mechanics, shopkeepers, teamsters, overseers, and in a variety of apprentice positions. The unmarried volunteers were in social limbo with regard to their standing in their communities. They had not yet found their place in society and were likely anxious to win some type of positive reputation. According to the father of one of the soldiers, an inherent restlessness was also a trait among the single volunteers: "Many of our young men are always ready for a fight, and when it is a 'free fight' some care but little upon which side they are engaged, as long as they are in [it]."[21]

Married men in the regiment were little better off than their unmarried counterparts. Most were recently wed, with perhaps one or two small children. The vast majority were farmers who worked only meager holdings as they struggled to feed their families. Both husbands and wives in these households were not far removed from their parents' charge and could count on communal support for their families as the husband left home to participate in what most believed would be a relatively short conflict. In the enlisted ranks of the 15th Mississippi there were few men who had firmly established themselves as the family patriarch of a large household. Of all the enlisted men, married and single, 43 percent were born in Mississippi, and just less than half came from slaveholding families, most of whom owned less than 10 slaves.[22]

---

[21] Wood, *Union and Secession in Mississippi*, 20; United States Census, 1860 (population and agricultural) Mississippi; Compiled Service Records: 15th Mississippi Infantry.

[22] United States Census, 1860 (population, agricultural and slave schedules), Mississippi; Compiled Service Records: 15th Mississippi Infantry.

Profile of Enlisted Men
15th Mississippi Infantry (1861)[23]

			Place of birth by %	
Average age:	23		Mississippi	43%
% unmarried:	74.6		Alabama	18%
Occupation by %:			South Carolina	15%
Farmer/Farm laborer		68%	Tennessee	8%
Overseer		3%	Georgia	6%
Student		3%	North Carolina	5%
Merchant		3%	Other	4%
Clerk		3%		
Mechanic		2%		
Carpenter		2%		

Other, including blacksmith,
brickmason, stage driver, miller,
wagon maker, druggist,
teacher/minister, grocer, tinsmith,
and various apprentice positions 16%

While the majority of enlisted men in the regiment fit these general profiles, there were exceptions. Thomas Jefferson Gates was the youngest member of the 15th Mississippi Infantry. He volunteered for service in the Grenada Rifles in April of 1861, a few days after his thirteenth birthday. Thomas J. Haines, a widower from Water Valley who worked as an overseer, joined the Water Valley Rifles at the age of fifty. The Water Valley Rifles also included forty-one-year-old farmer Edmond C. Badley, who enlisted alongside Thomas Badley, his twenty-year-old son. Although almost all of the men of the 15th Mississippi were born in the United States, a scattered few were first-generation immigrants from Ireland, England, Wales, and Prussia.[24]

The company officers were usually somewhat older, prominent community leaders, sons of prominent families, and in most cases men who had helped organize and finance the company. The officer corps of the 15th Mississippi companies reflected peacetime, class-based community hierarchies and included lawyers, doctors, merchants, and

---

[23] Ibid.

[24] United States Census, 1860, Mississippi; Compiled Service Records: 15th Mississippi Infantry.

planters' sons. The officers, or their families, were all significant property holders, both in land and slaves. The average captain in the 15th Mississippi owned several hundred acres of land and around 20 slaves. Thirty-year-old William F. Brantley of Company D earned a living as a lawyer, but he also owned a 480-acre farm on which 20 slaves toiled daily. According to the 1860 census he owned real and personal property valued at more than $60,000 dollars. Brantley was a well-established, politically connected community leader, and the men in his company elected him as their captain just as their county had elected him as a delegate to the secession convention. Similarly, while twenty-three-year-old Thomas Booth of Company B was among the youngest company captains and still lived in his father's household, the elder Booth was a local politician and the wealthy owner of 3,200 acres of land and 46 slaves. With few exceptions, lieutenants in each company also attained their positions with similar class-based political credentials.[25]

Conspicuous in the ranks of the volunteers were a small number of slaves. Several officers brought body servants with them into the army while others donated slaves for use by their individual companies. A few small groups of non-slaveholders pitched in to hire a slave to tend their common needs. The wealthy Binford brothers, John and James, brought three slaves with them from Carroll County—Elisha Binford, Chatham Binford, and Burt Bradley. They donated the latter for service to Company E. Slave Andrew McQuiston served the same company and Isaac Trotter served Company B. Several men from Company D paid the masters of Charles Geren and William Haskins for their services, and a group from Company K hired William Parker and Sol Poe.[26] Such arrangements were not unusual in the Confederate army, particularly during the first year of the war. Of course the Confederate government did not recognize slaves as members of any Southern regiment, and the bondsmen's duties were generally confined to cooking, cleaning, and tending horses. Several of the slaves who traveled with the 15th Mississippi would run away at the first opportunity once the war began in earnest.

---

[25] United States, Census, 1860 (population, agricultural and slave schedules), Mississippi; Compiled Service Records: 15th Mississippi Infantry; Blain, "William Felix Brantley, 1830–1870," 359–65.

[26] WPA History of Yalobusha County.

There was an interim of three to four weeks between the time that the companies destined for the 15th Mississippi were organized and the time that they actually left home. During this period each group held rudimentary drill sessions on their local village greens. Daily drills quickly became public spectacles, enhancing community pride as local residents gathered to view the awkward transformation from citizens to soldiers. These events bolstered the feeling that the service of each company was more of a community undertaking than a military exercise. Though the enlisted men possessed few military skills and the officers little knowledge of tactics and strategy, there was a sense that all were the torchbearers of a patriotic tradition passed down by previous generations of volunteers who served in the American Revolution, the War of 1812, and the Mexican War.[27]

Around the middle of May, the ten companies that would make up the 15th Mississippi received orders to report to Corinth for muster into state and, ultimately, Confederate service. Before the companies left home, however, each took part in a ritual universal throughout the South in the spring of 1861—the presentation of the local battle flag. Though they would function under a variety of army, corps, brigade, and regimental banners, the battle flag of the local company gave most soldiers immediate symbolic evidence of what they were fighting for. Women of the various communities sewed together the company battle flags with great care and presented them to each company in ceremonies that publicly affirmed the notion that the volunteers had taken up a virtuous crusade against a villainous foe. The ceremonies promoted the ideal of the noble soldier going into battle to protect the moral underpinnings of his homeland and reinforced the idea that the entire enterprise was divinely sanctioned.

In early May of 1861 the citizens of Water Valley, Mississippi, took respite from tending their homes, fields, and shops to attend the flag presentation ceremony of their local company, the Water Valley Rifles. The mood of the event was at once serious and celebratory. The crowd assembled around a wooden stage, on which stood some of the community's more prominent residents, in the center of town. Near the stage stood the young men who would soon leave the confines of the

---

[27] Robertson, *Soldiers Blue and Gray*, 5.

town for the first time. Others were leaving for the final time. Some were doing both.[28]

The ceremony began with the introductions and speeches of a political gathering but culminated as eleven women from the community, each representing one of the Southern states that had seceded up to that time, moved to the center of the stage to participate in the ritual. They were led by Althea Dawson, who walked to the podium with a five-foot square banner, "a beautiful bunting flag, with the name of the company and the inscription 'Our Country, Our Home' on it," folded over one of her arms. Dawson handed the flag to Lieutenant Robert A. Bankhead, a physician who was one of the company's officers, with appropriate remarks:

> The Water Valley Rifles—deep and thrilling are the feelings that cling and cluster around my heart as I gaze with soul-felt pride on the noble spirits who so gallantly resolve to strike for our altars, our firesides, God, and our native South.... Our glorious sister states are with you, their freemen are in arms; join them in their struggle for defense and let tyrants know there are men who can make them hear the ring and feel the weight of Southern steel.... I, on behalf of the ladies of Water Valley, present you this proudly waving banner of noble Mississippi. Will it not return to Water Valley with a halo gleaming from every sacred fold? The proud hopes that come trembling from the very depths of my soul murmur that it will.[29]

The ceremony, and particularly Dawson's remarks, reinforced the basic mission of the company and carried the message that the men were going into the field to do their manly duty as protectors of their mothers, sisters, wives, and sweethearts. Rather than fighting for an abstract political or social ideology, they believed they were literally protecting their women from the potential insults of invading Northern hordes. As such, each believed he was protecting the most intimate components of their community. The remarks also reminded the men that they were about to embark on what many considered a holy crusade, striking out for their *alters* and for their *God*. In the 15th Mississippi counties,

---

[28] *Water Valley Progress*, 3 June 1911.
[29] Ibid.

churches were a central element of community in both a social and religious context. The men were supposedly going to war to fight against an army assembled by Northern *tyrants* who would likely desecrate community churches and trample on basic religious freedoms—freedoms upon which the United States was founded—if given the opportunity. The implication was clear. In addition to doing their manly duty, the men were also doing their Christian duty, and whether they were all frequent churchgoers or not, God was definitely on the side of their collective effort. Finally, Dawson assured the men that the *freemen* of the other Southern states were united with them, evoking a sense of shared values based on individual freedom and property ownership. In essence, the men were fighting for their own freedom, the freedom of their comrades, and the freedom of their community against those who would pervert the foundational republican principle of property holding. As she concluded her remarks, Dawson pledged unwavering community support, reminding the men once more that "the cause of justice, of liberty and truth is yours. Remember then amid the tumult of strange, wild scenes there are loving friends at home offering up fervent prayers for your safety and success."[30]

While the flag presentation ceremony successfully promoted community unity, it was a class-based affair. Of the eleven female participants representing the different Southern states, most were daughters of prominent families in the area. The flag itself was presented to a company officer who also came from an established clan, as the enlisted men looked on from subordinate positions around the stage. The entire crowd cheered the company following the ceremony, but the occasion itself was social in nature, led by the community's more socially prominent residents. It represented an extension of the community hierarchy that had developed in Water Valley over the last twenty-five years.[31]

All the communities that produced the 15th Mississippi Infantry held similar ceremonies, after which citizens passed the hat on behalf of the companies. As local patriotism soared, one observer wrote soon after the surrender of Fort Sumter, "The people seem united for Southern independence, the company at Greensboro now numbers about 100, Will

---

[30] Ibid.

[31] Ibid.; United States Census, 1860 (population, agricultural, and slave schedules), Mississippi.

Brantley, captain…. the presentation of the flag to the Choctaw Guards was beautifully performed by Miss Mary E. Gore…. I gave $20 to the Wigfall Rifles."[32] Following ceremonies in Grenada, a local newspaper reported "The Grenada Rifles will take up their line of march on Monday. This truly noble and chivalric company will, if they have an opportunity, honor themselves, Grenada, their state, and the Confederacy…. May God be their constant shield and protection is our ardent prayer."[33] Unfortunately for all of the 15th Mississippi volunteers, the flag presentation ceremonies and their immediate aftermath represented the high point for the volunteers' emotional and psychological well-being as soldiers. At the time, their communities were united behind them, reveling in their commitment. Every soldier was a hero, but the glow of the moment would soon begin to fade. The men were yet to leave home, yet to receive orders from officers they did not know, yet to know the true deprivation of war, both within the Confederate army and at home, yet to watch friends and family die horribly in battle, and yet to kill another human being.

The volunteers arrived in Camp Clark at Corinth during the last week of May 1861. On 27 May, military authorities grouped the companies together, creating the 15th Mississippi Infantry. It was also at Corinth that the men received their true introduction to the rigors of army life. The 15th Mississippi was one of many new regiments preparing for war, and what little training its members had received at home paled in the face of more knowledgeable drill instructors. One member of the regiment's Company F later recalled, upon reaching Camp Clark, "The manual of arms had to be learned, in fact everything pertaining to the duties of a soldier in the way of drill and discipline had to be learned." The men also discovered the great physical price of their Confederate adventure as they suffered through a difficult series of drills twice each day. Speaking of his comrades, one member of Company E stated that "discipline was very galling to them, and as they would be brought under

---

[32] John W. Brannon, *The John F. Johnson Journal of 1902* (Eupora MS: Privately printed, 1984) 69.

[33] Rebecca Martin Stokes, "History of Grenada (1830–1880)" (master's thesis, University of Mississippi, 1929) 35.

rigid military discipline a large amount of swearing could be heard every day."[34]

On 6 June, after "a spirited canvas of the companies...by aspirants for regimental honors and their friends," the 15th Mississippi held elections for field officers. The men chose Walter Statham of Company G to command the regiment as colonel. They also elected J. W. Hemphill of Company I as lieutenant colonel and James Dennis of Company A as major. Those filling appointed positions were James R. Binford, Adjutant; C. G. Armistead, Quartermaster; James W. Wade, Commissary; and William Minter, Chaplain. On 21 July, Hemphill, a physician described by one contemporary as "an elegant gentleman...not made for a military man," resigned his commission, and Edward C. Walthall won the election to take his place.[35] Like company elections, regimental elections were primarily political rather than military exercises. They were carried out under the assumption that the traits of peacetime community leadership automatically equated to an ability to successfully lead men into battle. Such was the case in other Southern regiments and in regiments from the North as well.

Following regimental elections, shifts in leadership at the company level occurred as the 15th Mississippi struggled to streamline itself. Company G elected regimental surgeon E. R. Armistead to replace Statham as captain while Company I elected Robert C. Love to replace Hemphill. In Company E, Michael Farrell replaced Edgar Sykes, who resigned to join another unit. Over the course of the next four years numerous changes would take place in the leadership of the 15th Mississippi at both the regimental and company levels.

On 30 June 1861, the membership of the 15th Mississippi totaled 987 men. By 22 July that number had risen to 1,022, and for the next few months membership hovered around 1,000. Each week a few new men enlisted while others received discharges, usually for medical reasons. Because most of the soldiers had never been exposed to large groups, various illnesses—particularly those traditionally labeled "childhood" illnesses—took their toll on the regiment. On 30 May 1861, just three days after the 15th Mississippi was formed, Choctaw County farmer

---

[34] James R. Binford, "Recollections of the Fifteenth Mississippi Infantry, CSA," Patrick Henry Papers, Mississippi Department of Archives and History Library, Jackson, Mississippi, 2; "History of the Water Valley Rifles," 12–15.

[35] Rowland, *Military History of Mississippi*, 231; Binford, "Recollections," 2.

Robert DeShazo of Company D became the regiment's first casualty, succumbing to disease at the age of twenty. On 30 June, Joseph S. Guy of Company G wrote a female acquaintance in Grenada that "there are a good many boys sick in our regiment," and on 19 July the ranks were missing fourteen privates from Company E who were "sick at home with measles." From June through the rest of the year more than 60 men from the 15th Mississippi died from disease, and another 148 men received medical discharges. Although most of the regiment's losses during the period were the result of illness, William Nations of Company F was "drummed out of the service" for theft while at Corinth. Throughout the course of the war the 15th Mississippi gained men through additional enlistment and lost men through death, desertion, or discharge. Total membership at any given time declined steadily after the regiment began active combat. [36]

While they received better training in Corinth than they had at home, a lack of proper equipment handicapped the men of the 15th Mississippi. There was an initial shortage of supplies in camp, including rifles, tents, uniforms, and blankets. On 12 June, Statham reported that only 620 rifles were available to the regiment and that many of the men drilled using personal firearms. During this period Captain Aldridge of Company H complained in a letter to his wife, "We are in a wonderful state of confusion.... The government has not provided us with, nor have I been able to buy, blankets, and [we are] sleeping on the bare ground." Women in the 15th Mississippi counties formed sewing societies to supplement the men's clothing supply and military aid societies to raise money. Much like the flag presentation ceremonies, however, sewing and aid societies were generally class-based social functions that included only prominent community women who had the time and resources to participate. Women in poorer families usually contributed to the war effort by sending personal items to relatives and friends. The 15th Mississippi soon received adequate supplies, but the flow of provisions grew more tenuous as the war progressed. [37]

---

[36] Official Records, 15th Mississippi Infantry, CSA, Mississippi Department of Archives and History Library, Jackson, Mississippi. Cited afterwards as Official Records, 15th Mississippi Infantry; Joseph S. Guy, letter to Julia A. Berry, 30 June 1861, Grenada County Historical Society, Grenada, Mississippi.

[37] Walter S. Statham, letter to Staff Headquarters, 12 June 1861, Official Records, 15th Mississippi Infantry; F. M. Aldridge, letter to Lizzie, 18 June 1861, Francis Marion

Pay was also a problem for the men from the war's outset. By law, Confederate infantry and artillery privates received only $11 per month. Payments were routinely slow, and when money did arrive massive inflation had usually reduced it to a fraction of its original value. During the war's latter stages the pay for privates would be $18 per month, but this was little compensation at a time when a single pair of shoes might cost the average soldier more than $100. Inadequate pay would also affect morale in that soldiers had little or no money to send home to their struggling families. While officers received higher pay—$195 per month for Statham as colonel of the 15th Mississippi in 1861—they too saw money on an irregular basis. In December of 1861 one of the 15th Mississippi company captains complained to his wife that "the government is now due me for nearly four months service."[38]

Most of the young recruits at Corinth were away from home for the first time, and there was a considerable amount of horseplay in and around the camp. With each passing week the monotony of camp life found many men desperate to occupy their idle evening hours. Card or checker games, foot races and wrestling were popular pastimes as was singing around the campfire and, among those with the ability, reading books and writing letters. Armed with a few dollars brought from home, however, many soldiers chose drinking as a way to occupy their time. In an effort to curb excessive frivolity, authorities eventually forbid the soldiers of Camp Clark to visit Corinth without first receiving a pass signed by their colonel, and anyone found smuggling a bottle of whiskey into camp risked stern punishment. These measures failed to deter some of the men. One member of the 15th Mississippi's Company E later recalled that a few of his fellow soldiers, returning from guard duty in town, "remember[ed] that they would be searched when they got to the guard line around camp, conceived the idea of filling their gun barrels with whiskey, which they did, and it worked like a charm."[39]

Aldridge Papers, Mississippi Department of Archives and History Library, Jackson, Mississippi; E. Gray Dimond and Herman Hattaway, eds., *Letters from Forest Place: A Plantation Family's Correspondence* (Jackson: University Press of Mississippi, 1993) 243, 252.

[38] Robertson, *Soldiers Blue and Gray*, 79; Wiley, *The Life of Johnny Reb*, 136; Official Records, 15th Mississippi Infantry; F. M. Aldridge, letter to Lizzie, 13 December 1861, Francis Marion Aldridge Papers.

[39] Binford, "Recollections," 2.

The men of the 15th Mississippi trained at Corinth for several weeks, during which time their confidence grew, as did their concern that the war would end before they had seen any action. This concern bordered on panic after word of Bull Run reached Mississippi in July of 1861. According to one soldier, the men "longed for a fight with our enemies, and they would often say that the war would end and the 15th would go home disgraced never having seen battle."[40] Still believing that any fight with the Yankees would be easily won, most of the men of the 15th Mississippi failed to recognize the deficiencies of Southern bravado as an effective military tool. They did not realize that a war fought with weapons other than stubbornness, self-righteous appeals to honor, and inflammatory political rhetoric would be a fierce, bloody struggle in which men and resources in superior numbers would carry the day. As the great sectional tragedy unfolded, the men of the 15th Mississippi Infantry would recognize this as warfare's consummate lesson. The novice soldiers were ready to begin their Confederate adventure when orders finally arrived that took them away from Corinth, but as one veteran of the regiment later recalled, "Alas how utterly ignorant we were of actual warfare, and of the perils, hardships and sacrifice to follow for four weary years."[41]

---

[40] Ibid.

[41] "History of the Water Valley Rifles," 4.

CHAPTER 3

TENNESSEE AND KENTUCKY, 1861–1862

This was a hard trip for soldiers who had never marched before.[1]
James Dicken, Company A, 15th Mississippi Infantry

The war started slowly for the men of the 15th Mississippi Infantry. They left Corinth in the summer of 1861 and moved along the rail lines to Union City, Tennessee, about 100 miles north of Memphis. Local citizens welcomed the regiment, and the men spent several quiet weeks "admiring the large poplar trees and enjoying the hospitality of the fine people." Despite the warm welcome, the soldiers were skittish. On a moonless night during the first week of August, a false alarm in the form of gunfire from local hunters created bedlam in camp. Before learning the true origins of the shots, the men scrambled from their tents, believing that they were about to meet the Yankees for the first time. "The first thing I knew of it," Thomas Shuler of Company A told his sister in Attala County, "Jim [his brother] was up on his hands and knees hollaring 'boys, boys, fighting, fighting.' He soon had us all out in line...where we stayed but [a] few minutes." According to Shuler, "Some of the boys were excited so bad it took them two or three days to get over it." While reports of Union troops in the area proved false, the rumors motivated several slaves from the regiment to slip away from the camp under cover of darkness. One soldier informed his family during the period, "We are having a hard time here now since our mess negroes have both left us."[2]

---

[1] James T. Dicken, "Long Creek Rifles," *Kosciusko Star Ledger*, 1 January 1898.

[2] James R. Binford, "Recollections of the Fifteenth Mississippi Infantry, CSA," Patrick Henry Papers, Mississippi Department of Archives and History Library, Jackson,

In mid-August the 15th Mississippi received orders to move again. According to the rumor mill the regiment was bound for Virginia and service under General Robert E. Lee. A great tremor of excitement passed through the camp at the prospect of seeing real action. The excitement was short lived, however, as the rumor proved false. On 13 August, the 15th Mississippi moved to Knoxville and took its place with several other regiments in a brigade under the command of Brigadier General Felix Kirk Zollicoffer. On 15 September, the strength of the 15th Mississippi was 1,043 men.[3]

Like the makeshift soldiers in his newly created brigade, forty-nine-year-old Tennessean Felix Zollicoffer was a makeshift commanding general. A newspaper publisher and politician, Zollicoffer had limited military experience as a lieutenant of volunteers during the Seminole Wars. Born into an affluent family, he took advantage of his status and worked his way up the political ladder in Tennessee. He served as state comptroller from 1843–1849 and as a state senator from 1849–1850. In 1852 he won the election to the U.S. House of Representatives, where he served three terms. Following the surrender of Fort Sumter, Zollicoffer's political influence landed him a position as brigadier general in the Tennessee state forces. He was transferred to Confederate service with the same rank and given command of the District of East Tennessee, Department Number Two, on 1 August 1861. In addition to the 15th Mississippi, Zollicoffer's original command included the 16th Alabama and the 11th, 17th, 19th, and 20th Tennessee.[4]

Placement in Zollicoffer's brigade was an important milestone for the men of the 15th Mississippi. It was their first major assignment of the war, but it also marked their indoctrination into the Confederate army's military infrastructure. They would now function under a brigade commander from another state, alongside troops from other states. The

---

Mississippi, 3; T. J. Shuler, letter to Mary Ann Sallis, 12 August 1861, Gladys Boyette papers, Kosciusko, Mississippi, copy in possession of the author.

[3] Binford, "Recollections," 2–3; US War Department, comp., *The War of Rebellion: A Compilation of the Official Records of the Union and Confederate Armies*, 128 vols. (Washington, DC: 1880–1902) ser. 1, vol. 4:409. Afterwards this work is cited as *OR*, followed by the volume number, part number (when applicable), and page numbers. Unless otherwise noted, all references are to volumes from series 1.

[4] James C. Stamper, "Felix K. Zollicoffer: Tennessee Editor and Politician," *Tennessee Historical Quarterly* 24/4 (Winter 1969): 356; Stewart Sifakis, *Who Was Who in the Civil War* (New York: Facts on File, 1988) 740.

change represented more than just an expanded military horizon for the men. The soldiers of the 15th Mississippi had gone to war to protect their homes, but in Zollicoffer's brigade they were part of a larger effort with men who were not part of their communities. They were also operating in territory far removed from the family and friends that they had gone to war to defend. Before coming to Knoxville the 15th Mississippi had its own command structure based on community hierarchies. The men drilled with and answered to other men who shared a common bond based on the concept of community. While their regimental command structure remained intact, the soldiers would have to follow orders issued by officers they did not know and depend on soldiers from other regiments with whom they had no intrinsic connections. Although it would not happen immediately, placement in a brigade with soldiers from other states represented the first step in the erosion of the 15th Mississippi Infantry as a community enterprise.

Zollicoffer's troops chafed in the Knoxville camp. East Tennessee, a region of few slaveholders, was staunchly pro-Union. For the first time the men of the 15th Mississippi found themselves removed from the warm bosom of Confederate sympathy. During his stay in the area one soldier observed "the people are generally Lincolnites, and are perfectly horror-struck by the passing of our army through their country." Because the locals considered any Confederate encroachment as a threat to their homes, civilian snipers became a concern. In addition, many of the men of the 15th Mississippi remained anxious to participate in a major battle. Rather than a vehicle for displaying their honor, the soldiers' grand adventure in the Confederate army had become a daily exercise in tedium, punctuated by dismal weather, poor food, and a series of false reports of pending engagements. With each passing day of inactivity frustrations mounted. According to James Binford of Company E, "The boys were disappointed and mad, but they were determined to find some enemy of the South and go after them, for they had heard that many of that kind resided in this east Tennessee city."[5]

One evening, after receiving the appropriate permits, several soldiers from the 15th Mississippi ventured into Knoxville determined to find or create a fight. Upon reaching town they procured some alcohol and enlisted the help of some like-minded Texas soldiers who were

---

[5] Binford, "Recollections," 4; "16th Alabama Infantry," regimental history files, Alabama Department of Archives and History Library, Montgomery, Alabama.

stationed in the area. The group formed a posse of sorts, choosing William G. "Parson" Brownlow as their target. Brownlow was a well-known Unionist and critic of Southern policies who lived in Knoxville. The men proposed to find Brownlow's home, drag the "interstate South-hater" out into his yard, and hang him from the nearest tree. Fortunately for Brownlow, the inebriated guerrilla band never got a chance to carry out their plan. Upon learning that some of his men were drunk in town, Colonel Statham dispatched guards who arrested the group and brought them back to camp.[6]

On the surface the aborted search for Brownlow was little more than an alcohol-induced "boys will be boys" incident. It did, however, represent a significant breakdown in discipline among some of the men of the 15th Mississippi. Zollicoffer himself had issued specific orders that his troops were to do nothing to provoke the pro-Union civilian population of the region. The actions of the men, regardless of their condition, indicated a general disdain for orders issued by a non-Mississippian. The men had volunteered for service to fight Yankees in defense of their homes, and many of the soldiers believed that the general from Tennessee was holding them back. Their actions had not dishonored their own regimental and company commanders because those officers had not issued the orders restricting such activities. The men still functioned within community units, striking out more as Mississippians than as Confederates. While Statham could not ignore the incident, he and the other 15th Mississippi officers were likely proud that their men had shown such spirit. They too were suspicious of Zollicoffer's abilities. Francis Aldridge, one of the company captains, informed his wife that a new commander to replace the Tennessean would represent "a change much desired."[7]

On 13 September, Confederate authorities ordered Zollicoffer's brigade to Cumberland Gap, Tennessee. As there was no railroad line connecting the two points, the men of the 15th Mississippi began their first long march of the war. Augustus Mecklin, a private in Company I, later recalled that as the men packed for the move, "such noise and confusion greeted my ears—wagons rattling, drivers swearing and

---

[6] Binford, "Recollections," 4.

[7] F. M. Aldridge, letter to "My Dear Wife," 4 December 1861, Francis Marion Aldridge Papers, Mississippi Department of Archives and History Library, Jackson, Mississippi.

raving, men shouting and blaspheming, singing and whistling." The men strained under the burden of fully loaded packs, and the five-day journey was memorable for all. According to James Dicken of Company A, "This was a hard trip for soldiers who had never marched before, and there were many sore and blistered feet upon reaching our destination."[8]

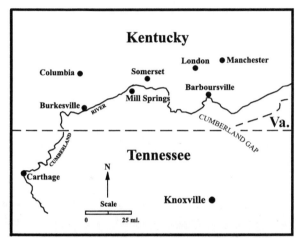

Map 2   Southeastern Kentucky-Tennessee Border, 1861

Many of the Mississippians, accustomed to the relatively flat terrain of their home state, were awestruck at the sight of the mountains. According to one observer, "Soon the boys were climbing the steep cliffs, and as they gained the summit would sit on some high rock." Exploring the mountain, however, proved dangerous. Hostile civilians, described by one member of the 15th Mississippi as "long-legged, long-haired men with long squirrel rifles ever ready to shoot a rebel when the opportunity was presented," continued to pose a problem for the Confederates. After snipers slightly wounded two men from ambush, Zollicoffer issued orders restricting all soldiers to camp.[9]

At Cumberland Gap, Zollicoffer's brigade was part of a grand scheme of Confederate defense. Protecting the Mississippi Valley was of vital importance to the Confederacy. Kentucky was the gateway to the

---

[8] Augustus Hervey Mecklin Papers, Mississippi Department of Archives and History Library, Jackson, Mississippi; Dicken, "Long Creek Rifles."

[9] Binford, "Recollections," 4–5.

Deep South, and losing it would leave the heart of the Confederacy vulnerable. Strong Unionist sentiment in eastern Kentucky and Tennessee also concerned Southern leaders. Consequently, the Confederate high command established a line of defense designed to keep the Mississippi Valley secure. The left flank of the line was anchored at Columbus, Kentucky, on the Mississippi River, while the center was established at Bowling Green. The right flank, of which Zollicoffer's brigade was now a part, concentrated around the Cumberland Gap. In Tennessee, the Confederates established Fort Henry on the Tennessee River and Fort Donelson on the Cumberland to secure those rivers from the threat of amphibious assault.[10]

After remaining at Cumberland Gap for several days, Zollicoffer and his men marched into Kentucky, where on 19 September they established camp at Cumberland Ford. Reflecting the importance of their new position, Zollicoffer's brigade finally saw limited action. On 26 September the general ordered a detachment of his command, including some of the men of the 15th Mississippi, to Laurel Bridge, where a small force of Federals was reportedly camped. At the same time, Zollicoffer ordered another group for salt at the Clay County salt works. Near Laurel Bridge the first detachment encountered a small contingent of Union troops. The Yankees exchanged a few shots with Confederate pickets and quickly retired to fight another day. By the time the main body of the Confederate detachment reached the Federal bivouacs they were empty. In their haste the Yankees left behind many of their supplies, which the Confederates hauled back to Cumberland Ford. On 30 September, Zollicoffer reported that his men captured "8,000 cartridges, 25,000 caps, 3 kegs of powder, 6 barrels of salt, 25 pair of shoes, 2 wagons and teams, 3 other horses and 3 prisoners, including 2 of their cavalry pickets."[11] As a result, the men of the 15th Mississippi could boast that their first great mission against the Yankees was a success.

Although they had not come under heavy fire at Laurel Bridge, the 15th Mississippi sustained one significant casualty the day after it marched into the Union camp. The men were still on alert when the rifle

---

[10] Edwin C. Bearss, *Decision in Mississippi: Mississippi's Important Role in the War Between the States* (Jackson: Mississippi Commission on the War Between the States, 1962) ix; James M. McPherson, *Battle Cry of Freedom: The Civil War Era* (New York: Ballantine Books, 1988) 284.

[11] *OR*, vol. 4:199–203.

of a careless Confederate cavalryman accidentally discharged. The bullet struck Colonel Statham in the shoulder, causing a bloody, painful wound. Despite the injury, Statham refused to leave the field for treatment until Colonel James E. Rains of the 11th Tennessee threatened to remove him forcibly. According to Bruce Henderson of the 15th Mississippi's Company A, Statham, while reeling in his saddle, told his men that "if we said so he would go but if not he would stay and die with us.... We told him to go. He then left but told us that he would watch and if we needed him he would come [back]."[12] The wound incapacitated Statham for some time and would nag him for the rest of his life.

In mid-October, Zollicoffer again ordered his force north toward a Federal encampment at Rockcastle Hills known as Camp Wildcat. There, on 21 October, men from the Tennessee regiments engaged Union cavalry under the command of Colonel Albin Schoepf. The Federals repulsed the Confederates and eventually withdrew in what amounted to an indecisive encounter. Zollicoffer's brigade suffered its first combat casualties during the fighting—11 killed and 48 wounded. The 15th Mississippi suffered no casualties. During the period, however, sixteen-year-old Francis M. Morris of Company I became one of the regiment's first deserters, quietly slipping away from camp one night.[13]

In the weeks following the skirmish with Schoepf's men, the Confederates were constantly on the march as Zollicoffer redeployed the bulk of his force to the west. "Our orders have just been received to pack up our duds," one soldier wrote. "Where we are to go, or for what purpose, I know not. It will be but a tramp, tramp, tramp." The men left Cumberland Ford on 6 November and, as inclement weather hampered their progress, slowly moved to Mill Springs, Kentucky, on the southern bank of the Cumberland River. After arriving at Mill Springs, Zollicoffer wrote to General Albert Sidney Johnston, overall commander of the troops in the region, "From this camp as a base of operations, I hope in mild weather to penetrate the country toward London and Danville [Kentucky]." To facilitate active reconnaissance of the area, Zollicoffer moved his men directly across the Cumberland to Beech Grove, placing the river at their backs. There, the men settled in for what most of the

[12] John K. Bettersworth, ed., *Mississippi in the Confederacy: As They Saw It* (Baton Rouge: Louisiana State University Press, 1961) 63–65.

[13] Dunbar Rowland, *Military History of Mississippi 1803–1898* (Spartanburg SC: The Reprint Company, 1988) 231.

soldiers assumed would be a winter break from marching. On 4 December, Francis Aldridge of the 15th Mississippi wrote to his wife, "This climate is too cold for a winter campaign. We have already had two light snows, a portion of the latter yet remaining upon the ground." Returns from Beech Grove at the end of 1861 listed the total strength of the 15th Mississippi at 1,025 men.[14]

As the year 1862 began, morale in the ranks of the 15th Mississippi waned. The men were tired of marching, many were homesick, and the weather was bitterly cold. One soldier expressed the prevailing sentiment in camp when he wrote home, "All I can now say is that it is my intention to go home as soon as I can with honor do so.... How happy we shall be when the independence of our country is established and peace restored in our domestic circles." Despite their circumstances, however, most of the men still harbored fears that they would return home without participating in a single major engagement. As he waited at Beech Grove, one Confederate corporal scribbled in his diary, "There is no open enemy about us. Don't know where they are. I am pretty sure I am eager to find them, for I am footsore and tired of hunting them. I am eager to get into a regular fight." During late 1861 Statham informed Confederate headquarters that his men wanted "to go to Virginia like the devil," and in early January of 1862, having lost all confidence in Zollicoffer, he requested a transfer for the 15th Mississippi to a more active theater. On 12 January, Assistant Adjutant William W. Mackall wrote to Statham that although Johnston denied the request, "The general

---

[14] Unknown Author, "History of the Water Valley Rifles, Company F, Fifteenth Mississippi Infantry," Supplement to the WPA Historical Research Project, Yalobusha County, 16 February 1937, Special Collections, J. D. Williams Library, University of Mississippi, Oxford, Mississippi, 19. Afterwards cited as "History of the Water Valley Rifles"; Lowell H. Harrison, "Mill Springs: 'The Brilliant Victory,'" *Civil War Times Illustrated* 10/9 (January 1972): 7; "16th Alabama Infantry," regimental history files; F. M. Aldridge, letter to "My Dear Wife," 4 December 1861; Robert Underwood Johnson and Clarence Clough Buel, eds., vol. 1 of *Battles and Leaders of the Civil War* (New York: The Century Company, 1887) 392. Afterwards this work is cited as *Battles and Leaders*, followed by the appropriate volume and page numbers; *OR*, vol. 7:824. On 8 December 1861 Maj. Gen. George B. Crittenden was given command of the District of East Tennessee, Department 2, which included Zollicoffer's brigade, Col. William A. Carroll's brigade, and a number of reserve troops.

is satisfied that you will soon have an opportunity under General Z[ollicoffer] of contributing to turn back the invaders of the South."[15]

Soon after receiving this message Statham received a short medical furlough, probably related to his still painful shoulder wound. As a result, he would miss leading the 15th Mississippi in its first opportunity "to turn back the invaders of the South." In Statham's absence, Lieutenant Colonel Edward Cary Walthall took command of the regiment.

In early January the Federals made the decision to move against the Confederates in eastern Kentucky and thus threaten the right flank of the Southern defense line. Union Brigadier General George H. Thomas, who commanded a force stationed near Lebanon, Kentucky, moved toward Somerset to concentrate with Schoepf's command. Due to heavy rains it took Thomas and his men more than a week to cover 40 miles. On 17 January, Thomas arrived at Logan's Crossroads, an intersection 9 miles west of Somerset and 8 miles north of the Zollicoffer's encampment. There, he was able to unite with three infantry regiments and an artillery battery sent by Schoepf. The combined force totaled more than 4,000 men.

During the same period Major General George B. Crittenden arrived at Mill Springs to take command of Confederate troops in the area. These included Zollicoffer and his men and another Confederate brigade commanded by Brigadier General William H. Carroll. On 16 January, the Confederates learned of Federal troop movements in the area. Two days later Crittenden decided to attack, hoping to catch Thomas before he could unite with Schoepf.[16] After receiving their orders, the men of Zollicoffer's and Carroll's brigades readied themselves to move out. The soldiers of the 15th Mississippi, on 18 January, fell in line "ready for the tramp" north. Zollicoffer's brigade, with the 15th Mississippi in front, led the procession, followed somewhat clumsily by Carroll's brigade. The troops, many of whom were skeptical as to whether they would

---

[15] Official Records, 15th Mississippi Infantry, CSA, Mississippi Department of Archives and History Library, Jackson, Mississippi. Cited afterwards as Official Records, 15th Mississippi Infantry; *OR*, vol. 7:828; F. M. Aldridge, letter to "My Dear Wife," 4 December 1861; "16th Alabama Infantry," regimental history files.

[16] Everette B. Long with Barbara Long, *The Civil War Day by Day: An Almanac 1861–1865* (Garden City NY: Doubleday and Company, 1971) 161; Harrison, "Mill Springs: 'The Brilliant Victory,'" 8.

actually meet a significant Yankee force, marched all night through sleet, snow, and fog. Just after dawn they found the enemy.[17]

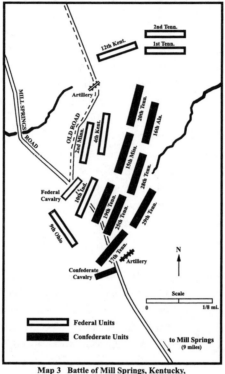

**Map 3   Battle of Mill Springs, Kentucky,
January 18, 1862**

Fighting began at the foot of a ridge less than 2 miles from Logan's Crossroads. Upon hearing the gunfire, Zollicoffer formed his brigade in a battle line with the 15th Mississippi and the 20th Tennessee in front, flanked by the 19th and 25th Tennessee to the left. Because of delays, Carroll's brigade initially offered little support. Zollicoffer's line advanced to engage the Union infantry, and within minutes the Battle of Mill Springs had begun. It was a confused battle fought in clouds of thick smoke and early morning fog. The terrain was rough, and heavy thickets made orderly movements almost impossible. To make matters worse for

---

[17] Ibid.

the Southerners, many of the Tennesseans carried only old flintlock muskets and squirrel rifles that frequently misfired in wet weather.[18]

Led by the 15th Mississippi under Walthall and the 20th Tennessee under Colonel Joel A. Battle, the Confederates applied significant pressure to the Federal center. Many of the Confederates fired from a heavily wooded ravine, which provided natural cover. Amid the fog and confusion, however, Zollicoffer mistakenly rode into the Union lines, believing he was joining part of his own command. Before realizing his mistake, a Union officer shot and killed the general.[19]

Disheartened by their commander's death and hampered by the misfires of their damp rifles, the 19th and 25th Tennessee regiments gave way, as did all semblance of battlefield discipline. Despite the chaos, the 15th Mississippi and the 20th Tennessee continued the fight at the fence in the center of the battle line. Too close to discharge their weapons, some of the men used their rifles as clubs while others slashed away with long "cane knives." The Southerners gave ground grudgingly, but after the left flank collapsed the Federals overwhelmed the two regiments, forcing them into a hasty retreat along with the rest of Confederate army. The defeat turned into a complete rout. The Confederates abandoned their artillery, cast aside their rifles, and retreated in a dead run back to their camp. A Union colonel later wrote of the retreat, "The road which the retreating force followed was strewn with evidences that the retreat had degenerated into a panic.... A piece of artillery was found in a mudhole, hundreds of muskets were strewn along the road and in the fields." According to a sergeant from the 10th Indiana, "It became evident that they [the Confederates] had made a perfect stampede, wagon loads of blankets, haversacks filled with provisions, were left strewn along the road for miles. As we had started without breakfast, we made a hearty meal from theirs."[20]

By nightfall what was left of Crittenden's command huddled behind their original fortifications at Beech Grove with Union troops surrounding them on three sides. Exhausted from the fight and

---

[18] Ibid., 4–9, 44–45.

[19] Ibid.

[20] Ibid.; *Battles and Leaders*, 1:390; Samuel McIlvaine, letter to J. B. Wilson, 21 January 1862, in Clayton E. Cramer, *By the Dim and Flaring Lamps: The Civil War Diary of Samuel McIlvaine, February through June, 1862* (Monroe NY: Library Research Associates, 1990) 78–82.

subsequent chase, the Federals chose to wait until the next morning to attack or demand a full surrender. Luckily for the Confederates, the *Noble Ellis*, a rickety steamboat previously used to carry provisions, was still docked near their camp. Throughout the night the army used it to cross the river, barely completing the task by daybreak. After the battered Confederates crossed the Cumberland, they set fire to the boat and continued their retreat. The Federals woke the next morning to find the rebel camp empty. Rather than attempt to ford the river, Thomas chose not to pursue.[21]

The Battle of Mill Springs (also known as the Battle of Fishing Creek, Logan's Crossroad, or Somerset) lasted a little over three hours, and one participant from the 15th Mississippi described it as "a succession of blunder from the beginning." About 4,000 Confederates took part in actual combat. Confederate casualties outnumbered those of the Union forces by more than two to one. The Southerners losses were 125 killed, 309 wounded, and 99 missing, for a total of 533. The Federals losses were 40 killed, 207 wounded, and 15 missing, for a total of 262. By virtue of its position in the middle of the fight, the 15th Mississippi sustained more casualties than any other regiment. Its losses were 44 killed, 115 wounded, and 29 missing, or about 35 percent of the Confederate total. The Federals sent wounded Confederate prisoners to a field hospital in Somerset and buried the dead unceremoniously in a mass grave near the spot where Zollicoffer fell.[22]

The men of the 15th Mississippi fled the area with little more than the shirts on their backs. All their equipment was lost, as were more than 1,000 of the army's horses and mules. Soon after the battle one member of the regiment's Company H wrote to his wife that "many of our men left money in their trunks. Fortunately I left none of your letters…but your miniature and that of our children were in my trunk, now Yankee property." When the smoke cleared a member of a Federal regiment from Minnesota told his family, "Our boys had a great time in pillaging the tents. They found clothing of all kind and quality, watches, jewelry, swords, knifes, pistols, daguerreotypes, letters, keepsakes, and most everything you can think of…. I got me a nice gray coat which belonged to a lieutenant in the secesh army." Some Confederate "property" did not wait to be captured. A slave belonging to Captain William F. Brantley of

---

[21] Binford, "Recollections," 21.

[22] "History of the Water Valley Rifles," 21; *Battles and Leaders*, 1:392.

the 15th Mississippi's Company D took advantage of the confusion during the fight and fled into the Union lines.[23]

The humiliating defeat left the men of the 15th Mississippi Infantry in a psychological quandary. If their cause was honorable, just, and divinely sanctioned, as they had been told, and if it was indeed true that "one rebel can whip a half dozen Yankees," why did they lose the battle? More importantly, how would they explain the loss to their relatives and friends in Mississippi who had sent them off to war with such fanfare? How could they keep their honor? A number of the men from the 15th Mississippi wrote letters home in which they rationalized the defeat. Two themes were common in their correspondence, both of which were factually inaccurate. First, although the two forces were evenly matched at around 4,000 men each, the Confederates maintained that they had fought an honorable fight, succumbing only to superior Federal numbers. Second, most of the Mississippians placed the blame squarely on the shoulders of the two Tennessee regiments that had broken and exposed the army's left flank. Two cousins, Charles and James Frierson of the 15th Mississippi's Company F, wrote home that their regiment had done most of the actual fighting against a Union force that numbered in the tens of thousands. Charles explained in one letter, "We went out with the intention of attacking three [regiments]...so we expected to bag them at once, but when we came up we met 25,000 men." He also claimed that the Federals suffered 1300 casualties during the battle and that "the Mississippians are down on the Tenn[esseans] for running, leaving them exposed ... our men shot well and were much opposed to the retreat." In one of his letters, James explained that the 15th Mississippi "fought single-handedly 36,000 Yankees for 3 hours and 15 minutes," while Francis Aldridge of Company H wrote that "the truth is the Tennesseans [from the 19th and 25th regiments] acted with great cowardice." The letters also emphasized the large number of Mississippi casualties as proof that "the Mississippians sustained their noble character." None of the correspondence mentioned that most of the men of the 15th

---

[23] F. M. Aldridge, letter to Lizzie, 30 January 1862, Francis Marion Aldridge Papers; Samuel McIlvaine, letter to J. B. Wilson, 21 January 1862, in Cramer, *By the Dim and Flaring Lamps.*

Mississippi threw down their rifles at the end of the fight as they fled the battlefield in sheer panic.[24]

Back home, citizens of the 15th Mississippi communities also lived in collective denial of the exact nature of the Confederate defeat. Newspapers published accounts that generally confirmed what the men had written in their letters, particularly with regard to troop strength. One newspaper assured its readers that the Confederates "fought 25,000 troops with 5,000—drove them back a mile in three separate charges, and after three hours' conflict were forced to retreat only by overpowering numbers." The newspaper went on to describe the retreat as "a most masterly one, and Gen. Crittenden is entitled to great credit for the manner in which it was made." Another account stated that the 15th Mississippi "rescued our army from total annihilation.... Lieut. Col. Walthall was conspicuous for his skill, coolness, and unflinching courage." Little mention was made of the supposed cowardice of other regiments or that some regiments had "acted badly" during the fight.[25]

Crittenden was also at a loss when trying to explain the rout to his superiors. Like the soldiers' letters and the newspaper accounts, the general's written report, dated 13 February 1862, rationalized the defeat by exaggerating Federal troop strength. He claimed that at Mill Springs his force had met a Federal contingent of about 12,000 men. He also exaggerated Federal losses, claiming that about 700 of the enemy were killed or wounded during the struggle. Crittenden did his best to minimize the defeat and, in doing so, highlighted the conduct of the 15th Mississippi during the battle, earning the regiment and its interim leader Edward Walthall significant notoriety in Confederate command circles. According to the report, the regiment "was most gallantly led by Lieutenant-Colonel Walthall. The reputation of the Mississippians for heroism was fully sustained by this regiment. Its loss in killed and wounded, which was by far greater than that of any other regiment, tells sufficiently the story of discipline and courage."[26]

---

[24] Charles Frierson, letter to Parents, 28 January 1862, Gay Carter papers, Houston, Texas, copy in possession of the author; James Frierson, letter to Mother, 28 January 1862, Gay Carter papers, copy in possession of the author; F. M. Aldridge to Lizzie, 30 January 1862.

[25] *Natchez Daily Courier*, 25 January 1862, 1 February 1862, 8 February 1862.

[26] *OR*, vol. 7:109.

The reaction to the defeat at Mill Springs on the part of the soldiers of the 15th Mississippi, the citizens back home, and Crittenden himself was indicative of the delusional nature of the early Confederate war effort. Just as they had denied the superiority of Northern resources, the fighting ability of the average Northern soldier, and the fact that the war effort was not actually sanctioned by God, all involved struggled to deny the defeat. The soldiers had taken part in the defeat and panicked retreat, yet the men were honor-bound to their communities and had to place the blame on other factors to maintain their psychological well-being as soldiers. The burden of representing their communities would not allow them to admit to themselves, much less to anyone else, that they had lost and run away from a fair fight. As a result, it was relatively simple for the men to include gross exaggerations in their letters back home. It was also easy for those back home to believe the letters' contents. The 15th Mississippi communities could not tolerate the thought that community sons might act in a dishonorable way. Such an admission would dishonor the soldiers and the communities themselves. By highlighting the large number of casualties from the 15th Mississippi in his report, Crittenden won praise for the regiment but also discounted the cold, hard reality that losing less men than the enemy is one of the primary goals of warfare. Had all of the regiments under Crittenden's command fought with the same "discipline and courage" and sustained as many casualties, his entire force might have been wiped out.

The Battle of Mill Springs was a disaster for the Confederacy. With the defeat, the right wing of the Southern defense line collapsed. A joint land-water invasion led by Ulysses S. Grant and Andrew Foote resulted in the fall of Fort Henry of 6 February. Fort Donelson fell ten days later. Outflanked, the Confederates abandoned Kentucky and much of Tennessee in hopes of constructing a second line of defense at points further south. Though subsequent events overshadowed its importance, the loss at Mill Springs was a significant Confederate setback.

The battle also ended the grumbling in the ranks of the 15th Mississippi from soldiers anxious to see combat. The men emerged from the fight as combat veterans and first-hand witnesses of the consequences of war. After a relatively small battle, one in five of the farm boys who left Mississippi less than a year earlier was dead or wounded. Their battle flags, carefully sewn by the women of their communities and presented to each company with such fanfare, were gone. The regiment's first brigade commander was dead, and many still suffered from a variety of maladies as a result of an inadequate diet and exposure to the elements. While they did not realize it at the time, the war had barely begun. "I said I did not believe the Yankees would fight if they had the chance," one soldier wrote soon after the Battle of Mill Springs, "but I retract. They will."[27]

---

[27] Charles Frierson, letter to Parents, 28 January 1862.

CHAPTER 4

SHILOH, 1862

Now my mind is agitated, and as I think of what I have seen today visions dark and bloody float before my eyes.[1]
Augustus H. Mecklin, Company I, 15th Mississippi Infantry,
6 April 1862

As the winter of 1861–1862 ended, the Confederate West was in disarray. Following the setbacks at Mill Springs, Fort Henry, and Fort Donelson, Union General Samuel R. Curtis defeated Earl Van Dorn's command at Pea Ridge, Arkansas, in early March. The Confederate defense line in Kentucky collapsed for good as Albert Sidney Johnston abandoned its center at Bowling Green, falling back through Tennessee. With Kentucky and much of Tennessee gone, the Confederates scrambled to establish a new line of defense and to protect one of the most strategically important points on the Southern map.[2]

In 1862 Corinth, Mississippi, had a population of about 2,000. With the collapse of Southern defenses in Kentucky, however, holding the northeast Mississippi town became crucial. Corinth was a major railroad center. The Mobile and Ohio Railroad ran north-south through the settlement, and the Memphis and Charleston—called by many the "vertebrae of the Confederacy"—ran east-west. Johnston eventually concentrated his army around Corinth and put out the call for more troops. Soldiers from various locations throughout the South answered the summons, and by late March Johnston's army numbered about

---

[1] Augustus Hervey Mecklin Papers, Mississippi Department of Archives and History Library, Jackson, Mississippi.

[2] James Lee McDonough, *Shiloh—in Hell before Night* (Knoxville: The University of Tennessee Press, 1977) 6–7.

40,000. Meanwhile, after his victory at Fort Donelson, Grant moved freely through Tennessee, finally halting at Pittsburg Landing, where he went into camp with around 42,000 men. He planned to wait there for the arrival of Don Carlos Buell's 20,000-man Army of the Ohio. The combined Union force would then move south, attempt to capture Corinth, and, if successful, plunge into the heart of Mississippi, dealing the Southern rebellion a mortal blow.[3]

The 15th Mississippi was among Johnston's force around Corinth. Following the Battle of Mill Springs the defeated Confederates moved first through Monticello, Kentucky, and then "continued [their] weary march footsore and sad hearted, weary and hungry" into Tennessee without wagons, horses, or supplies. One soldier wrote that the withdrawal, "as it stretched along the road, looked like a great funeral procession." After living on little more than a handful of cornbread per day for almost a week, the retreating Confederates arrived at Carthage, Tennessee, on the Cumberland. A supply boat met them there, and the soldiers enjoyed their first significant meal since fleeing the Mill Springs battlefield.[4]

The 15th Mississippi remained at Carthage for about a month, during which time the men slowly recovered from their first battle. Though the regiment was nominally resupplied, provisions ran low. Immediately after their arrival the Confederates set up a crude hospital. "This hospital is an affair hastily gotten up," one ailing soldier recorded in his diary. "Two meals a day and they not fit to eat. Soup for the sick that a hog would hardly eat. Raw salty pickled pork and hotcakes that are enough to make a man sick." Conditions improved somewhat during the second week of February when the local Ladies Aid Society took an active interest in the army's welfare. The women cooked for the men in the camp and served as nurses in the hospital. One surprised but grateful soldier from the 15th Mississippi reported, "The ladies make arrangements to do all our cooking.... This is better than we have reason

---

[3] Ibid.; Thomas L. Livermore, *Numbers and Losses in the Civil War in America: 1861–1865* (Bloomington: Indiana University Press, 1957) 79–80.

[4] James R. Binford, "Recollections of the Fifteenth Mississippi Infantry, CSA," Patrick Henry Papers, Mississippi Department of Archives and History Library, Jackson, Mississippi, 21; "16th Alabama Infantry," regimental history files, Alabama Department of Archives and History Library, Montgomery, Alabama.

to expect. We shall ever cherish in our hearts the memory of these noble ladies."[5]

While the society took care of many of the camp necessities, it could do little to boost morale among the men of the 15th Mississippi, particularly after word of the fall of Fort Donelson reached the area on 18 February. "Many long faces in Carthage," one soldier from Company I wrote. "Our boys scarcely moved all evening. I never saw them so completely down." During the stay at Carthage several members died in the hospital, some from disease and others from wounds they received at Mill Springs. Those men with debilitating wounds received discharges to go home, while T. J. Belcher of Company F deserted, quietly slipping out of camp one night as his comrades slept.[6]

Despite their circumstances, many of the men looked to the future. On 19 February officers from the 15th Mississippi and 20th Tennessee signed a joint letter to Confederate president Jefferson Davis. In it they requested "that these two regiments continue to serve together" and further informed the president that "this would be highly gratifying to these two regiments."[7] At Mill Springs the 15th Mississippi had seen men die, and they had seen men break and run for their lives. They left the battlefield deflated, with the knowledge that success depended on cooperation with other units. While many of the soldiers from the 15th Mississippi blamed the 19th and 25th Tennessee regiments for the defeat, the shared experience of combat bonded the Mississippians with the men of the 20th Tennessee. Shoulder to shoulder the two regiments had led the fight against the Federals, and they had been the last Confederate regiments to abandon the battlefield. This subtly altered the nature of the ties that bound the men of the 15th Mississippi together. Under fire, military considerations were paramount, and the Mississippians were now willing to place their complete trust in strangers from a "foreign" unit. While their self-perception as defenders of their homes remained intact, the men of the 15th Mississippi had developed a greater awareness of their place in a much larger military enterprise.

---

[5] Augustus Hervey Mecklin diary, 13–16 February 1862, Augustus Hervey Mecklin Papers.

[6] Ibid., 17 February–6 March 1862.

[7] Official Records, 15th Mississippi Infantry, CSA, Mississippi Department of Archives and History Library, Jackson, Mississippi. Cited afterwards as Official Records, 15th Mississippi Infantry.

Leaving Carthage on 25 February, the 15th Mississippi and the rest of the Confederate force moved west to Lebanon and then south through Murfreesboro, finally arriving at Athens, Alabama, on 10 March. The men remained in low spirits, and at times it seemed as if Mother Nature had declared war on their army. "It rained hard all night, raining this morning," one soldier wrote while at Athens. "The wagons all [in] mud before they reach the road. We have a great deal of pulling and hauling and swearing." After a particularly grueling day another man turned his frustrations on the officers corps when he angrily complained, "It does look to me that our field officers do not consider the welfare of their men as they should." Despite a constant battle against the elements, the Confederates marched south toward Decatur, wading creeks along the way. According to one soldier, "The rain was falling all the time and our blankets felt like they weighed fifty pounds. For the remainder of the march we lost all regard for mud and water. We walked through every pool and waded every pond that came our way."[8] The men reached Decatur on 13 March, then moved by rail to Iuka, Mississippi, and finally to Burnsville, a few miles from Corinth, where the 15th Mississippi became part of Johnston's army.

Once in camp, many of the men of the 15th Mississippi again grew anxious, speculating as to what was about to occur. "I know not definitely why we have come to this place," Francis Aldridge wrote to his wife on 26 March. "The impression must be that the main force of the Federals will attack in the vicinity of Corinth.... I presume a fight is inevitable on this line and I have a fixed belief that we shall be victorious." On the night of 3 April, Augustus Mecklin scribbled in his journal, "I know nothing of the intention of the enemy, or of our army. But from all preparations it is evident to my view that a great battle is pending."[9] Mecklin would live to see the great battle's outcome. Aldridge would not.

As a result of events at Mill Springs, several significant command changes took place within the 15th Mississippi and the brigade to which it was attached. Statham regained his health, and Confederate authorities gave him command of Zollicoffer's old brigade. Walthall left the 15th

---

[8] Augustus Hervey Mecklin diary, 12–13 March 1862.

[9] Augustus Hervey Mecklin Papers; F. M. Aldridge, letter to Lizzie, 26 March 1862, Francis Marion Aldridge Papers, Mississippi Department of Archives and History Library, Jackson, Mississippi.

Mississippi after being summoned to Richmond. While the battle was lost, reports of the position of the regiment at the center of the fight at Mill Springs earned its acting commander much praise. Walthall eventually received his own command and a promotion to brigadier general. After Statham's promotion to the head of the brigade, command of the 15th Mississippi fell to Choctaw County lawyer William F. Brantley of Company D.[10]

Upon reaching the vicinity of Corinth, Statham's brigade joined Brigadier General John C. Breckinridge's Reserve Corps in Albert Sidney Johnston's Army of the Mississippi. In addition to the 15th Mississippi under Brantley, Statham's brigade was reorganized to include the 22nd Mississippi, the 19th, 20th, 28th, and 45th Tennessee, and Rutledge's Tennessee battery. The total strength of Statham's brigade was around 3,700 men.[11]

By early April the Confederate high command in Richmond was desperate to stop the Federal advance in the West. After studying reconnaissance reports of Grant's and Buell's movements, Jefferson Davis instructed Johnston to move quickly against the Union forces. Davis and his military advisors, including Robert E. Lee, believed that if Buell successfully united with Grant, their combined force would be difficult to fend off. "If you can meet the division of the enemy before it can make a juncture," Davis wrote in his dispatch, "the future will be brighter. If this cannot be done, our only hope is that the people of the Southwest will rally en masse...to oppose the vast army which will threaten the destruction of our country."[12]

With his object clearly defined, Johnston ordered his army north to face Grant. Three corps, commanded respectively by Major General Leonidas Polk, Major General Braxton Bragg, and Major General William J. Hardee, left Corinth on the afternoon of 3 April. Breckinridge's corps, including the 15th Mississippi in Statham's brigade, followed from Burnsville the next day. The approach was difficult. The Confederates advanced over ground that was heavily

---

[10] Binford, "Recollections," 23; Dunbar Rowland, *Military History of Mississippi 1803–1898* (Spartanburg SC: The Reprint Company, 1988) 229.

[11] McDonough, *Shiloh—in Hell before Night*, 246–47; David G. Martin, *The Shiloh Campaign, March–April, 1862* (Conshohocken PA: Combined Books, 1996) 231.

[12] Wiley Sword, *Shiloh: Bloody April* (New York: William Morrow and Co., 1974) 91.

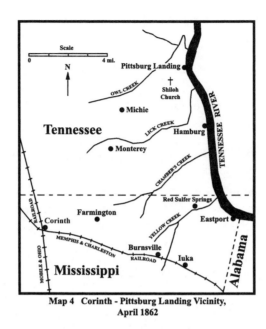

**Map 4   Corinth - Pittsburg Landing Vicinity,
April 1862**

wooded and broken by creeks, ravines, swamps, and a confusing network of simple dirt roads. Breckinridge's corps was delayed temporarily after the artillery bogged down in mud. By 5 April most of the Confederate army was camped near Pittsburg Landing, where Johnston announced that the attack on Grant would commence the next morning at daybreak.[13]

On the evening of 5 April 1862 the men of the 15th Mississippi Infantry faced the prospect of yet another uncomfortable night's sleep. Their accommodations were meager. Many of the men slept on blankets on the bare ground, using cartridge boxes for pillows. Tired from the ponderous march north, the regiment retired and the night passed quickly. The men rose the next morning to a clear sky and a hasty breakfast.[14] They knew a major engagement was likely but, despite their experience at Mill Springs, still had no frame of reference with which to gauge warfare's true ferocity. Within distant earshot of the Confederate army to which the 15th Mississippi was attached, Grant's soldiers also greeted the new day. Their camp was on the western side of the

---

[13] McDonough, *Shiloh—in Hell before Night*, 76–81.

[14] Augustus Hervey Mecklin Papers.

Tennessee River near a small Methodist meeting house that would ultimately give the day's events a name. The church was called Shiloh.

The Battle of Shiloh was among the first major bloodbaths of the Civil War. During the two-day fight on 6–7 April 1862, Shiloh produced more casualties than all prior American wars combined. Around 13,000 Union troops fell, along with a like number of Confederates. It was a savage, confused battle, involving many men who were barely soldiers and who had never discharged a weapon at anything capable of returning fire. For the North, Shiloh made it evident that the Federal army would not easily defeat the Confederates. For the South, it served painful notice that long-winded rhetoric about ideals and honor had little effect in the face of rifles, cannons, and bayonets. After the battle it was apparent to all that the Civil War would be an exceedingly bloody affair driven by resources, casualty counts, and the collective will of the participants. "Up to the battle of Shiloh," Grant later wrote, "I, as well as thousands of other citizens, believed that the rebellion against the government would collapse suddenly and soon if a decisive victory could be gained over any of its armies . . . but [afterwards] I gave up all ideas of saving the Union except by complete conquest."[15]

On the morning of 6 April, as Grant waited for Buell's arrival, Johnston attacked. Although Grant and his subordinate commanders knew that Johnston's army was close by, the Confederates caught the Union army by surprise and eventually overran the Federal positions. After several hours of particularly fierce combat near the center of a 3-mile front—a spot known as the "Hornet's Nest"—the Southerners retired, holding the field.

As part of the Reserve Corps, the 15th Mississippi was not engaged on the first day until the battle was well under way. Around noon, Breckinridge's corps began assembling on the right for an attack. As the men of the 15th Mississippi approached the battlefield, they could hear the roar of artillery and small arms fire up ahead, and they passed over ground that had been heavily contested earlier in the day. "We passed several wounded men and occasionally whole squads of wounded Yankees," one soldier wrote immediately following the battle. "Soon we were on the battlefield, here and there we saw the bodies of dead men, friend and foe alike, lying together. Some torn to mince meat by cannon

---

[15] Livermore, *Numbers and Losses*, 79–80; Ulysses Simpson Grant, *Personal Memoirs of U. S. Grant* (Mineola NY: Dover Publications, 1995) 142–43.

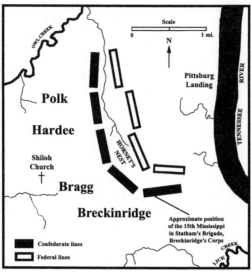

Map 5   Shiloh Battlefield, April 6, 1862

balls. Some still writhing in the agonies of death…on all sides lay the dead and dying."[16]

The men advanced and then paused temporarily in the midst of one of the old Yankee camps to wait for orders. A mixture of trepidation and excitement gripped the ranks. Surrounded by tents, smoldering campfires, and tables of food that offered evidence of a hasty Federal withdrawal, some of the men began to pray. Others were anxious to get into the fight, while still others would probably have turned and run had they had the opportunity. As they stood at ease the men heard reports of Confederate victory. At one point Johnston passed by on horseback, and the men "greeted his appearance by deafening cheers."[17] At about two o'clock the men of the 15th Mississippi went into action. Just prior to his death, Johnston personally ordered Statham's brigade, along with brigades commanded by John S. Bowen and John R. Jackson, to strike. The men swung left and charged over an open field toward the left of the Union center. There, the enemy lay partially concealed by thick underbrush. An Iowa soldier who witnessed the charge described it as "a splendid sight.… The field officers were seen waving their hats, a shout

---

[16] Augustus Hervey Mecklin Papers.
[17] Ibid.

arose, and the brigade [Statham's] moved on magnificently." The attack was one in a series of Confederate assaults on the Hornet's Nest by various commands. Statham's, Bowen's, and Jackson's brigades swept several Federal units from the field until a counterattack slowed their efforts.[18]

As the men of the 15th Mississippi charged, they were met by "a perfect storm of shot and shell and the deadly minnies, thinning out our ranks at every discharge." The regiment had gone only a short distance when its commanding officer William Brantley fell wounded, as did Captain John J. Gage of Company G. In Company H, Federal fire killed Captain Francis Aldridge. Augustus Mecklin made the charge with neighbors and relatives from Choctaw County, including his brother. "For the first time in my life, I heard the whistle of bullets," he wrote later that night in his diary, "I was near the front and firing. Soon men were falling on all sides. Two in Company E just in front of me fell dead, shot through the brain. On my left in our own company William Wilson, William Thompson, Ben Stewart, Brother George [Mecklin] and James Boskins were wounded.... The mini balls were falling thickly around us.... Many of our boys fell in this charge. Never was there such firing."[19]

Sharp fighting continued throughout the day. The men of the 15th Mississippi were engaged for more than two hours, withdrawing just before five o'clock. While they were encouraged by Confederate success, they ended the day with full knowledge that they had driven the Federals from their original positions at a great price. As they fell back following the fight, the men of the 15th Mississippi stumbled through a litter of mangled corpses, some of whom they recognized as the remains of childhood friends or relatives. Many of the men were wounded, and all the survivors were exhausted and thirsty. Some gathered with other Confederates to drink from a tiny body of water that would become known as the Bloody Pond. Ignoring dead men and horses lying in and

---

[18] Augustus Hervey Mecklin Papers; McDonough, *Shiloh—in Hell before Night*, 133; Robert Underwood Johnson and Clarence Clough Buel, eds., vol. 1 of *Battles and Leaders of the Civil War* (New York: The Century Company, 1887) 589. Afterwards this work is cited as *Battles and Leaders*, followed by the appropriate volume and page numbers; Martin, *The Shiloh Campaign*, 127–36; Larry J. Daniel, *Shiloh: The Battle That Changed the Civil War* (New York: Simon and Schuster, 1997) 218.

[19] Augustus Hervey Mecklin Papers.

around the water, the men cupped their hands and drank in haste.[20] Soon word circulated through the ranks of the death of Albert Sidney Johnston.[21]

Following the battle, confusion reigned behind the Confederate lines. As darkness fell, so did a heavy rain, hampering efforts to reorganize the ranks. In some quarters discipline broke down completely as rebel soldiers ransacked the old Union camps. According to one soldier from the 15th Mississippi's Company F, "a mania" seized some of his comrades, "and thus began a system of straggling and plunder" by men looking for food, clothing, or anything else of value. Civilian looters who lived in the region added to the mayhem. Efforts to reorganize were further slowed by the condition of the men. Tired and wounded, most were also traumatized to one degree or another by what they had witnessed over the last few hours. "Now my mind is agitated," Mecklin recorded in his journal, "and as I think of what I have seen today visions dark and bloody float before my eyes." As the rain fell, Confederate soldiers sought cover in Federal tents that became so crowded that the men could not lie down to sleep. The sounds of rainfall, thunder, shelling from Federal gunboats on the Tennessee River, and the tortured laments of dying men left in the field echoed through the darkness. Lightning flashed, periodically illuminating the battlefield and the "dead heaped and piled upon one another." The screams and moans of wounded soldiers served as an oral testament to the savageness of the struggle. While the Confederates had gained a victory during the day, there were few celebrations during the evening.[22]

The Federals had been driven back to the river, but Buell's army arrived during the night, and suddenly the Union possessed a far superior force. By daybreak the Confederates, now commanded by Beauregard, remained disorganized and generally "fought out." First light again revealed to the men the true cost of their previous day's victory. "Wherever I turned," one survivor from the 15th Mississippi stated, "I

---

[20] Ibid.

[21] Historians continue to argue about the precise effect that Johnston's death had on the battle's outcome. Some make the case that had Johnston not died, the Confederates may have defeated the Federals decisively on the first day. Others suggest that had the general lived, the battle's outcome would not have been significantly altered.

[22] Augustus Hervey Mecklin Papers; McDonough, *Shiloh—in Hell before Night*, 184–95; Daniel, *Shiloh: The Battle That Changed the Civil War*, 262–64.

saw men pale in death, saw pale faces upturned and besmeared with mud and water, hair matted with gore." While casualty counts were incomplete, the 15th Mississippi in Statham's brigade sustained major losses during the first day's fight. With Brantley wounded and out of action, command of the regiment fell to Lampkin S. Terry of Company A.[23]

On the morning of 7 April, the reinforced Federals launched a massive counterattack, driving the weary Southerners back in confusion to their original camps and eventually into full retreat toward Corinth. As the Federals attacked, Statham's brigade advanced to meet them but soon had to abandon the fight in the face of fresh Union troops. "I saw our men falling back one by one," Mecklin later recorded. "Then I saw whole squads retreating. Soon the whole regiment was in full retreat. The retreat was a perfect rout. The men scattered in every direction. Our regiment never again formed itself." John W. Taylor of Company E wrote to his parents soon after the battle that "we was badly scattered. I never seen any of my regiment until night. I fell in with the 22 Louisiana regiment and we run till I give out. I escaped the balls but I do not know how it was for the men fell all around me."[24]

Breckinridge's corps was the last to withdraw, forming the rear guard. Casualty counts on the second day from the 15th Mississippi were incomplete, but losses were again significant. During the two-day battle the regiment probably lost around 200 men out of almost 600 engaged. Years later one survivor estimated the effective strength of the 15th Mississippi at Shiloh at about 500 men, of which almost half were casualties of the battle. Another maintained that among the 15th Mississippi, few men "escaped without a wound of some character, many of them painful and serious, and some of them were taken prisoner." Officially, Breckinridge's corps suffered 31 percent casualties while one in four of all Confederates fell during the struggle. On 8 and 9 April,

---

[23] Ibid.

[24] Augustus Hervey Mecklin Papers; John W. Taylor, letter to Father and Mother, 11 April 1862, on file at the University of North Carolina Library, Chapel Hill, North Carolina.

Union troops pitched most of the Confederate dead, including men from the 15th Mississippi, into hastily dug trenches on the battlefield.[25]

It was perhaps the last few lines of Augustus Mecklin's 7 April journal entry that were the most telling with regard to the aftermath of the battle. Admitting that the struggle of the second day was "a complete rout," he ended with the claim that "our loss was great, though not as great as the enemy. We left the enemy in possession of the field. Our men destroyed several of their campgrounds. All things compared we have gained a dearly fought victory." Mecklin's interpretation of the battle's outcome as a victory for the Confederates was consistent with one of the great flaws that plagued the Southern cause throughout the war, a tragic inability to reign in emotions in the face of stark reality. By denying defeat and claiming victory in the face of contrary evidence, many Confederates maintained the illusion in their own minds that the war could be won. Such skewed perceptions ultimately kept many soldiers fighting well after the war was probably lost. After Shiloh, the long, excruciating decay of the Confederate West began in earnest. On a given day, such as 6 April 1862, the South might win a battle, but ultimately the superior resources of the North, as was the case on 7 April 1862, were destined to carry the day. "No day in my life has been so full of stirring, terrible events as this," one soldier wrote immediately following the battle. "Never may I see another."[26]

---

[25] *Battles and Leaders*, vol. 1:593; Binford, "Recollections," 27; Yalobusha County Historical Society, *Yalobusha County History* (Dallas TX: National Share Graphics, 1982) 32–33; Sword, *Shiloh*, 461.

[26] Augustus Hervey Mecklin Papers.

CHAPTER 5

MISSISSIPPI AND LOUISIANA, 1862

Mississippi is in a critical condition at present.[1]
Richard Walpole, Company D,
15th Mississippi Infantry, December 1862

Following the Battle of Shiloh, Beauregard's tattered army limped back to Corinth. Breckinridge's men covered the rear of the retreat, and soldiers from the 15th Mississippi were among those who exchanged a few final shots with the enemy. On the night of 7 April, the regiment camped just 2 miles from the battlefield. Moving steadily but slowly south, the Confederates were within a few miles of Corinth by 10 April. According to one soldier, "The roads were wretched, almost impossible. All along the way we saw wagons mired and caissons." The 15th Mississippi finally marched into Corinth on 11 April. Weakened from the fight, the Federals did not immediately pursue following Shiloh, and it would be nearly a month before they moved again on their original objective. In the meantime, Major General Henry W. Halleck assumed from Grant command of the Union troops that had taken part in the battle.[2]

The arrival of the Confederate army transformed Corinth from a railroad center into an enormous makeshift field hospital. The Confederates set up overcrowded quarters for more than 8,000 wounded

---

[1] Richard Walpole, letter to Anna Bowman, 18 December 1862, Special Collections, Robert W. Woodruff Library, Emory University, Atlanta, Georgia.

[2] Augustus Hervey Mecklin Papers, Mississippi Department of Archives and History Library, Jackson, Mississippi; Wiley Sword, *Shiloh: Bloody April* (New York: William Morrow and Co., 1974) 464.

in churches, schools, hotels, and private homes. Doctors were in short
supply, as were the crude medical necessities of the day. The
Confederates quickly exhausted their stores of pain killers, primarily
opium and morphine, and from every corner of the town men cried out in
agony. The quickest cure for a serious bullet wound in an extremity was
amputation, a procedure that likely killed more soldiers than it saved.
Regardless, bloody tubs filled with severed limbs soon filled those
quarters set aside for the procedure.[3]

Among the wounded from the 15th Mississippi was James Binford
of Company E. On the first day at Shiloh he received a serious bayonet
wound to his thigh. That evening other soldiers placed Binford in a
wagon, jostled him over rugged terrain several miles south of the
battlefield, and finally deposited him with a number of other soldiers in a
corncrib. "I could not turn without great pain," he later recalled, "and the
ears of corn would seem to almost break my back." Binford's wound
festered as he traveled south by wagon with the rest of the army. At
Corinth a hospital detail placed him in a tent, where after some time an
overworked Confederate physician appeared and administered hurried
medical care. According to the wounded man, "A surgeon came in [and]
looked at my wound, which was now much inflamed and gaped open in
the shape of a three-cornered bayonet, so the bone could almost be seen.
He poured some turpentine in the wound and bandaged it." The doctor
then rushed Binford to recover in a boxcar lined with blood-soaked hay.
Compared to many of his comrades, Binford was lucky in that he lost
neither his leg nor his life.[4]

At Corinth, Beauregard called in soldiers from around the South and
assembled an army numbering approximately 80,000. The men,
however, suffered greatly from a lack of proper sanitation. At any given
time almost 25 percent of the Confederates assembled around the town
were sick, and the "pestilential air and unwholesome water of that
swamp-surrounded village" left few men unaffected. During this period
one soldier from the 15th Mississippi reported, "Some of our sick were
sent off today. [I] saw a great many wagons loaded with them. Judging

---

[3] James Lee McDonough, *Shiloh—in Hell before Night* (Knoxville: The University
of Tennessee Press, 1977) 214.

[4] James R. Binford, "Recollections of the Fifteenth Mississippi Infantry, CSA,"
Patrick Henry Papers, Mississippi Department of Archives and History Library, Jackson,
Mississippi, 25–28.

from all appearances there must be a great deal of sickness in camp." In short, although Beauregard managed to assemble a significant army in the weeks following Shiloh, it was not necessarily a battle-ready force.[5]

While at Corinth the original one-year enlistments for the men of the 15th Mississippi drew to a close, but their service to the Confederacy would not end. On 16 April, Jefferson Davis approved an act for the conscription of every able-bodied white male between the ages of eighteen and thirty-five for three years' service. This mandate by the Richmond government caused great controversy in the South, where many viewed it as a grievous violation of individual rights and of states' rights principles that had been the rhetorical foundation for secession. From a practical standpoint the act obligated most of the men of the 15th Mississippi to an additional two years in the Confederate army. This was unwelcome news to volunteer soldiers less than two weeks removed from Shiloh. "The passage of the 'conscript act' confirmed," Augustus Mecklin recorded in his journal on 19 April. "Quite a sensation in camp. Many of the boys talking bitterly against it as an arbitrary use of power.... We are doomed men two years longer."[6]

While the Conscription Act forced most of the men of the 15th Mississippi into additional service, it gave some soldiers a legal device to exit the Confederate army. The law contained a number of exemptions, including minimum and maximum age requirements and for federal and state officials, ministers, schoolteachers, iron-furnace laborers, foundry laborers, and railroad workers.[7] Because they were primarily farmers, most of the men in the 15th Mississippi did not meet the exemption requirements. However, a few members of the regiment received discharges soon after the law went into effect. Several teenagers received discharges, as did a number of older men. A. G. Noah of Company A had his name placed on the ballot for sheriff in Attala County, won the election, and left the army to return home and take office. Some loopholes in the act favored the wealthy. Men could avoid the army by hiring a substitute, and the so-called "twenty-negro provision" in the law exempted major slaveholders. However, few soldiers from the 15th

---

[5] John G. Biel, "The Evacuation of Corinth," *Journal of Mississippi History* 24/24 (Spring 1962): 43; Augustus Hervey Mecklin Papers.

[6] Augustus Hervey Mecklin Papers.

[7] Emory M. Thomas, *The Confederate Nation: 1861–1865* (New York: Harper & Row, 1979) 152–53.

Mississippi were wealthy enough to use these avenues to escape further service. The day after he heard of the passage of the Conscription Act, one soldier wrote, "If there is any chance to procure a discharge, I shall endeavor to obtain it."[8]

After passage of the Conscription Act, the 15th Mississippi was reorganized, and the men again chose Statham to command the regiment as colonel and elected Michael Farrell of Company E lieutenant colonel. James Binford, recovering from his wound, was elected major, and his brother John was elected adjutant. J. T. Lay (commissary), B. J. Dudley (quartermaster), John Wright (surgeon), and T. R. Trotter (assistant surgeon) filled other regimental posts.[9]

The tenuous nature of command within a Confederate regiment was reflected in the fact that after a single year of service most of the original company captains of the 15th Mississippi Infantry were gone. Only Lampkin Terry of Company A retained his position at the head of his company:

15th Mississippi Infantry
Company Command Changes (1861–1862)

Co.	Captain, May 1861	Status	Captain, May 1862
A	Lampkin S. Terry	re-elected	Lampkin S. Terry
B	Thomas J. Booth	wounded at Mill Springs	Hugh O. Freeman
C	James W. Wade	resigned, physically unfit	Patrick H. Norton
D	William F. Brantley	promoted, wounded at Shiloh	A. W. Middleton
E	Edgar Sykes	resigned to join another unit	J. F. Smith
F	Burrell H. Collins	resigned due to ill health	Harry Patton
G	Walter S. Statham	promoted	Jonah Drummond
H	Francis M. Aldridge	killed at Shiloh	Wm. M. Reasons
I	J. W. Hemphill	resigned, personal reasons	Russell G. Prewitt
K	Thomas Foard	resigned due to ill health	M. W. Rose[10]

---

[8] Compiled Service Records of Confederate Soldiers who served in Organizations from the State of Mississippi: 15th Mississippi Infantry, Mississippi Department of Archives and History Library, Jackson, Mississippi, microfilm. Cited afterwards as Compiled Service Records: 15th Mississippi Infantry; Augustus Hervey Mecklin Papers.

[9] Binford, "Recollections," 28–29; Dunbar Rowland, *Military History of Mississippi 1803–1898* (Spartenburg SC: The Reprint Company, 1988) 229–30; Compiled Service Records: 15th Mississippi Infantry.

[10] Binford, "Recollections," 28-29.

Following regimental elections, Statham again received an appointment to brigade commander. Upon Statham's promotion, command of the 15th Mississippi passed to Michael Farrell. Farrell was an Irish immigrant whose booming voice and thick accent were a source of both amusement and respect among the men under his command. A brickmason by trade, he had served in the US Army and was stationed in St. Louis before moving to Yalobusha County a few months before the beginning of the war. His actual army experience set him apart from his comrades, as did his behavior under fire. One soldier from Company E wrote home soon after Shiloh, "Capt. M. Farrell was with our company throughout the fight and conducted himself most nobly and best of all he did not get hurt. He showed himself to be among the best officers in the field." At one point during the battle, Farrell personally halted a group of retreating Confederates at gunpoint, threatening to shoot the next man who took another step. James Binford called him "a brave and impulsive Irishman," adding, "I have never seen his equal as a drill officer." Another soldier from the 15th Mississippi described Farrell as "a full blooded Irishman…six feet tall with dark blue eyes and strait black hair, as strait in his athletic frame as an Indian, and retaining that brogue peculiar to his nationality."[11]

While most of the men united behind Farrell, the regimental elections caused bitterness in some quarters. The proceedings particularly upset William Collins of Company C. Like Farrell, Collins was one of a handful of Irish immigrants in the regiment, having come to the United States in August of 1860 and settling at Richland in Holmes County. Respected by his fellow soldiers, Collins later replaced James Wade as company captain. After he lost the election for regimental commander to Statham during the reorganization, he requested and received a transfer to another unit, claiming that he was the victim of prejudice. According to Collins, his Irish descent and "the littleness that resides in the breasts of some men who cannot see how anything good, virtuous, or worthy of honor could come from that dark, desolate and

---

[11] Ibid., 2, 27–29; Augustus, letter to T. J. Edmondson, 9 April 1862, Gladys Boyette papers, Kosciusko, Mississippi, copy in possession of the author. Although Augustus's last name is not given in the letter, the contents of the letter confirm that he was a member of Company E; John L. Collins, "Gallant Mike Farrell," *Confederate Veteran* 34/10 (October 1926): 372.

downtrodden land that gave me birth" caused his defeat.[12] In reality, the men of the 15th Mississippi held little prejudice against the Irish in their ranks, as Farrell's election as lieutenant colonel and Collins' own election to company posts proved.

In the year since the 15th Mississippi entered Confederate service the character of the regiment had changed dramatically. The men had participated in two battles. The deaths of friends and relatives had proven that the soldiers had entered the service under a host of false and fatal misconceptions. Northern men would indeed fight and kill if pressed, and the war was turning into a protracted struggle that would keep survivors away from their homes for an extended period of time. The dangers of war had become painfully clear to the men as they came face to face with their own mortality. With each passing day Federal armies crept closer to their home counties, and supplies were becoming more difficult to come by. The Southern volunteers of 1776 had emerged victorious from their struggle, and their exploits had passed into legend, but for the men of the 15th Mississippi Infantry the revolution of 1861 was not going as planned.

The nature of the war also changed the nature of the men's service. They were no longer volunteers charged with protecting their communities. The Conscription Act forced the men into longer service and at the same time allowed a lucky few to escape. Their service was originally a local enterprise, but the men were now part of the Confederate mission to protect all the Southern states as a single political entity. They had become what they were fighting to avoid, slaves to the commands of officers they did not know and dependent on the actions of men from other parts of the country. The original community commitment could no longer be practically applied. For many of the men their new situation fostered second thoughts with regard to their service and to the war effort in general. Soon after his arrival at Corinth, one Choctaw County soldier stated, "I have said that I wished to escape all participation in another battle. I never want to fire another gun at a human being." In Company I, Augustus Mecklin began having doubts about the "divine" nature of the Confederate crusade. "A few leading characters have been the chief instigators of this war," he wrote during

---

[12] Compiled Service Records: 15th Mississippi Infantry.

the period. "The more I see of this war, the more fully satisfied am I that there is not religion about it."[13]

Growing dissatisfaction in the ranks affected desertion rates in the army. After Shiloh many of the men believed that they had done their share for the Southern rebellion. Their units had been organized as local undertakings, and many refused to accept the concept of Confederate nationalism as a reason to continue fighting. As a result, some soldiers responded to their condition by walking away. During the week before Shiloh, Johnston's army reported 1,334 enlisted men absent without leave. After the battle that number quickly doubled to almost 2,700, or roughly 5 percent of the total. Like the rest of the army, the 15th Mississippi experienced its first significant rash of desertions following Shiloh. Whereas the regiment lost less than five men to desertion in the nine months prior to the battle, fifteen men disappeared during the two-month period following passage of the Conscription Act. Many who remained with the regiment still considered themselves honor-bound to do their duty, but they no longer held visions of the war as an idealized adventure. Other soldiers felt trapped. "We are bound to re-enlist in our old regiment or be sent elsewhere," a 15th Mississippi private wrote. "I am desirous to escape, but do not know how."[14]

Command changes within the regiment also reflected the erosion of the 15th Mississippi as a community enterprise. While some company officers were retained, in 1862 several companies elected men who had gained the confidence of their peers during battle. These elections broke down the original community hierarchies within the individual companies. The men now recognized the war as a literal matter of life and death and placed their confidence in those who seemed to perform well under fire. Local, class-based political considerations carried little weight in the face of Yankee bullets and bayonets. Farrell's election to command the 15th Mississippi bore this point. The Irishman was one of the few military veterans in the regiment. He had only recently moved to Yalobusha County. He was not wealthy and had no long-standing ties to his company's community. As the men elected officers at Corinth in 1861 Farrell was not even considered as a candidate for regimental

---

[13] Ibid.; Augustus Mecklin diary, 26 May 1862, Augustus Hervey Mecklin Papers.

[14] Larry J. Daniel, *Soldiering in the Army of Tennessee* (Chapel Hill: The University of North Carolina Press, 1991) 127–29; Compiled Service Records: 15th Mississippi Infantry; Augustus Mecklin diary, 22 April 1862.

command positions because he lacked the appropriate social and political connections. At Corinth in 1862, however, he possessed the primary qualities that the men were looking for. He was tough, cool under fire, and his conduct on the battlefield inspired trust.

As the Confederates waited at Corinth, Union general Henry W. Halleck assembled a force of about 120,000 men in the vicinity of Pittsburg Landing and on 30 April 1862 began a slow advance toward the town. Plagued by bad weather and disease problems of their own, the Federals took almost a month to cover 30 miles. Meanwhile, Beauregard took advantage of the slow approach to strengthen his defenses, flanking Corinth with a semicircle of entrenchments. The Confederates twice sent out detachments to skirmish with Union pickets, but they accomplished little.

The Confederates would remain at Corinth for more than a month. The men drilled from time to time, but little took place inside the town's defenses. "Nothing of interest transpired today," one soldier from the 15th Mississippi wrote. "This day has passed as many others in camp. Men lying around asleep, some talking idly. Others engaged in card playing. Do nothing is the order of the day." In some quarters inactivity bred discontent and a fair amount of grumbling among the soldiers. Minor quarrels between the men occasionally led to fist fights and a night in the stockade for the combatants. Some of the enlisted men blamed their dismal situation on the officer corps. One frustrated soldier complained, "I have had occasion to observe the neglect of our officers to discharge their duties.... How could our men do their duty on the field of battle under such circumstances?" On 19 May, the 15th Mississippi received 100 new recruits into its ranks, providing momentary entertainment for some of the regiment's battle-tested veterans. Augustus Mecklin in particular found it "quite amusing to hear them talk. They can easily be distinguished from the old, experienced soldiers by their remarks and observations upon things they see around them."[15]

By 25 May, Halleck was establishing a 5-mile battle line facing Corinth, complete with siege guns, and sporadic firing began around the town's perimeter. That same day Beauregard called together his subordinate commanders to discuss the prospect of abandoning the town. The need to evacuate Corinth in the face of a significantly larger and

---

[15] Augustus Mecklin diary, 19 May 1862.

better-equipped Union army was apparent to everyone, and that evening Beauregard issued the necessary orders.[16]

The Confederates conducted the four-day evacuation with considerable skill and under the utmost secrecy. As some troops moved south, Beauregard ordered others to the front as if he planned to move on Federal positions. Supplies moved south via the railroad. During the evenings, as empty trains returned to Corinth for reloading, Confederate commanders ordered their men to cheer loudly as if the cars carried reinforcements. At one point during the evacuation, Brigadier General John Pope sent word to Halleck: "The enemy are reinforcing heavily in my front and on the left. The cars are running constantly, and the cheering is immense every time that they unload in front of me. I have no doubt that I shall be attacked in heavy force by daylight." The Federals were completely deceived. By dawn on 30 May the entire Confederate force, with the exception of some cavalry, had withdrawn. The Federals briefly pursued Beauregard's retreating army before Halleck settled in Corinth and became "engaged in the congenial business of reorganizing and disciplining" his troops.[17]

The 15th Mississippi left Corinth on 28 May, and by nightfall the regiment was camped a few miles south of the town. They rested there the next day until orders came to move out again. While the weather was dry, problems with broken wagons slowed the withdrawal. The regiment traveled through the night and most of the next day, when the weather turned hot. According to one soldier, "This retreat is scarcely less disastrous than the one from Mill Springs. The men are somewhat better supplied with food, but here it is so much warmer that they cannot stand it." As they marched the troops became more dejected. Soon after the evacuation, John W. Taylor of Company E reported to his parents in Carroll County, "I have seen hard times since I left home." A number of Confederates deserted, including at least eight from the 15th Mississippi, who simply "left the regiment, and no one could say where they were."[18]

---

[16] Sword, *Shiloh*, 436; Biel, "The Evacuation of Corinth," 44.

[17] Sword, *Shiloh*, 436; Biel, "The Evacuation of Corinth," 44; Robert Underwood Johnson and Clarence Clough Buel, eds., vol. 2 of *Battles and Leaders of the Civil War* (New York: The Century Company, 1887) 720. Afterwards this work is cited as *Battles and Leaders*, followed by the appropriate volume and page numbers.

[18] Augustus Hervey Mecklin Papers.

The fall of Corinth further destabilized the Confederate West. To make matters worse for the Southerners, as they evacuated the northeast Mississippi railroad center, the Union navy, under the command of Admiral David G. Farragut, steamed up the Mississippi River. The Federals had captured New Orleans in late April, and soon after Baton Rouge and Natchez surrendered. By late June the Union fleet threatened Vicksburg, the most coveted point along the river. Strategists on both sides knew that the capture of Vicksburg would split the Confederacy, disrupt Southern supply lines, and allow Federal ships safe passage up and down the river. As early as November of 1861 Lincoln had stated emphatically, "Vicksburg is the key. The war can never be brought to a close until that key is in our pocket." As Farragut's ships approached during the summer of 1862, however, the city was well fortified and defiant. In response to demands for surrender, Confederate leaders in Vicksburg sent word that "Mississippians don't know, and refuse to learn, how to surrender.... If Commodore Farragut...can teach them, let [him] come try."[19]

As a result of these events, the activities of the 15th Mississippi shifted west. Following the evacuation of Corinth, the regiment camped at Tupelo for several days and then moved northwest to Holly Springs. As Farragut moved up the river, Breckinridge's division, to which the 15th Mississippi in Statham's brigade remained attached, was ordered to Vicksburg, where it became part of a 10,000-man force commanded by Major General Earl Van Dorn. At the time Van Dorn was in charge of the district of Mississippi lying along the eastern bank of the Mississippi River.[20]

Although they held New Orleans, Baton Rouge, and Natchez, the Federals would have to wait another year for Vicksburg. Farragut moved his ships into position and as the end of June approached began shelling the city. Vicksburg rested on a 200-foot bluff, however, and the batteries that defended the city opened fire and would not be silenced. With each passing day it became more apparent to Farragut that his attempt to capture Vicksburg was ill-timed. Trading blows with the Confederate guns accomplished little, and Union commanders deemed an infantry assault from the river without support from a significant land-based force

---

[19] James M. McPherson, *Battle Cry of Freedom: The Civil War Era* (New York: Ballantine Books, 1988) 420–21.

[20] Binford, "Recollections," 29; *Battles and Leaders*, vol. 2:275.

suicidal. In addition, due to a summer drought, the Mississippi dropped several inches each day and soon threatened to strand several of Farragut's deep-draft vessels.[21]

Map 6   Mississippi - Louisiana, 1862

The men of the 15th Mississippi were in position to watch these events unfold. For more than two weeks they camped on the bluffs at Vicksburg and periodically did sniper duty in the woods along the river. Soldiers from the regiment were among a group of about 200 Confederates sent on an unsuccessful mission to harass the Federal fleet from just below the city. The men set out one evening at dusk, and in trying to gain advantageous positions along the shore most of the soldiers became hopelessly lost. The area below Vicksburg was swampy, and the men had to move through a "mass of tangled vines, swamp grass, timber...lakes, sloughs and marshes." According to one participant,

[21] McPherson, *Battle Cry of Freedom*, 420–21.

"Where we struck the swamp with its dense timber clad with vines and festooned with long moss, the darkness grew into inky blackness so that one could not see his file leader.... We floundered in mud and darkness all night long." The group finally gave up the mission, straggling back into camp on the bluffs just before sunrise.[22]

Toward the middle of July the Federals gave up their initial attempt to capture Vicksburg, but not before the Confederates delivered a parting blow from upstream. On 15 July, the *Arkansas*, an ironclad constructed above Vicksburg on the Yazoo River, steamed down and harassed the Federal fleet. To one 15th Mississippi private who watched the unusual craft approach, the *Arkansas* "seemed more like a monster turtle swimming along down the river than a gunboat." As it neared Vicksburg the ironclad crippled the *Carondelet*, forcing the ship to run ashore. It then moved in among the Federal fleet and began "firing rapidly at every point on the circumference." Recovering from the surprise of such a bold action, the Union navy fired on the *Arkansas*, inflicting heavy damage. "A flash of a report," one witness to the Federal barrage later wrote, "and then another and another. Now all joined the chorus, making the very earth tremble for miles around by the rapid explosions of the huge guns. Everything was dire and confused. We could not discern friend from foe for a while." Despite the massive counterattack, the Confederate ship was still able to sink a Federal ram before finally drifting into port under the protection of the Vicksburg guns. Thousands of Confederate soldiers and citizens who witnessed the spectacle from the heights greeted the *Arkansas* with cheers. Louis P. Carr of the 15th Mississippi's Company F later remembered the exchange on the river as "the grandest sight I ever saw.... [The *Arkansas*] was among the Yankee fleet giving broadside after broadside." After inspecting the battered ironclad the following day, another soldier from the regiment observed that "numerous shots and pieces of shell could be seen on all sides of the vessel where they had wedged themselves in between bars of iron in their vain attempt to penetrate her armor.... Her smoke stack was literally

---

[22] Unknown Author, "History of the Water Valley Rifles, Company F, Fifteenth Mississippi Infantry," Supplement to the WPA Historical Research Project, Yalobusha County, 16 February 1937, Special Collections, J. D. Williams Library, University of Mississippi, Oxford, Mississippi, 31–33. Afterwards cited as "History of the Water Valley Rifles."

riddled by the enemy's grape and canister." Soon after the battle with the *Arkansas*, the Federals withdrew.[23]

During the summer of 1862 the Confederates were able to drive Farragut away from Vicksburg, but they were powerless to impede the progress of their deadliest enemy—disease. Dysentery and a variety of maladies placed under the broad medical heading of "fever" plagued the Confederate camp. According to James Binford, the routine of the men of the 15th Mississippi while at Vicksburg included "drinking stagnant water and fighting huge mosquitoes" in heat that sometimes reached 100 degrees. "We had recruited our ranks with convalescent sick and wounded and new recruits and numbered around 500," he later wrote, "but soon the men began to fall as victims to the deadly malaria until many were prostrated." No one was immune. Among men from the 15th Mississippi both Statham and Farrell fell desperately ill. Farrell would recover, but on 27 July 1862, just days before he was to receive a promotion to brigadier general, Statham died of what official reports described simply as "a hot fever." His body was sent back to Grenada for burial.[24]

In Farrell's absence, Binford assumed command of the 15th Mississippi Infantry and held that position when the regiment was ordered to Baton Rouge with the rest of Breckinridge's division in late July. Buoyed by the successful defense of Vicksburg, the Confederates hoped to attack and defeat the Federal garrison there and reclaim another vital point along the river. The trip was difficult. About 250 men from the 15th Mississippi were healthy enough to make the march into

---

[23] "History of the Water Valley Rifles," 31–34; Richard Wheeler, *The Siege of Vicksburg* (New York: Thomas Y. Crowell Co., 1978) 58–64; Veterans' Survey, Louis P. Carr, 1902, Official Records, 15th Mississippi Infantry, CSA, Mississippi Department of Archives and History Library, Jackson, Mississippi. Cited afterwards as Official Records, 15th Mississippi Infantry.

[24] US War Department, comp., *The War of Rebellion: A Compilation of the Official Records of the Union and Confederate Armies*, 128 vols. (Washington, DC: 1880–1902) ser. 1, vol. 15:1122. Afterwards this work is cited as *OR*, followed by the volume number, part number (when applicable), and page numbers. Unless otherwise noted, all references are to volumes from series 1; Binford, "Recollections," 28–30; Compiled Service Records: 15th Mississippi Infantry. There is a slight discrepancy with regard to the exact date of Statham's death. His service record, used here by the author, indicates that he died on 27 July 1862. However, Statham's gravestone in Old Fellows Cemetery in Grenada gives his death date as 30 June 1862.

Louisiana, but many fell ill along the way. Several men died and were buried in unmarked graves along the marching route. By the time the regiment arrived in the vicinity of the Louisiana capital, illness had significantly thinned its ranks. In addition to Statham, at least twenty-five men from the 15th Mississippi died from disease during the summer of 1862[25]

The Battle of Baton Rouge took place on 5 August 1862, and the men of the 15th Mississippi did not actively participate. Originally deployed as skirmishers, Breckinridge ordered the regiment to stand down during the actual battle. He later wrote in his official report, "The Fifteenth Mississippi…was not brought into action. This admirable regiment, much reduced by long and gallant service, was held in reserve." The men of the 15th Mississippi spent most of the battle in the middle of a sugar cane field. The Federals repulsed the Confederate attack, and the Southerners fell back to the Comite River. Breckinridge then took his troops to nearby Port Hudson, where they camped for two weeks.[26]

On 19 August, Breckinridge's force left Port Hudson after being ordered to Jackson, Mississippi. At Jackson, Lieutenant Colonel Farrell reported back to the 15th Mississippi, as did a number of other soldiers who had been hospitalized in Vicksburg. Upon his return, Farrell assumed command of the regiment. While stationed at the state capital, the regiment also received about sixty "conscripts" from the recruiting station at Brookhaven. According to James Binford, the 15th Mississippi's recruiting officer, most of these men were of little use. "Among this number of recruits," he later wrote, "were the old and the young, the halt, the lame, the blind; but none were too dumb to tell their tale of woe, why they were not fit to be soldiers and the pressing necessity for them at home. We selected the best material out of this number and directed the surgeon to discharge the balance."[27]

Over the next few weeks the Confederates moved north, first to Holly Springs, then Davis' Mill (now Michigan City), and finally across the Tennessee state line to Grand Junction and Bolivar. At Davis' Mill, Confederate authorities placed the 15th Mississippi in Brigadier General John S. Bowen's brigade, Major General Mansfield Lovell's division, in

---

[25] McPherson, *Battle Cry of Freedom*, 422; Binford, "Recollections," 29.

[26] *OR*, vol. 15:81; Binford, "Recollections," 31–32.

[27] Binford, "Recollections," 33.

Van Dorn's Army of West Tennessee. Lovell's division was designated the Army of the District of the Mississippi. In addition to the 15th Mississippi, Bowen's brigade included the 6th and 22nd Mississippi, Caruther's Mississippi battalion of sharpshooters, the 1st Missouri, and Watson's Louisiana battery.[28]

Throughout August and early September, Van Dorn communicated with Major General Sterling Price with regard to combining their troops and attempting to drive the Federals away from Corinth. Price's command was engaged at Iuka on 19 September and eventually fell back to the west. Van Dorn moved his men back into Mississippi, and the two forces concentrated at Ripley on 28 September. The next day, with Van Dorn commanding the entire force, the Confederates moved east toward Corinth.[29]

Major General William S. Rosecrans, commander of the 21,000-man Union army at Corinth, occupied the town on 26 September and immediately deployed several detachments of "colored engineer troops" to dig a network of breastworks inside the old breastworks that had been left by the Confederates. By 1 October, Corinth was well fortified. "I knew that the enemy intended a strong movement," Rosecrans later remembered, "and I thought that they must have the impression that our defensive works at Corinth would be pretty formidable."[30]

Van Dorn's force totaled around 22,000 men, including Lovell's division and two divisions under Price. On 2 October, the army crossed the Tuscumbia River and moved to Chewalla, where the men camped for the night. The next day the Confederates moved into position and attacked Corinth from the north. Lovell's division occupied the Confederate right, with Bowen's brigade positioned in the center between brigades commanded by Albert Rust and John Villepigue. Bowen deployed his men with Caruther's battalion, the 33rd Mississippi and the 1st Missouri in front, and the 6th, 15th, and 22nd Mississippi in support. The Confederate attack began on 3 October. On the right, the 15th Mississippi crossed the Memphis and Charleston Railroad with the rest of Lovell's division and clashed with Federal troops. The Southerners were initially successful, driving back several Federal regiments under the command of Brigadier General John McArthur.

---

[28] *OR*, vol. 17(1):375.

[29] *Battles and Leaders*, 2:738, 743; Binford, "Recollections," 33–34.

[30] McPherson, *Battle Cry of Freedom*, 522–23; *Battles and Leaders*, 2:740–43.

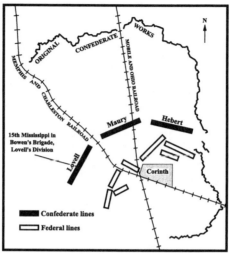

Map 7   Battle of Corinth, October 3 - 4, 1862
(Troop positions October 4)

After driving the Federals back, however, Lovell broke off the engagement and ordered his men to re-form. Lovell's subordinate commanders were incensed, believing that in concert with the Confederate attack on the left, Corinth could be taken. According to one frustrated Confederate participant, after the men re-formed, "The battle raged with redoubled fury. We remained there; not a regiment of the brigade or of the division engaged." By nightfall the Federals were well positioned in their internal defenses, which would prove impenetrable. The next morning Price's two divisions made a fierce and costly assault on the town but ultimately fell prey to exhaustion and thirst in the 90-degree heat. Lovell's division skirmished on the right, but the general again withheld orders to advance, nominally following a directive from Van Dorn to "move cautiously." The Confederates were repulsed and by that afternoon were retreating to the west. Because his division did not take part in the second day's assault, Lovell's casualties for the two-day battle were relatively light—77 killed, 285 wounded, and 208 missing out of around 7,000 men engaged. Bowen's brigade lost "about 50 men killed and wounded," including several soldiers from the 15th Mississippi. Losses in Price's two divisions were far greater—428 killed,

1,865 wounded, and 1,449 missing out of almost 14,000 men engaged. Federal casualties totaled 355 killed, 1,841 wounded, and 324 missing.[31]

Lovell's lack of action caused significant controversy after the battle. His subordinate commanders blamed him for the defeat, as did most of the troops. "With little dissent," said one Confederate after the debacle, "the opinion of the participants...is that the loss of the battle of Corinth...was mainly owing to the misconduct of General Lovell and the inaction on the right wing." Another angry soldier called the defeat "another victory lost the Confederates by the inactivity of one man." Unmoved by the criticism, Lovell never apologized for any decisions made during the struggle. Charges of insubordination against Lovell were discussed but rejected because of potential damage to Confederate morale. In the end, the Southern press blamed Van Dorn for the defeat, and the general would soon be removed from command.[32]

After the battle, Bowen's brigade, including the 15th Mississippi, helped cover the Confederate withdrawal as the army recrossed the Tuscumbia River. Bowen assembled his men on the crest of a hill near the bridge and formed a skirmish line across the road over which the Confederates had marched. They waited in ambush for any Federal troops that might come along. Soon, advance pickets from a half-hearted Federal pursuit appeared and moved into range, at which point the 15th Mississippi "rose quick as a thought and poured a volley into them that effectually put a stop to any further annoyance that night from that source." Before falling back, the Federals answered the volley, wounding several men and killing three, including Attala County farmer Purdom Carpenter of the 15th Mississippi's Company A. Following the encounter, Bowen's brigade crossed the bridge, burned it, and joined the rest of the army in retreat. Lovell later wrote in his report that the 15th Mississippi "distinguished itself particularly at Tuscumbia River Bridge." Bowen, however, who was in command at the bridge, noted four isolated acts of what he considered cowardice in the ranks. While his report was not specific with regard to charges, he recommended "that Second Lieut. T. J. Clark, Company A, Fifteenth Mississippi Regiment, be dismissed in disgrace, and that Corporal Bennett and Privates

---

[31] *OR*, vol. 17 (1):411–13; Peter Cozzens, *The Darkest Days of the War: The Battles of Iuka & Corinth* (Chapel Hill: The University of North Carolina Press, 1997) 166–74, 305–06.

[32] Cozzens, *The Darkest Days of the War*, 305–10.

Applegate and Spivey, Company B, be drummed out of the service."
Bowen stated that he knew of no better way to reward the rest of the
regiment than "by casting out the two or three cowards that happen to be
among them." The general's orders were carried out.[33]

The defeat at Corinth was the final major engagement of 1862
involving the men of the 15th Mississippi Infantry. Following the battle
the Confederate retreat took the men to Ripley and then to Holly Springs.
Rations were scarce, and hunger forced some soldiers to "go where the
horses had been fed and rake up the scattered corn." Again, morale
plummeted, and during the next two months the 15th Mississippi would
lose a dozen more men to desertion. During the period an angry private
who stayed at his post with the regiment wrote that although no
engagements were pending, "There is no telling what our fool officers
intend doing." The army finally went into camp at Coldwater, 4 miles
north of Holly Springs, where it spent several weeks after being
resupplied. Confederate command positions were again shuffled as
Lieutenant General John C. Pemberton took charge of Van Dorn's army.
Bowen received a transfer, and Albert Rust took charge of the brigade to
which the 15th Mississippi was attached. During the first week of
December the dispirited regiment went into winter quarters at Grenada,
where it would remain for the next several weeks. As he passed his
second Christmas season in the Confederate army, Richard Walpole of
Company D could sense the inevitable. "Mississippi is in a critical
condition at present," he wrote to a friend. "We cannot think of holding
the state much longer."[34]

---

[33] *OR*, vol. 17 (1):413–14.

[34] *OR*, vol. 17 (1):404–08; McPherson, *Battle Cry of Freedom*, 523; *Battles and
Leaders*, 2:747–50; Richard Walpole, letter to "Esteemed Friends," 4 November 1862
and Richard Walpole, letter to Anna Bowman, 18 December 1862, Special Collections,
Robert W. Woodruff Library; Compiled Service Records: 15th Mississippi Infantry;
Binford, "Recollections," 34.

CHAPTER 6

WINTER QUARTERS, PORT HUDSON, AND THE
VICKSBURG CAMPAIGN, 1863

> The Yankee army brings desolation on our country
> wherever they march. This I have witnessed.[1]
> *Albert G. Fraser, Company H, 15th Mississippi Infantry*
> *November 1863*

Although there were exceptions, winters during the Civil War generally
brought about a brief, unofficial suspension of hostilities. Commanders
on both sides were hesitant to continue the struggle during months in
which freezing rain or an occasional heavy snow could suddenly bring
their armies to a shivering standstill. At some point during late
November, December, or January, most Confederate and Federal forces
went into winter quarters to await warmer temperatures. Troop locations
and the severity of the weather dictated the length of these military
hibernations.[2]

Structures built to house soldiers during the winter months were
more permanent in nature, and winter quarters usually took on the
appearance of a rustic village. When orders arrived to go into winter
quarters, soldiers worked quickly to prepare their shelters. After

---

[1] Albert G. Fraser, letter to Emma and Martha, 22 June 1863, WPA History of
Yalobusha County, Mississippi Department of Archives and History Library, Jackson,
Mississippi, microfilm.

[2] Bell Irvin Wiley, *The Life of Johnny Reb* (Baton Rouge: Louisiana State
University Press, 1978) 60–63; James I. Robertson Jr., *Soldiers Blue and Gray*
(Columbia: University of South Carolina Press, 1988) 74–77.

choosing a suitable location, the men fanned out in every direction to fell trees to construct log huts. These huts, each of which lodged as many as a dozen soldiers, were arranged in an orderly fashion along company and regimental streets and alleys. Local homes, by invitation of the owner or otherwise, sometimes served as headquarters for ranking officers. An army usually maintained an open field for drilling, parade, or general recreation purposes. Where wood was scarce, the men stitched together standard issue tents or confiscated building materials from surrounding communities. In extreme cases, soldiers simply dug holes in the ground and covered them with blankets.[3]

Time spent in winter quarters was usually monotonous, and many soldiers grew weary of the inactivity and confinement. For the 15th Mississippi Infantry, however, the mild winter of 1862–1863 was a relatively pleasant period. The regiment was fortunate in that it was sequestered only a short distance from the homes of most of the soldiers. The men of Company G hailed from Grenada while those of the other companies came from the same or adjacent counties. Family and friends visited the winter camp, resupplying many soldiers with personal articles from home, and some men received furloughs that allowed them to sleep in their own beds.[4] After spending a few weeks at Grenada, the regiment moved to Coffeeville, which was home to the men of Company F. There, local citizens tried to cheer the soldiers with "dinner invitations and dancing parties." The active roster of the 15th Mississippi increased during the regiment's stay at Grenada and Coffeeville. A number of sick soldiers recovered in the less hostile environment while the Confederates recruited new men locally. Coming out of winter quarters the strength of the regiment was around 500 effectives.[5]

---

[3] Ibid.

[4] James R. Binford, "Recollections of the Fifteenth Mississippi Infantry, CSA," Patrick Henry Papers, Mississippi Department of Archives and History Library, Jackson, Mississippi, 37.

[5] US War Department, comp., *The War of Rebellion: A Compilation of the Official Records of the Union and Confederate Armies*, 128 vols. (Washington, DC: 1880–1902) ser. 1, vol. 24(3):546. Afterwards this work is cited as *OR*, followed by the volume number, part number (when applicable), and page numbers. Unless otherwise noted, all references are to volumes from series 1. Roll numbers are incomplete for the period. However, in April of 1863 returns state that the strength of the regiment was 517 with 484 present for duty.

The men of the 15th Mississippi remained at Coffeeville for only ten days before the reality of their situation was thrust back upon them. On the night of 29 January they received orders to cook several days' rations and pack their belongings. On 1 February the regiment, with the rest of Rust's brigade, boarded a troop train bound for Jackson. Two days later the 15th Mississippi went into camp just outside the state capital and remained there for almost a week. On 9 February, Rust's brigade moved west to Edwards Depot near the Big Black River in Hinds County. The brigade returned to Jackson, and on 22 February Rust's men were ordered south by Pemberton to strengthen the defenses at Port Hudson, Louisiana. As the only Confederate-held outpost on the Mississippi River between Vicksburg and Baton Rouge, Port Hudson was of great strategic importance and, because of its location, was vulnerable to Federal attack. [6]

The 15th Mississippi left Jackson on the morning of 23 February. Moving by train, they arrived at Osyka, Mississippi, later in the day and prepared for the grueling, 70-mile march to Port Hudson. Before the march began, however, an incident took place involving the regiment's commander. Within Rust's brigade it was well known that Michael Farrell did not care for Rust and that the feeling was mutual. Unfortunately, the hard feelings finally manifested themselves in the form of a controversy concerning several brigade supply wagons. When the 15th Mississippi detrained at Osyka, Farrell discovered that no wagons had been provided to haul his regiment's supplies. The "brave and impulsive Irishman" immediately commandeered several wagons belonging to Rust's staff, had the 15th Mississippi's gear loaded, and ordered the regiment in line for the march. Upon hearing that Farrell had taken the brigade wagons without orders, Rust confronted the lieutenant colonel. The two men exchanged heated words, after which Rust had Farrell arrested and threatened to court martial him. While Rust never filed official disciplinary charges, he relieved Farrell as the 15th Mississippi's commander, and James Binford again took charge of the regiment.[7]

Rust's brigade left Osyka on 24 February, and over the next two days the men covered 30 miles. A hard rain began to fall on 26 February,

[6] Dunbar Rowland, *Military History of Mississippi 1803–1898* (Spartenburg SC: The Reprint Company, 1988) 233.

[7] Binford, "Recollections," 38.

slowing their progress. The 15th Mississippi finally arrived at Port Hudson on 3 March and set up camp "in the bottoms amongst the cane." Accommodations were meager. Both food and tents were in short supply. During their stay most of the men paired up and slept on beds made of brush. One soldier later recalled that the makeshift bunks "made a tolerably comfortable bed, that at least kept us out of mud. For a covering and shelter from the rain that fell almost every day, a blanket was stretched over the bed." During the period a member of Company E recorded his experience on picket duty in his diary: "Commenced raining at 4 o'clock A.M. and rained [all day] until 1 o'clock at night. No tents. We waded branches waist deep to get to camp—wet, wet soldiers." As a result of the hostile climate sickness again dogged the men in camp, "dysentery and malaria fever" being the most common maladies. Several cases of small pox also appeared in the 15th Mississippi's Company G, and doctors ordered the afflicted soldiers quarantined until the disease ran its course.[8]

A Federal land-based attack on Port Hudson was rumored but never materialized. By the middle of March, however, David Farragut was moving his fleet upriver from Baton Rouge in hopes of running the formidable Port Hudson batteries. Conventional wisdom among the Federal high command held that if the ships could pass Port Hudson, the Union fleet could continue operations on the Mississippi and Red Rivers and cripple the Southern armies by cutting off their supplies from Texas. Such a move would also put Farragut in position to once again threaten Vicksburg.[9]

On the afternoon of 14 March, Union warships began exchanging heavy fire with the Port Hudson batteries, and later that night seven ships made their move up river. Farragut's flagship, the *Hartford*, led the group, followed by the *Albatross, Richmond, Genesee, Monongahela, Kineo,* and the side-wheeler *Mississippi*. The *Mississippi*, the oldest of the seven ships, was the same vessel that had carried Commodore

---

[8] Unknown Author, "History of the Water Valley Rifles, Company F, Fifteenth Mississippi Infantry," Supplement to the WPA Historical Research Project, Yalobusha County, 16 February 1937, Special Collections, J. D. Williams Library, University of Mississippi, Oxford, Mississippi, 44. Afterwards cited as "History of the Water Valley Rifles"; Joel Calvin Watson diary, Grenada Public Library, Grenada, Mississippi, 7–8.

[9] Edward Cunningham, *The Port Hudson Campaign* (Baton Rouge: Louisiana State University Press, 1963) 21–25.

Matthew C. Perry to Japan in 1854. Just as they viewed the attack of the *Arkansas* at Vicksburg, the men of the 15th Mississippi watched the bombardment of the Union ships from the heights at Port Hudson. According to James Binford, "With the burning shells from their gunboats and mortars and the shells from our artillery the whole atmosphere seemed a network of fire.... One continuous roar was caused by burning shells. It was simply indescribable."[10]

Amid a great deal of smoke and confusion, only the *Hartford* and *Albatross* successfully ran the batteries. Fire from Port Hudson damaged four Federal ships and completely destroyed the *Mississippi*. During the fracas the side-wheeler ran aground and became a stationary target for Confederate shells. The Port Hudson batteries pounded the disabled ship until it caught fire and drifted slowly downstream. About 5 miles above Baton Rouge fire reached the *Mississippi's* magazine, resulting in a spectacular explosion that sent sheets of flame high into the air. The concussion from the blast shook houses 20 miles away, and Federal guards on duty in New Orleans saw the flash from the blast. According to an observer in Baton Rouge, when the ship's magazine ignited, the sky "lit from horizon to horizon in fiery splendor. The stars sank in an ocean of flames." At Port Hudson the men of the 15th Mississippi witnessed the illumination of the night sky, followed immediately by "a low, rumbling sound that resembled the peal of distant thunder." Among the Union sailors who escaped the *Mississippi* in lifeboats was future naval hero George Dewey, the doomed vessel's executive officer.[11]

The 15th Mississippi remained in camp at Port Hudson for three more weeks, during which time the men survived on "burnt molasses, very inferior brown sugar, and cow peas." Their diet occasionally included "hickory shad," which one member of the regiment disparaged as "a fish with several thousand bones to the inch and about as destitute of flesh as any fish might well be." The weather cleared, and the men relaxed in camp as the immediate danger passed. Although Farragut steered ships past Port Hudson, the naval action in March of 1863 proved that river fire alone could not silence the Confederate batteries. The

---

[10] Cunningham, *The Port Hudson Campaign*, 23; Binford, "Recollections," 38–39; Lawrence Lee Hewitt, *Port Hudson, Confederate Bastion on the Mississippi* (Baton Rouge: Louisiana State University Press, 1987) 93.

[11] "History of the Water Valley Rifles," 45; Cunningham, *The Port Hudson Campaign*, 30–31.

Federals would have to use a land-based force to take the port, and Union commanders were not yet prepared to make such an assault.[12]

With no apparent threat of attack at Port Hudson, Pemberton ordered Rust's brigade, along with a number of other troops, back into Mississippi. Rust's men left Port Hudson for Jackson on 5 April, retracing the route that had brought them into Louisiana a few weeks earlier. Covering about 15 miles per day, the weary soldiers marched back into Osyka on 10 April and boarded railroad cars. The next evening the 15th Mississippi went into camp just southwest of Jackson, and a number of the men drew assignments to provost duty in the city. Confederate authorities posted soldiers from block to block with orders to check the permits of anyone on the streets. It was rumored that Union spies were in the city, but only one man was ever detained for questioning. After several Confederate officers were stopped and inconvenienced and a brigadier general was momentarily detained, procedures for policing the streets were relaxed. While in Jackson, Rust received a transfer to another department and Brigadier General Lloyd Tilghman took command of the regiment to which the 15th Mississippi was attached. This was good news to Michael Farrell, who resumed his place as regimental commander. After another reorganization, Tilghman's command formed a "Mississippi brigade" made up of the 6th, 14th, 15th, 20th, 23rd, 26th, 37th, and 40th Mississippi infantry regiments.[13]

During the spring of 1863 Confederate forces in Mississippi were on the defensive, reacting frantically to rumored and actual Union troop movements. As Grant moved down the west bank of the Mississippi River in the early stages of his campaign for Vicksburg, Union colonel Benjamin H. Grierson began a cavalry raid that would take him through much of the eastern half of Mississippi. Grierson's raid was designed to disrupt Confederate supply and communication lines that serviced Vicksburg and siphon off Confederate troops that could be used in Vicksburg's defense. Among other things, Grant charged Grierson with "destroying all telegraph wires, burning provisions, and doing all

---

[12] Binford, "Recollections," 38–39; Cunningham, *The Port Hudson Campaign,* 30–32; James M. McPherson, *Battle Cry of Freedom: The Civil War Era* (New York: Ballantine Books, 1988) 637–38.

[13] Edwin C. Bearss, vol. 2 of *The Vicksburg Campaign* (Dayton OH: Morningside House, 1986) 92–93; Binford, "Recollections," 39–40; *OR,* vol. 24(3):746.

mischief possible." As they carried out their orders, Grierson's men left a "smoldering path of destruction" through many Mississippi communities.[14]

As a result of these events, the 15th Mississippi moved to various locations during the month of April, as contradictory reports of Federal activity throughout the South came in. Confusion reigned at Pemberton's headquarters. On 14 April the general ordered Tilghman's brigade to Tullahoma, Tennessee, to help reinforce Braxton Bragg. The next day the 15th Mississippi boarded railroad cars with the rest of Tilghman's men at Jackson. As there was no direct route to Tullahoma, the men sped east on the Southern Railroad to Meridian, arriving 16 April, and that night moved south to Mobile, Alabama on the Mobile and Ohio line. The men then switched trains again, following a northern line to Montgomery. The soldiers arrived at the Alabama state capital on 18 April only to find out that Pemberton wanted them back in Mississippi. As the threat to Vicksburg became apparent, the general sought to consolidate his forces. Retracing their route, the 15th Mississippi finally went into camp just outside of Jackson on 22 April.[15]

The men were not idle for long. On the afternoon 24 April, in response to Grierson's raid, the 15th Mississippi moved east to Lake Station with Brigadier General John Adams "to stop the enemy from tearing up the railroad." According to J. C. Watson of Company K, the regiment arrived too late: "We got to Morton and telegraphed up the rode and found out that the wires were cut. We went on up the road and found everything tore up and the Yankees gone." Within a few days the 15th Mississippi was back with Tilghman's brigade at Edwards Depot.[16]

On 30 April the Union campaign for Vicksburg began in earnest as Grant and 23,000 Federals crossed the river into Mississippi at Bruinsburg and proceeded northeast toward Jackson. On 1 May the Federals secured their bridgehead across the river by defeating 6,000 Confederates at the Battle of Port Gibson. Grant then called for William T. Sherman and his troops, bringing total Federal strength east of the

---

[14] William T. Blain, "Banner Unionism in Choctaw County," *Mississippi Quarterly* 29/2 (Spring 1976): 213; D. Alexander Brown, *Grierson's Raid* (Urbana: University of Illinois Press, 1954) 5; Samuel Carter III, *The Final Fortress: The Campaign for Vicksburg, 1862–1863* (New York: St. Martin's Press, 1980) 164–65.

[15] Joel Calvin Watson diary, 9–10.

[16] Bearss, *The Vicksburg Campaign*, 2:93, 222, 226; Joel Calvin Watson diary, 10.

Map 8 Vicksburg Vicinity, May - June 1863

Mississippi River to more than 40,000 men. Pemberton's 30,000 troops were scattered in various detachments and proved little impediment to Grant's swift progress. On 12 May a Confederate force under the command of Brigadier General John Gregg met defeat at the Battle of Raymond, and two days later Union troops drove the Confederates out of Jackson. Leaving Sherman's corps to destroy the city as a supply and transportation center, Grant turned his full attention toward Vicksburg.[17]

Union and Confederate troops clashed in the decisive battle of the Vicksburg campaign on 16 May at Champion Hill, near Edwards Depot. There, Grant concentrated 29,000 men against 23,000 under Pemberton. Grant's men were organized into two corps, commanded respectively by Major Generals John A. McClernand and James B. McPherson. Pemberton's command was made up of three divisions under Bowen, Major General Carter L. Stevenson, and Major General William W.

---

[17] McPherson, *Battle Cry of Freedom*, 628–30; Edwin C. Bearss and Warren Grabau, *The Battle of Jackson, May 14, 1863; The Siege of Jackson, July 10–17, 1863; Three Other Post-Vicksburg Actions* (Baltimore: Gateway Press, 1981) 1.

Loring. The 15th Mississippi, in Tilghman's brigade, was part of Loring's division.[18]

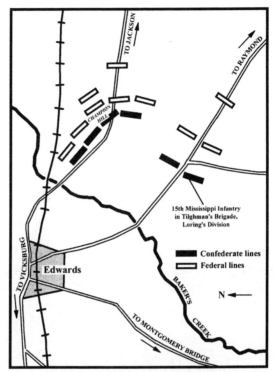

Map 9   Battle of Champion Hill, May 16, 1863

Early on the morning of 16 May, Pemberton deployed his men. At about 10:30 A.M. Grant launched an assault on the Confederate positions. During several hours of hard fighting, Champion Hill changed hands three times. The outnumbered Confederates eventually lost the field and that evening retreated to the west, leaving behind twenty-seven cannons and hundreds of prisoners. Tilghman's brigade, including the 15th Mississippi, was not engaged during the heat of the fight. Loring's division covered the retreat, with Tilghman's men occupying a ridge along the Raymond road. As the retreat progressed, Tilghman's artillery dueled six guns from the Chicago Mercantile Battery and two from the

---

[18] Bearss, *The Vicksburg Campaign*, vol. 2:564, 594–95, 642–51; Carter, *The Final Fortress*, 17; McPherson, *Battle Cry of Freedom*, 630–31.

17th Ohio Battery, both part of Brigadier General Stephen J. Burbridge's Federal brigade. At about 5:20 P.M., shrapnel from a Yankee shell struck and instantly killed Tilghman, who was standing near the 15th Mississippi's position. According to one witness, the Federal shell "exploded about fifty feet in front" of Tilghman, and "a ragged fragment of this shell struck the general in the breast, passing entirely through him and killing the horse of his adjutant a little further to the rear." After Tilghman's death, command of his brigade passed to Colonel Arthur E. Reynolds of the 26th Mississippi. The Confederates suffered 3,840 casualties at the Battle of Champion Hill to 2,441 for the Union. Although casualty returns for individual regiments were incomplete, the 15th Mississippi lost several men who were on detached service during the battle, most of whom eventually ended up in Vicksburg with Pemberton.[19]

As they covered the Confederate retreat, Loring's division was cut off from the rest of Pemberton's force that would eventually fall back into Vicksburg. Unable to reunite with Pemberton, the men retreated toward Crystal Springs. Enlisting the aid of a local farmer as a guide, Loring's force "marched all night through woods and by-paths, wading all the creeks we came to." In the process, they abandoned their artillery and other equipment in the darkness. According to a soldier from the 15th Mississippi's Company K, "We had to make our way through dismal swamps after night. Lost all our artillery, wagons, knapsacks, blankets, and everything we had. We left the field at sundown and marched all night." The next morning the men crossed the road leading from Jackson to Raymond, at which time local citizens warned them that Federal forces were still in the area. Not looking for a fight, Loring kept his soldiers on the march throughout the day on 17 May, finally stopping to set up camp near Crystal Springs. The men had been marching steadily for nearly twenty-four hours without food or rest, and a number

---

[19] Binford, "Recollections," 42; Bearss, *The Vicksburg Campaign*, vol. 2:580–82, 594–96, 627, 642; Compiled Service Records of Confederate Soldiers who served in Organizations from the State of Mississippi: 15th Mississippi Infantry, Mississippi Department of Archives and History Library, Jackson, Mississippi, microfilm. Cited afterwards as Compiled Service Records: 15th Mississippi Infantry.

of stragglers, including at least a half dozen from the 15th Mississippi, never returned to the ranks.[20]

From Crystal Springs, Loring's division marched north, arriving in Jackson on 19 May, where they united with General Joseph Johnston. After pillaging the state's capital, Sherman's corps had abandoned the city, leaving it free for occupation by the Confederates. Johnston organized his "Army of Relief" there during the following week, ostensibly to come to Pemberton's aid in Vicksburg. At Jackson, the 15th Mississippi was placed in John Adams's brigade in Loring's division along with the 6th, 14th, 20th, 23rd, and 26th Mississippi Infantry regiments, Forney's 1st Confederate Infantry Battalion, and Barry's Lookout Tennessee Artillery.[21]

Because Grant positioned seven divisions behind the Federal siege lines at Vicksburg, specifically to prevent relief of the city, Johnston's effort to aid Pemberton never materialized. Throughout June the 15th Mississippi and the rest of Johnston's force "did a great deal of marching up and down the Big Black [River]" with little effect. The men camped at Canton (1–4 June), Yazoo City (5 June), Benton (7–9 June), Moore's Bluff (10–13 June), Benton (14–23 June), and Beattie's Bluff (24–29 June). On 2 July the Confederates went into camp at Porter's Creek, where, three days later, "astonishing news came that Vicksburg had capitulated." Believing rightly that part of the Federal army would double back, Johnston moved his force toward Jackson. At the same time Sherman moved his men toward the capital city. According to one soldier, "Then followed consternation and confusion for a time as…a footrace was at once inaugurated between Johnston and Sherman to see who would reach Jackson first." As they marched, Johnston's men poisoned the wells in the area. Central Mississippi had not seen rain for weeks, and the Confederates hoped that a water shortage might hamper Sherman's progress. The Confederates beat the Federals to Jackson, and on 10 July, as Sherman's larger and better-equipped army approached the city, the men of the 15th Mississippi listened as Johnston made a rare address to the troops, speaking of pride, sacrifice, and victory. Despite the appeals to patriotism, Johnston's men were powerless to halt the

---

[20] Bearss, *The Vicksburg Campaign*, vol. 2:637; Binford, "Recollections," 42. Joel Calvin Watson diary, 12.

[21] Edwin C. Bearss, vol. 3 of *The Vicksburg Campaign* (Dayton OH: Morningside House, 1986) 1150.

Union advance. Sherman laid partial siege to the city for several days as the men of the 15th Mississippi "lay in the entrenchments all the time [July] 13th, 14th, 15th, and 16th." As the Federals pressed, there was heavy skirmishing around the lines. According to a private from the regiment, "It was now a mere matter of time as to how long we could hold out against an enemy that outnumbered us." Johnston finally ordered the evacuation of Jackson on 16 July, and the Confederates fell back to the east through Brandon and Morton.[22]

After the fall of Vicksburg, the state of Mississippi was no longer a focal point of Federal strategy. The Union accomplished its primary objective by capturing the city, which split the Confederacy in two and freed the Mississippi River for Federal traffic. Events in Georgia and Tennessee would dictate troop movements in Mississippi for the remainder of the war. Coupled with Lee's defeat at Gettysburg, the fall of Vicksburg marked the beginning of the end of the Southern rebellion.[23]

By the end of 1863 the Confederacy's severe military setbacks had further demoralized the already bleak Southern home front. The economic noose had begun to tighten around the South from the first shots at Fort Sumter, and after two years of fighting, desperate families populated much of the Southern countryside. From an economic standpoint the Confederacy had entered the war woefully unprepared. The South had looked to European imports for many of its commodities, and the Federal blockade had left the region dependent on its own resources. At the war's outset the rebellious states as a whole had sparse manufacturing and an underdeveloped railroad system, and since 1861 speculators had hoarded many important items in hopes of selling them at enormous profits as demand grew. The South relied on agriculture, with cotton being the primary cash crop, yet the Confederate cause had depleted much of the region's agricultural labor force. Thousands of non-

---

[22] Bearss and Grabau, *The Battle of Jackson, May 14, 1863*, 51, 55, 63; Edwin C. Bearss, "The Armed Conflict," vol. 1 of *A History of Mississippi*, ed. Richard A. McLemore (Hattiesburg: University and College Press of Mississippi, 1973) 478–79; Official Records, 15th Mississippi Infantry, CSA, Mississippi Department of Archives and History Library, Jackson, Mississippi. Cited afterwards as Official Records, 15th Mississippi Infantry; "History of the Water Valley Rifles," 49–51; Joel Calvin Watson diary, 14; Craig L. Symonds, *Joseph Johnston: A Civil War Biography* (New York: W. W. Norton, 1992) 216.

[23] Bearss, "The Armed Conflict," 479.

slaveholding yeomen farmers, many of whom had been the sole family breadwinner at home, were in the army or dead. Thousands of slaves had run away as Federal troops moved through the Confederacy. Many fields that had flourished in 1860 grew little but weeds in 1863. Meanwhile, the Richmond government and the state governments lacked the resources to feed all the soldiers in the field, as well as their destitute families at home. Programs to aid the poor had little widespread effect due to poor administration and a general deterioration of the South's fiscal infrastructure. At depots throughout the Confederacy, perishable foodstuffs rotted as workmen waited to load them onto freight cars that would never arrive over the South's fragile railroad network.[24]

Mississippi suffered these conditions along with the other Southern states. Efforts by state officials to increase food production during the war met with only limited success. From 1861 state leaders had encouraged farmers to plant less cotton and devote more acreage to cereal grains, which initially increased the production of corn and wheat. However, a severe drought in 1862 ruined much of Mississippi's corn crop, and the general disorder produced by the war resulted in many crops being left in the field unharvested. Meat was relatively plentiful in the state during the war's first year, but shortages of salt hampered meat production, and the supply of domestic livestock dwindled. Eventually, most families learned to improvise, producing homemade coffee from parched corn or okra, tea from dried raspberry leaves, and consuming on a regular basis a variety of boiled roots, berries, and foliage previously considered of little culinary value. Because of the war, one Mississippian conceded during 1863, "Our civilized conventionalities must once more give place to primitive necessities and simplicities."[25]

By the midpoint of the war the state's economy was already in a downward spiral from which it would never recover. With most of Mississippi's wealth tied up in land, slaves, and cotton, the government and the public operated largely on constantly deflating paper. The state legislature tried to solve the state's fiscal problems by simply printing more money, which ultimately drove the value of the state's notes and bonds down and greatly inflated prices on all goods. After the fall of the

---

[24] Paul D. Escott, "'The Cry of the Sufferers': The Problem of Welfare in the Confederacy," *Civil War History* (September 1977): 228–34.

[25] John K. Bettersworth, "The Home Front, 1861–1865," vol. 1 of *A History of Mississippi*, ed. Richard A. McLemore, 504–08.

state capital, records were so confused that it was impossible for a full accounting of the state's finances. Apparently stricken by the pressures of his job, state treasurer M. D. Haynes committed suicide. To make matters worse, as Mississippi's economy deteriorated so did the rule of law in many parts of the state. Vigilantes policed some communities, and local courts met on an irregular basis, if at all. In addition to anxieties brought on by hunger and poverty, many Mississippi whites lived in constant fear of slave insurrections, particularly after Federal troops entered the state. Slaves made up a majority of the state's population, and rumors of rebellion caused alarm even in those regions where slaves were in the minority.[26]

Concerns about the home front weighed heavily on the minds of the soldiers in the army, causing many men to question their military commitment. The year 1863 marked the point at which the desertion rate of the 15th Mississippi began to significantly increase. Coming out of winter quarters in Grenada and Coffeeville a number of men decided that they had had enough of the Confederate army. While camped near their homes, the men viewed wartime hardships in their communities. When they went back on the march, reports continued coming in concerning deprivations in the 15th Mississippi counties. "What awful times we are passing through," a Carroll County woman wrote. "It is just as much as we can do here to get enough to eat. I feel thankful for anything to live on." Inflation was rampant, and merchants were admonished for selling goods "at enormous prices, at such prices that the poor families cannot purchase [them], and will be compelled to suffer." During the period $150 in Confederate currency brought in exchange only $10 in gold. From the home of Company A word reached the regiment that because so many local men were absent, "there are a great many poor families in the county of Attala that are almost destitute of the necessities of life." Conditions were similar in the home county of Companies D, I, and K. "Meat is not to be had in Choctaw County," one man reported. "Two-thirds of the working class are in the army and their families are helpless."[27]

---

[26] Ibid., 497–99.

[27] Blain, "Banner Unionism in Choctaw County," 208–11; James P. Coleman, *Choctaw County Chronicles* (Ackerman MS: James P. Coleman, 1974) 69–70; Jason Niles Scrapbook, Southern Historical Collection, University of North Carolina Library,

The original volunteers had signed on firm in the belief that the war would be over before they completed their full tour of duty. They had left communities yet to know the deprivations of war and had drawn strength from the encouragement their communities provided. By the end of 1863, however, there were no more cheering crowds in the 15th Mississippi counties. Wartime difficulties had dampened enthusiasm for the war at home, which in turn dampened the spirits of the men. Nearly everyone in the communities that produced the regiment had a friend or relative in army, and as a result nearly everyone had lost a friend or relative by the end of 1863. One area resident lamented, "The plow has been left standing in the furrow of many a poor conscript's field, and his aged father, or poor little barefooted sister, are left to work out with the hoe." One newspaper was more succinct, informing its readers that "the condition of North Mississippi is deplorable." The soldiers of the 15th Mississippi had entered the service to defend their communities, but by the end of 1863 their communities needed them back. Some survivors from the regiment acted accordingly.[28]

The initial flurry of desertions actually began when five men left the regiment while it was in winter quarters. On 1 January 1863, Private Wash Lewis of Company D became the regiment's first deserter of the new year. By the end of March twenty more soldiers were absent without permission. Many of the men returned home to hide out for the remainder of the war. From the 15th Mississippi counties, reports would soon surface that deserters from various regiments, and angry local citizens, were threatening Confederate conscription officers. During the period, an area resident noted that Choctaw County had become a haven for deserters and that runaway slaves there had supposedly found "the woods so full of white men that there was no room for them."[29] In April, officers from the 15th Mississippi began placing advertisements in newspapers with the names and descriptions of deserters from the

---

Chapel Hill, North Carolina; John W. Wood, *Union and Secession in Mississippi* (Memphis: Saunders, Farrish and Whitmore Printers, 1863) 6.

[28] Blain, "Banner Unionism in Choctaw County," 208–11; Coleman, *Choctaw County Chronicles*, 69–70; Wood, *Union and Secession in Mississippi*, 6; *Memphis Daily Appeal*, 27 June 1863.

[29] Blain, "Banner Unionism in Choctaw County," 208–11; Jason Niles Scrapbook; Compiled Service Records: 15th Mississippi Infantry; *Memphis Daily Appeal*, 10 April 1863; *Canton American Citizen*, 3 October 1863.

regiment. An announcement concerning one Choctaw County private
was typical:

> JOE JOHNSON, Company D, 23 years of age, six feet four
> inches high, dark hair, blue eyes, weighs 170 pounds, resides at
> Greensboro, Miss., absent from January, 25, 1863.[30]

While deprivations at home and the erosion of domestic support for
the war influenced some to flee the army, many of the men had grown
disillusioned with the general nature of their Confederate experience.
The original members of the 15th Mississippi were volunteers, but the
Richmond government had forced them into service for an extended
period. One soldier from Company I was firm in his belief that
Confederate lawmakers had severely overstepped their bounds "when it
comes to pressing the twelve month volunteers into service for two or
more years without giving them the privilege of going home as free
men." The soldiers had been told that Northern abolitionists were a threat
to their independence, yet the Confederate government had stolen their
independence through the Conscription Act and through its inability to
assist the men's suffering families. The government also could not keep
its armies adequately supplied. Some deserters were simply tired of
fighting a war that already seemed lost. Northern soldiers now tread
confidently on Mississippi soil. For some soldiers who had entered the
service as part of a community enterprise, it was the enemy occupation
of their home state in 1863, not the subsequent fall of Richmond or the
surrender at Appomattox, that marked the end of the war. As a result, a
second, more dramatic wave of desertions took place during the ten-
week period following the Battle of Champion Hill. Men began leaving
the 15th Mississippi immediately after the battle as they made their way
toward Crystal Springs with the rest of Loring's division. By the end of
June another twenty-five soldiers from the regiment were listed as absent
without leave. After the fall of Vicksburg, desertions peaked. Joel
Watson of Company K recorded in his diary that on 18 July, during the
course of a grueling 18-mile march, several men from the regiment
"[ran] away and went home." In July and August thirty soldiers fled, and
another dozen left during the next four months, bringing total reported

---

[30] *Memphis Daily Appeal*, 10 April 1863.

desertions from the 15th Mississippi for 1863 to 88 men, or approximately 20 percent of the regiment's average total membership during the year.[31]

Number of Reported Desertions by Year
15th Mississippi Infantry, 1861–1863

Year	# of reported desertions
1861 (June–December)	2
1862	40
1863	88
Total	130

Attempts to apprehend deserters from the 15th Mississippi met with little success. Due to manpower shortages the Confederate army could send few troops into the field on such missions. Authorities sometimes used volunteer militia to round up men who had left the army, paying $30 per capture, but these efforts often met local resistance. In June, as he tried to accumulate troops for his Army of Relief, Joseph Johnston offered amnesty to any absent soldier who would return voluntarily. The order was published, along with pleas from local newspapers that the absent men should remember their duty and "remove from their shoulders a load of obloquy which will followed them and their children to the grave."[32]

Amnesties and appeals to duty had little effect on deserters from the 15th Mississippi. Only three men who deserted the regiment during 1863 returned to the army, and even those who remained found it difficult to justify their commitment to the Confederate cause. After hearing false rumors that Confederate authorities planned to transfer the 15th Mississippi to the eastern theater, a private from Company G wrote to his family in Grenada, "I hear it whispered that they are fixing to send us to

---

[31] Augustus Hervey Mecklin Papers, Mississippi Department of Archives and History Library, Jackson, Mississippi; Joel Calvin Watson diary, 14; Compiled Service Records: 15th Mississippi Infantry.

[32] *Natchez Daily Courier*, 23 June 1863

Virginia to aid General Lee. I don't think that fair, either. I think we have been called on too much already."[33]

The men who did not abandon the 15th Mississippi remained in their home state for the rest of 1863, but their combat activity for the year ended with the evacuation of Jackson. Operating mainly in the eastern part of the state, the regiment camped at various locations in response to rumors of Federal activity. On 27 July the men moved to Forest and a few days later to Newton, where they remained for the month of August. They spent most of September in Meridian, moving west to Brandon on 1 October. Finally, the 15th Mississippi marched to Canton, where it remained through the winter. On 16 December, Joseph Johnston received a transfer, and Lieutenant General Leonidas Polk took command of the Department of Mississippi and East Louisiana, to which the regiment remained attached. As the year 1863 drew to a close, Albert G. Fraser of the 15th Mississippi's Company H, in a letter that reflected his Confederate experience over the course of the last few months, warned his sister in Yalobusha County that "the Yankee army brings desolation on our country wherever they march. This I have witnessed. It is painful to see the destruction that follows them. Should they ever get to Yalobusha, you all had better stay at home."[34]

---

[33] Ed Jones Boushe, letter to Grand Ma, undated, WPA History of Grenada County, Mississippi Department of Archives and History Library, Jackson, Mississippi, microfilm.

[34] Official Records, 15th Mississippi Infantry; Albert G. Fraser, letter to Emma and Martha, 22 June 1863.

CHAPTER 7

RETREAT FROM MISSISSIPPI AND THE ATLANTA CAMPAIGN, 1864

> Parson Reese sang a hymn and made a few appropriate remarks. It was a solemn spectacle to witness; about a dozen of his comrades standing around the grave and the pale moon looking down on us.[1]
>
> *W. B. Wagner, Company F, 15th Mississippi Infantry, 25 August 1864*

During the winter of 1863–1864, the men of the 15th Mississippi Infantry camped at Canton, only a few hours by rail from Grenada, where they spent the previous winter. Again the men were fortunate in that they were able to see friends and relatives. Some obtained passes to visit their homes. Most furloughs were for twenty days and came with the stern warning that if a soldier failed to return to the regiment on time, he would be treated as a deserter. Despite the admonition, some men never found their way back to the regiment and remained in hiding as the war ran its course. Although one soldier later recalled that the 15th Mississippi was "in the swim at Canton," the men faced a melancholy present and an uncertain future.[2] The twin blows of Gettysburg and

---

[1] W. B. Wagner, letter to Ella Young, 15 August 1864, Yalobusha County Historical Society, *Yalobusha County History* (Dallas TX: National Share Graphics, 1982) C35–C36.

[2] Official Records, 15th Mississippi Infantry, CSA, Mississippi Department of Archives and History Library, Jackson, Mississippi. Cited afterwards as Official Records, 15th Mississippi Infantry; James R. Binford, "Recollections of the Fifteenth Mississippi

Vicksburg had staggered the Confederacy. The soldiers knew that their army and their country might be living on borrowed time.

At Canton the 15th Mississippi did take part in one celebrated confrontation, but not a single Union soldier was involved. The central event of the regiment's stay in the city was a drill contest between Farrell's Mississippians and men from Colonel A. P. Thompson's 3rd Kentucky Infantry. It is unclear which side issued the challenge, but the contest apparently evolved from a mixture of boredom and bravado that had accumulated in camp during weeks of inactivity. Confederate commanders promoted the idea as a means to bolster the morale of the troops and to raise the spirits of local citizens. Before the contest took place, word spread throughout Canton, and the exercise became a major community occasion. "As an incentive toward heightening the ambition and inspiration of the contestants," wrote one participant, "some ladies of Canton, headed by Mrs. D. Lattimer, proposed to present the victorious regiment with a fine silk flag."[3]

On the day of the contest soldiers and citizens gathered at the parade ground near the Confederate camp, and a small collection of officers and local dignitaries took their place on a hastily constructed stage. Generals William H. Jackson of Tennessee and Thomas M. Johnson of Louisiana served as judges for the event. Just after noon, John Adams's Mississippi brigade, with the 15th Mississippi in the lead, marched onto the drill ground, followed by several Kentucky regiments, led by the 3rd Kentucky. According to one soldier who watched the proceedings, "The Mississippi Regiment took the lead, going through many movements. Then the Kentuckians moved out and went through the same, each without a jostle. Thus they alternated for hours without any apparent advantage to either side.... However, Col. Farrell had several fancy movements.... They were unique and the regiment of Mississippians carried the day." The judges declared the men of the 15th Mississippi winners of the contest, and Farrell received the flag on behalf the regiment.[4] That evening, the "keys to Canton" were turned over to Farrell and Thompson, and the entire city celebrated at a party honoring both

Infantry, CSA," Patrick Henry Papers, Mississippi Department of Archives and History Library, Jackson, Mississippi, 43.

[3] John L. Collins, "Mississippi and Kentucky in a Contest," *Confederate Veteran* 17/9 (September 1909): 460.

[4] Ibid.

regiments. One member of the 3rd Kentucky later recalled that the 15th Mississippi "had many friends in and around Canton, especially among the ladies. Nearly all of the girls had a friend, relative, or sweetheart in the Fifteenth. It was their pet regiment."[5]

The men had little time to savor their victory. On 3 February 1864, Sherman left Vicksburg and moved east with a force numbering around 20,000, intent on capturing Meridian. With the loss of Vicksburg, Meridian had become the most strategic Confederate-held location in Mississippi. The Mobile and Ohio Railroad crossed the Southern Railroad there, and the city included a large number of railroad shops, magazines, and hospitals. The Federals advanced across the center of the state in what proved to be a testing ground for the total war strategy that Sherman later employed during his famous march to the sea.[6]

Although Confederate cavalry occasionally engaged Sherman's men, the outnumbered Southerners could muster little resistance. As the Federals approached Jackson on 5 February, the 15th Mississippi and the rest of Loring's division left Canton and crossed the Pearl River at Grant's Ferry. The following evening the men camped 14 miles west of Morton, eventually entering the little railroad town on 7 February. There, Loring's division united with a division under the command of Major General Samuel G. French, but even the combined force could not challenge the great blue tide sweeping eastward.[7]

On 8 February, unfounded rumors swept through the Federal columns that the Confederates had massed at Morton for an attack. That afternoon, however, Confederate commanders decided to fall back in the face of the superior Union force. Polk's entire infantry fell back to the east, retreating through Meridian into Alabama. On 14 February, Sherman's men entered Meridian without a fight. For five days they dedicated themselves to destroying the city, until Sherman finally

---

[5] Henry Ewell Hord, "Prize Drill in the Army," *Confederate Veteran* 10/1 (January 1902): 548–49.

[6] Edwin C. Bearss, "The Armed Conflict," vol. 1 of *A History of Mississippi*, ed. Richard A. McLemore (Hattiesburg: University and College Press of Mississippi, 1973) 480; Everette B. Long with Barbara Long, *The Civil War Day by Day: An Almanac 1861–1865* (Garden City NY: Doubleday and Company, 1971) 460–61.

[7] Margie Riddle Bearss, *Sherman's Forgotten Campaign: The Meridian Expedition* (Baltimore: Gateway Press, 1987) 80, 96; Thomas L. Livermore, *Numbers and Losses in the Civil War in America: 1861–1865* (Bloomington: Indiana University Press, 1957) 119.

reported that "Meridian, with its depots, warehouses, arsenals, hospitals, offices, hotels, and cantonments no longer exists." During the course of the expedition across central Mississippi, Sherman's force destroyed 115 miles of railroad, 61 bridges, 20 locomotives, and countless businesses and homes. In the process the 15th Mississippi and the rest of the Confederate infantry had not fired a shot in opposition.[8]

After abandoning Meridian, the 15th Mississippi crossed a pontoon bridge over the Tombigbee River, moving to Demopolis, Alabama, where the army camped for several weeks. On 3 April the regiment left Demopolis and the next few days made a series of difficult marches through several Alabama towns, including Greensboro, Jericho, and Centreville. On 8 April one exhausted soldier from the 15th Mississippi reported that he and his comrades "marched 14 miles and all the creeks from shoe to waist deep. Boys all wet...rested very little." On 10 April the men arrived at Montevallo, where they camped for several weeks.[9]

Since coming out of winter quarters the ranks of the 15th Mississippi continued to dwindle. The final retreat out of Mississippi particularly demoralized those men who had remained with the regiment despite the previous year's setbacks. February saw more desertion from the regiment than any other month during the war. Eighty men fled the 15th Mississippi during a four-week period, almost equaling the total number of desertion for all of 1863. As was the case during the previous winter, the men went back on the march in 1864 after visiting with friends and relative in winter quarters and hearing of the deteriorating home front. The dismal retreat from their home state also solidified the idea that the cause was truly lost. Four soldiers left the regiment during March and another fifteen in April, bringing the total number of desertions for the four-month period to ninety-nine.[10]

The first four months of 1864 also saw periodic breakdowns in discipline, with one incident in particular illustrating conditions in the Confederate camp. During their stay in Alabama the 15th Mississippi

---

[8] Bearss, *Sherman's Forgotten Campaign*, 103, 161, 173; Long and Long, *The Civil War Day by Day*, 464; Binford, "Recollections," 45.

[9] Joel Calvin Watson diary, Grenada Public Library, Grenada, Mississippi, 16–17.

[10] Compiled Service Records of Confederate Soldiers who served in Organizations from the State of Mississippi: 15th Mississippi Infantry, Mississippi Department of Archives and History Library, Jackson, Mississippi, microfilm. Cited afterwards as Compiled Service Records: 15th Mississippi Infantry.

and the rest of the army were placed on short rations. According to one sympathetic observer, "As the days rolled by their hunger increased and their complaints, still unheeded…until it had come to the point where forbearance had ceased to be a virtue." One evening in late February about 150 enlisted men, mostly from the 15th Mississippi, took matters into their own hands, charging the commissary for Adams's brigade and liberating a large quantity of foodstuffs. James Binford, alone in his tent, heard the raid begin and, according to his account, raised his tent flap "just in time to see the large tent of the commissary topple over as if struck by a cyclone, and then began the capture of prisoners which proved to be sacks of flour, sugar, sides of bacon, etc." The next day, acting on Adams's orders, Farrell rounded up most of the men involved and had them placed under guard, where they remained for several days. Adams threatened the soldiers with court martials but ultimately deemed it more prudent to release the men and forget the incident. Some of the food was recovered, and discipline was restored. The men eventually left Montevallo on 5 May, boarding a train headed east to face Sherman again.[11]

With Mississippi secure, the Federals had turned their attention squarely toward Georgia. On 18 March 1864 Sherman officially assumed command of the Military Division of the Mississippi, comprised of George H. Thomas' Army of the Cumberland, James B. McPherson's Army of the Tennessee, and John Schofield's Army of the Ohio—a total force numbering about 100,000 men. Three weeks later Grant ordered Sherman to move on Joseph Johnston's Confederate force in Georgia. The Union objective was Atlanta. In early May, Sherman moved south from Chattanooga to challenge the outnumbered Confederates, who would wage a defensive campaign. Polk's Army of Mississippi, including the 15th Mississippi Infantry, was ordered to reinforce Johnston. Upon its arrival at Resaca, Georgia, during the second week of May, Polk's command became Polk's corps in Johnston's Army of Tennessee. The 15th Mississippi remained in Adams's brigade, Loring's division. With the addition of the Army of Mississippi, Johnston had at his disposal about 80,000 men.[12]

---

[11] Binford, "Recollections," 45; Joel Calvin Watson diary, 16–17.

[12] Long and Long, *The Civil War Day by Day*, 483, 500; James M. McPherson, *Battle Cry of Freedom: The Civil War Era* (New York: Ballantine Books, 1988) 744;

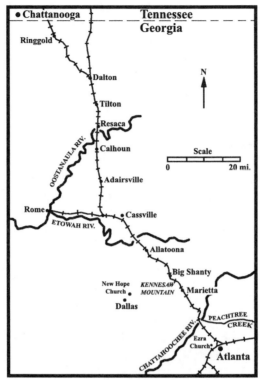

Map 10   Northwest Georgia, 1864

Polk's force, 10,000 infantry and 4,000 cavalry, arrived at Resaca on the evening of 11 May, just in time to aid Johnston. Johnston deployed his army west of the town, with Lieutenant General John Bell Hood's corps on the right, Lieutenant General William J. Hardee's men in the center, and Polk's new arrivals on the left. The 15th Mississippi occupied ground near the Oostanaula River. After intermittent skirmishing on 13 May, Hood attacked the Federal left the following afternoon. On the Confederate left McPherson attacked Polk's corps, failing to break the rebel line. The fighting continued the next day with neither army gaining a distinct advantage. During the evening Johnston received word that the Federals would be threatening the Confederate's left flank by morning. In response, the general ordered his army to fall

Albert Castel, *Decision in the West: The Atlanta Campaign of 1864* (Lawrence: University Press of Kansas, 1992) 145–47.

back, ending the Battle of Resaca. Later that night the Confederates crossed the Oostenaula on pontoon bridges, completing the withdrawal just before daybreak. One member of the 15th Mississippi's Company F called the battle "our debut or introduction to the famous Georgia campaign, that was followed by a series of hardships, battles, and skirmishing for several months afterwards, picket fire never ceasing day or night."[13]

In the face of a superior force, Johnston's overall strategy involved retreating slowly and in good order, destroying bridges and railroads along the way and engaging the enemy only with the advantage of well-protected entrenchments. Falling back steadily, different parts of the Confederate army skirmished almost constantly with Sherman's men. Major engagements took place at New Hope Church (25–28 May), Picket's Mill (27 May), Dallas (28 May), Kolb's Farm (22 June), and Kennesaw Mountain (27 June). On 14 June an artillery shell struck and killed Polk as he observed Union troop movements with other Confederate commanders. Polk's death moved Johnston to tears. "In this distinguished leader we have lost the most courteous of gentlemen, the most gallant of soldiers," the commanding general said in an emotional address to the troops. "The Christian, patriot, soldier has neither lived nor died in vain. His example is before you; his mantle rests with you." After several days Lieutenant General Alexander P. Stewart took command of Polk's corps, to which the 15th Mississippi remained attached.[14]

Johnston successfully avoided open warfare, but by mid-July Jefferson Davis had grown frustrated with both the general and the continued Federal advance. On 17 July, Davis removed Johnston from command of the Army of Tennessee and replaced him with John Bell Hood. The removal of Johnston distressed many of the men in the ranks, including soldiers from the 15th Mississippi. "From the hour the news of the change of commander reached the men in the pits, a mark of sentiment was discernable," Tom Gore of Company F wrote. "Whatever

---

[13] Castel, *Decision in the West,* 145–75; William R. Scaife, *The Campaign for Atlanta* (Atlanta: William R. Scaife, 1985) 16–23.

[14] Long and Long, *The Civil War Day by Day,* 522; Robert Underwood Johnson and Clarence Clough Buel, eds., vol. 4 of *Battles and Leaders of the Civil War* (New York: The Century Company, 1887) 270. Afterwards this work is cited as *Battles and Leaders,* followed by the appropriate volume and page numbers; Castel, *Decisions in the West,* 337–38.

may have been said or may be said in the future...General Johnston at least had the unqualified confidence of his men." James Binford later reflected that during the Georgia campaign, "President Davis never made a more serious mistake than he did by removing General Johnston." Several of Johnston's subordinate commanders bristled at Hood's appointment. Hardee, who was in line for the promotion himself, claimed that Hood was incompetent to command while Stewart called Davis's decision "the final coup de grace to the Confederate cause." During his service to the Confederacy, Hood had excelled as a brigade and division leader with the Army of Northern Virginia and as a corps commander under Johnston in Georgia. He distinguished himself at Antietam and Fredericksburg, suffered a crippling wound to his arm at Gettysburg, and lost a leg at Chickamauga. Despite his record, however, Hood's appointment as commander of the Army of Tennessee would have disastrous consequences. Years later Sherman wrote that in changing commanders "at this critical moment, the Confederate Government rendered us most valuable service.... I confess I was pleased."[15]

By the time of the Atlanta Campaign, two men who began their military careers with the 15th Mississippi were in command positions in the Army of Tennessee. Edward C. Walthall, originally a member of Company H during the war's first year, left the regiment after the Battle of Mill Springs in 1862 to lead the 29th Mississippi Infantry. He became a major general and division commander. William F. Brantley, the original captain of Company D and regimental commander at Shiloh, left the 15th Mississippi to serve under Walthall. He eventually achieved the rank of brigadier general. For the remainder of the war both men served in the Army of Tennessee along with the soldiers of their old regiment.[16]

During Sherman's advance the 15th Mississippi saw limited action at New Hope Church and Kennesaw Mountain, sustaining several casualties. The regiment was most heavily engaged at Peachtree Creek on 20 July. Abandoning Johnston's defensive strategy, Hood saw his

[15] Stewart Sifakis, *Who Was Who in the Civil War* (New York: Facts on File, 1988) 316–17; *Battles and Leaders*, vol. 4:253; Unknown Author, "History of the Water Valley Rifles, Company F, Fifteenth Mississippi Infantry," Supplement to the WPA Historical Research Project, Yalobusha County, 16 February 1937, Special Collections, J. D. Williams Library, University of Mississippi, Oxford, Mississippi, 52, 57; Binford, "Recollections," 50; Stanley F. Horn, *The Army of Tennessee* (Norman: The University of Oklahoma Press, 1952) 343–46.

[16] Sifakis, *Who Was Who*, 70, 689.

chance as George H. Thomas moved his Army of the Cumberland across the creek a few miles north of Atlanta. Hood hoped to increase his odds for victory by engaging Thomas separately from the rest of Sherman's army. "My objective," the Confederate commander later wrote, "was to crush Thomas' Army before he could [cross the creek and] fortify himself, and then turn upon Schofield and McPherson

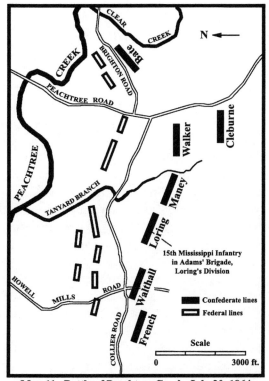

Map 11   Battle of Peachtree Creek, July 20, 1864

Hood's plan was doomed from the start. Miscommunication and indecisiveness caused numerous delays. At 4:30 P.M.—three hours behind schedule—on the afternoon of 20 July, the 15th Mississippi, with the rest of Stewart's corps, flung itself "with an insidious rebel yell" at Thomas's hastily constructed breastworks. Stewart's men initially drove the Federals back, but the thrust was poorly coordinated. After a fierce struggle, Union troops mounted a countercharge. Thomas also brought up artillery and began "pumping death into the ranks of the attackers."

Confusion reigned as the Confederates withdrew, losing around 5,000 men.[17]

The 15th Mississippi was fully involved in the chaos. Although under heavy fire, the regiment left the field with a number of prisoners. Michael Farrell narrowly avoided capture while waiting for support from Brigadier General D. H. Reynolds's Arkansas brigade. James Binford took part in the battle and reported that the Yankees crossed Peachtree Creek in considerable force, piled up their knapsacks, and began throwing up breastworks when Farrell ordered the 15th Mississippi to charge. According to Binford, "We drove the enemy back...capturing 193 prisoners, together with a number of guns, all their knapsacks, spades, picks, etc., but it cost us considerable, for in the charge we lost over 40 men and among them several officers.... Lt. Hugh Montgomery of Company I was among the number killed." In his journal Joel Watson recorded that after the Federals "crossed the creek and drove back our skirmishers and formed a line on our side of the creek," the 15th Mississippi "charged and drove them to the creek and killed a great many of them." Following the battle, reports came in from the field that Reynolds's Arkansas brigade had failed to support the 15th Mississippi's efforts. According to the Mississippians, the failure had almost allowed the Yankees to capture Farrell and had squandered an opportunity for the Confederates to capture an entire regiment of Federal prisoners.[18]

The incident was a source of controversy following the battle. John Adams, in his report of 19 July, indicated that Reynolds's hesitation was costly. Adams wrote, "Had Reynolds cooperated and connected with Colonel Farrell, a thousand prisoners might easily have been taken. As it was, however, I lost heavily in killed and wounded." Reynolds vehemently disputed this assessment in his report, claiming that Farrell repeatedly failed to move as directed and that "as to the regiment of infantry having surrendered to Col. Farrell and he being compelled to leave it, I would say that it is very strange indeed.... I think the statement simply unworthy of serious denial. There are other errors and sage

---

[17] Carter, *The Siege of Atlanta, 1864*, 204; Castel, *Decision in the West*, 378; Richard McMurry, *John Bell Hood and the War for Southern Independence* (Lincoln: University of Nebraska Press, 1982) 128.

[18] Binford, "Recollections," 48–49; Joel Calvin Watson diary, 21.

suggestions in Adams' report that I do not deem necessary to notice."[19] The controversy, while relatively minor in the face of subsequent events, was indicative of the finger-pointing that would take place at every level during Hood's tenure as commander of the Army of Tennessee.

During the battle the 15th Mississippi suffered numerous casualties, among them a soldier from Company F named Ben Hervey, who was hit as he escorted a prisoner from the field. Hervey's wound was especially unfortunate because it was the result of friendly fire. According to a fellow soldier who saw Hervey fall, "A soldier from the 9th Arkansas Regiment had followed up the 15th and spied the prisoner in his blue suit and, not seeing his captor who was behind him, fired at the Yankee." The bullet missed its intended target and instead passed through Hervey's right thigh.[20]

From Peachtree Creek the Confederates moved into Atlanta, and on 22 July part of Hood's force under Hardee and Cheatham took part in the Battle of Atlanta, another Confederate defeat. Six days later Hood again failed to drive the Federals back at Ezra Church. Although not on the front line, the 15th Mississippi was involved at Ezra Church as part of Stewart's corps. The regiment suffered few casualties. One soldier from Company E later recalled, "A minnie ball passed between us, so near Colonel Farrell's eye that it stung it, and he was compelled to keep it closed for several minutes."[21]

After defeating the Confederates at Ezra Church, Sherman laid partial siege to Atlanta for several weeks. Hood's already limited supplies dwindled, and it was only a matter of time until he would be forced to either surrender his command or abandon the city. According to one soldier from the 15th Mississippi, "Time wore on, but brought no relief to the half-starved, ragged Confederates who laid in ditches so long unwashed, unshaven, hair uncut, their rations consisting of a little salt meat and cornbread." During the siege the Federals hoisted shells over the Confederate fortifications, and sniper bullets flew sporadically as

---

[19] US War Department, comp., *The War of Rebellion: A Compilation of the Official Records of the Union and Confederate Armies*, 128 vols. (Washington, DC: 1880–1902) ser. 1, vol. 38(3):891–94. Afterwards this work is cited as *OR*, followed by the volume number, part number (when applicable), and page numbers. Unless otherwise noted, all references are to volumes from series 1.

[20] "History of the Water Valley Rifles," 56.

[21] Long and Long, *The Civil War Day by Day*, 543–47; "History of the Water Valley Rifles," 51.

Sherman's men expanded their works around the city. The 15th Mississippi suffered more casualties. According to one private, the regiment was "so near the picket lines…that for one to show his head above the works…meant certain death to one so negligent." E. L. Trask and Charles Bankhead of Company F "were visitors of this terrible malady, though both had only slight wounds. Trask received a slight abrasion from a piece of shell on the shoulder. Bankhead lost two fingers on his left hand, the little finger and the one next to it." On 10 August, Joel Watson recorded in his diary that three men were killed from the regiment, with three more killed on 13 August. James Dicken later remembered that in Company A, "losses were heavy from stray balls" fired by Federal soldiers around the Atlanta perimeter.[22]

Among those killed from Company E were childhood friends and Choctaw County farmers John Young and Willie Buford. Both men were popular among their fellow soldiers, and their loss was especially difficult. According to one of the soldiers, while "accustomed to the sight of blood and death in every form, the sight of these two boys as they lay cold and motionless, their pale faces upturned to heaven, fairly made us recoil for an instant." Young and Buford were buried in a common grave, marked by a wooden plank with a pocketknife inscription: "Comrades in arms, Comrades in death."[23] W.B. Wagner, a relative of Young's also serving in Company E, reported the death to Young's sister in a letter dated 25 August 1864:

> Your noble and brave brother John was killed yesterday morning. I have just finished a letter to our dear mother acquainting her with our great misfortune. John was shot by a minnie ball over the right temple. We were in the act of preparing breakfast when the fatal shot struck him. The ball passed directly over my right shoulder. Had I been a few inches to the right it would have killed us both. Willie Buford was killed at about the same time and the shot struck him at about the same place.… I had them buried in the same grave, but different vaults and was fortunate enough [to get] two nice coffins from

---

[22] "History of the Water Valley Rifles," 52, 56; McPherson, *Battle Cry of Freedom*, 754–56; Castel, *Decision in the West*, 462–68; James T. Dicken, "Long Creek Rifles," *Kosciusko Star Ledger*, 1 January 1898; Joel Calvin Watson diary, 22–23.

[23] "History of the Water Valley Rifles," 53–56.

the quartermaster's corps.... Parson Reese sang a hymn and made a few appropriate remarks. It was a solemn spectacle to witness; about a dozen of his comrades standing around the grave and the pale moon looking down on us. Frank Young of the 10th Tennessee was present. Console yourself that he is gone to heaven.[24]

On 26 August, Sherman swung most of his men south of Atlanta to cut the last open railroad line out of the city. Hood originally misinterpreted Sherman's intentions, believing that the Federals were withdrawing. He learned the truth too late, eventually sending two corps south to meet the threat. The Federals repulsed the Confederates at Jonesboro on 30 August, and the next day Sherman mounted a successful counterattack. On 1 September, Hood ordered the evacuation of Atlanta as Federal troops moved to completely encircle the city. The following day Union soldiers marched into the city unmolested. After his men raised the American flag over city hall, Sherman wired Washington that "Atlanta is ours, and fairly won." Meanwhile, the 15th Mississippi limped south to Lovejoy Station and eventually moved west to Palmetto, where they rested and regrouped.[25]

Atlanta was another disaster for the Confederacy. Although precise casualty counts of the Army of Tennessee were elusive, a survey of total infantry strength during the period shed light on the magnitude of Confederate losses. Estimates stated that Johnston's infantry at the beginning of the campaign numbered around 55,000, but by early September the Confederates could muster barely 23,000 effectives. In the eight-day period during which the two armies fought at Peachtree Creek, Atlanta, and Ezra Church, the Confederates lost about 15,000 men. In many quarters Confederate losses from desertion reached epidemic proportion as morale again plummeted. The 15th Mississippi turned in no official casualty reports from Atlanta. Various estimates indicated that

---

[24] W. B. Wagner, letter to Ella Young, 15 August 1864.

[25] McPherson, *Battle Cry of Freedom*, 774.

following the evacuation of Atlanta, the regiment numbered around 200 men. While official records were sketchy, as many as two to three dozen men from the 15th Mississippi deserted during the campaign.[26]

---

[26] James Lee McDonough and Thomas L. Connelly, *Five Tragic Hours: The Battle of Franklin* (Knoxville: University of Tennessee Press, 1983) 5; McPherson, *Battle Cry of Freedom*, 755; *Battles and Leaders*, vol. 4:289; Compiled Service Records: 15th Mississippi Infantry.

CHAPTER 8

POST-ATLANTA MOVEMENTS AND THE BATTLE OF FRANKLIN, 1864

The war ought to be stopped.[1]
Edwin J. Boushe, Company G, 15th Mississippi Infantry,
November 1864

By autumn 1864, the 15th Mississippi Infantry was filled with beaten men. Their collective faith in the Confederacy was threadbare. To many of the soldiers the quest for Southern independence had already failed. Their state was lost to the Federals, and reports from home still emphasized family hardships. Many of the friends and relatives with whom they began their Confederate adventure were dead, their remains deposited in hastily prepared graves throughout the South. Sickness and hunger followed the survivors on long, painful marches and into lonely, tattered camps. The men of the 15th Mississippi had not joined the Confederate army to endure such tests of will. The regiment had not been organized to lose the war, but as the winter of 1864 approached most of its members were gone. Those who remained carried on the struggle as they tenuously clung to the honor-bound community commitment that originally brought them into war. "If it were not for the disgrace to my family," one soldier from the regiment wrote, "I would not hesitate to desert."[2]

---

[1] Ed Jones Boushe, letter to Grand Ma, undated, WPA History of Grenada County, Mississippi Department of Archives and History Library, Jackson, Mississippi, microfilm.
[2] Ibid.

As they struggled to make sense of their situation, a number of men in the 15th Mississippi turned to religion. Throughout the war revival movements periodically swept through the Confederate armies in both the East and West, and following the defeats at Vicksburg and Gettysburg these movements became more intense. On the whole, Southern soldiers tended to be more enthusiastic than their Northern counterparts in demonstrating their religious commitment. The evangelical tradition of the South, with its emphasis on the individual soul, was more conducive to spontaneous professions of faith, particularly during trying times. As the war progressed the average soldier was confronted with his own mortality on a daily basis. What had once been a community enterprise had become a constant struggle for individual survival, in turn creating a need for spiritual solace. For many the eternal triumph of the individual soul salved the psychological wounds of more immediate defeats on the battlefield. By 1864 the revival movements were also tied to the perception among many Southerners that their severe military reversals were a punishment from God, the result of excessive "backsliding" and a general neglect of religious concerns. The soldiers had been told again and again that they were participating in a holy crusade. Because God could not be wrong, many Southern ministers promoted the notion that military victories by the "Godless Northern hordes" must be linked to spiritual shortcomings in the Southern ranks. This allowed the soldiers to reconcile their dire circumstances with the presumption that God continued to sanction the Confederate cause.[3]

In the West, Confederate revivalism peaked during the winter of 1863–1864 at Dalton, Georgia, in the camps of the Army of Tennessee. Numerous conversions took place in almost every brigade. The demand for preachers was high, and due to a shortage of army chaplains, local ministers or Christian laymen from the ranks sometimes led services. While Baptists, Methodists, and Presbyterians were the dominant faiths,

---

[3] James I. Robertson Jr., *Soldiers Blue and Gray* (Columbia: University of South Carolina Press, 1988) 186–88; Gardiner H. Shattuck Jr., *A Shield and Hiding Place: The Religious Life of the Civil War Armies* (Macon GA: Mercer University Press, 1987) 100–09; G. Clinton Prim Jr., "Born Again in the Trenches: Revivals in the Army of Tennessee," *Tennessee Historical Quarterly* 43/3 (Fall 1984): 256–67; Larry J. Daniel, *Soldiering in the Army of Tennessee* (Chapel Hill: The University of North Carolina Press, 1991) 115–25.

there was little denominational rivalry when it came to saving souls. The religious outpouring also transcended rank. While at Dalton, Leonidas Polk, an Episcopal bishop in civilian life, baptized Generals Johnston, Hardee, and Hood. "Religion is the theme," one soldier wrote to his sister during the period. "Everywhere, you hear around the campfires the sweet song of Zion. The spirit pervades the whole army."[4]

While not all soldiers converted, the spirit of revivalism in the Army of Tennessee continued throughout 1864. After the Atlanta Campaign a number of conversions took place in the 15th Mississippi during revival meetings. On 12 September, Joel Watson recorded in his diary that he "went and saw 12 or 15 baptized" from the regiment, and three days later he attended "a sermon preached by Parson Cooper on the condition of our country and that it was our own sins that caused it." For some of the regiment's soldiers spiritual renewal was a final attempt to find the strength and comfort they needed to sustain themselves. They could no longer count on support from close friends who had died or deserted the army, nor could they count on significant support from home. While the soldiers may have made a sincere religious statement by converting, it is likely that the act itself was, to varying degrees, a function of emotional and psychological desperation.[5]

On the morning of 26 September 1864 at Palmetto, Georgia, the men of the 15th Mississippi came face to face with their commander in chief. Jefferson Davis had arrived in camp the previous day. Alarmed by reports from Georgia, he traveled south to review Hood's troops and confer with Confederate commanders on problems with organization and morale. As he surveyed the Army of Tennessee, he saw despair in the men's thin faces. Sullen silence marked the review, broken occasionally by shouts from the ranks: "Give us Joe Johnston! Give us our old commander!" While in the Confederate camp, Davis heard numerous complaints about Hood's leadership, but he could not replace the general without admitting his own mistake. Relieving Hood would amount to a

---

[4] Shattuck, *A Shield and Hiding Place: The Religious Life of the Civil War Armies*, 100–09; Prim, "Born Again in the Trenches: Revivals in the Army of Tennessee," 262–67; Sidney J. Romero, *Religion in the Rebel Ranks* (Lanham MD: University Press of America, 1983) 116–21.

[5] Joel Calvin Watson diary, Grenada Public Library, Grenada, Mississippi, 24–25; Daniel, *Soldiering in the Army of Tennessee*, 115–25; Shattuck, *A Shield and Hiding Place: The Religious Life of the Civil War Armies*, 104–09.

concession that placing him in command in the first place had been a grievous error. After two days, Davis left Palmetto. Unfortunately for the men of the 15th Mississippi and their fellow soldiers, John Bell Hood remained in command.[6]

Following the president's visit, Hood mobilized his haggard force for what proved to be a prolonged, tragic pipe dream. Having lost Atlanta, Hood planned to circle the city to Sherman's rear and cut the Western and Atlantic Railroad, the Federals' supposedly vital supply and communication link to Chattanooga. If successful, he surmised that he could eventually attack the disheveled and starving Federal army at his leisure. Davis, with similar grand delusions, backed the plan, stating that "Sherman can not keep up his long line of communication, and retreat, sooner or later, he must. And when that time comes, the fate that befell the Army of the French Empire in its retreat from Moscow will be reenacted." When Grant got word of Davis's remarks, he reportedly posed the question, "Who is to furnish the snow for this Moscow retreat?"[7]

On 29–30 September, Hood's Confederates built pontoon bridges and crossed the Chattahoochie River near Campbellton. Moving north, they destroyed a significant portion of track and captured several hundred Federal prisoners. On 3 October, Stewart's corps reached Ackworth, where the 15th Mississippi and other soldiers from Adams's brigade took part in a minor siege against a small Union detachment. Adams's men surrounded the house and under a flag of truce sent in demands for an unconditional surrender. While the Federals were woefully outnumbered, a refusal meant that the Confederates would have to take the house by force and, in so doing, probably sustain a number of casualties.[8] James Binford of the 15th Mississippi was uneasy about the prospect. "The order almost made me shudder," he later wrote, "as I looked at that house with many bricks knocked out of it to furnish holes

---

[6] Albert Castel, *Decision in the West: The Atlanta Campaign of 1864* (Lawrence: University Press of Kansas, 1992) 551–52; Richard McMurry, *John Bell Hood and the War for Southern Independence* (Lincoln: University of Nebraska Press, 1982) 157–58.

[7] Castel, *Decision in the West*, 550–51; James M. McPherson, *Battle Cry of Freedom: The Civil War Era* (New York: Ballantine Books, 1988) 807–08.

[8] McMurry, *John Bell Hood and the War for Southern Independence*, 159; James R. Binford, "Recollections of the Fifteenth Mississippi Infantry, CSA," Patrick Henry Papers, Mississippi Department of Archives and History Library, Jackson, Mississippi, 54.

for enemy rifles, and realizing that there were neither trees nor shrubs between us and a wide, deep ditch to cross, I saw at once that if we made the charge it would be the last one many of us ever made."[9] Binford's fears never materialized. After a few minutes of negotiation the Federals surrendered. Because the 15th Mississippi was first in line to charge the house, Adams ordered the regiment to receive the prisoners. The Union soldiers marched out and stacked their arms. Upon examination, the Southerners found that the Federals "had bent nearly every gun barrel, rendering them unfit for service."[10]

The Confederates captured another Federal garrison at Dalton, and among the Union prisoners taken were a number of black troops. According to one member of the 15th Mississippi, "These sable soldiers were at first a white elephant on our hands. We did not recognize them as prisoners of war, or in the light of soldiers, but as property subject to be claimed by their owners." Rather than detain the black troops with their white counterparts, the Confederates put then to work repairing railroad lines between Tuscumbia, Alabama, and Corinth.[11]

Sherman initially pursued the Confederates north but soon realized that such a course would accomplish little. Far from crippled by Hood's movements, he regrouped most of his forces in Atlanta and, on 16 November, set out to "make Georgia howl" on his march to the sea. Meanwhile, Hood wandered through northern Georgia into Alabama. Instead of starving the Federals or luring them into some type of ambush, Hood's men quickly grew weary, footsore, and distanced from their own supply lines.[12]

The men of the 15th Mississippi suffered along with the rest of the troops as provisions ran perilously low. On 16 October, Thomas Jefferson Kent of Company E wrote to his parents in Duck Hill, "My feet is very sore and my shoes is worn out but I expect to keep up as long as I can make a track." In another letter, written two weeks later, he informed his family, "I am as good as barefoot, nothing except the tops of some

---

[9] Binford, "Recollections," 54–55.

[10] Ibid.

[11] Unknown Author, "History of the Water Valley Rifles, Company F, Fifteenth Mississippi Infantry," Supplement to the WPA Historical Research Project, Yalobusha County, 16 February 1937, Special Collections, J. D. Williams Library, University of Mississippi, Oxford, Mississippi, 58.

[12] Castel, *Decision in the West*, 552–53.

shoes on and no soles in them.... I don't think we can go very far
because our army is in very bad condition, no clothes or shoes." Another
soldier from Company F reported, "There was a distribution of blankets
and shoes in the army.... Four blankets and four pairs of shoes to a
company that perhaps had 25 men in it without shoes on their feet....
[The men] had to cast lots to see who should receive the shoes and
blankets." James Binford later recalled, "It was no uncommon thing for
us to have nothing, or but little to eat" for several days at a time before
the men "received the usual small ration of one pound of beef, one pound
of corn meal, and a small quantity of salt." Some soldiers substituted
parched acorns for corn and boiled vines of various descriptions for
cabbage.[13]

During the last two weeks of October, Hood made new plans.
Unable to engage the Federals, he set upon a wild course that would
undo his military career and virtually destroy what was left of the Army
of Tennessee. Hood planned to drive through central Tennessee, occupy
Nashville, and then proceed into Kentucky. From there the army would
move east to join Robert E. Lee. Together, Hood fantasized, he and Lee
could defeat Grant and then turn south to annihilate Sherman. "I
conceived the plan of marching into Tennessee," Hood later wrote, "with
the hope to establish our line eventually through Kentucky.... I hoped
then to be in condition to offer battle; and, if successful, to send
reinforcements to General Lee in Virginia." [14] Even with a tightly
organized and well-equipped force, the odds for success in such a
campaign were long. For Hood's battered army, a successful invasion of
Tennessee would prove impossible.

Miscommunication and general confusion again plagued Hood's
command on this new venture. Ostensibly in search of an adequate spot
to cross the Tennessee River, the Confederates marched aimlessly
through northern Alabama during late October and early November,
occasionally skirmishing with Federal detachments. The 15th Mississippi

---

[13] Montgomery County Historical Society, *History of Montgomery County* (Dallas
TX: Curtis Media Corp., 1993) 35; "History of the Water Valley Rifles," 58; Binford,
"Recollections," 56.

[14] McMurry, *John Bell Hood and the War for Southern Independence*, 161–63;
McPherson, *Battle Cry of Freedom*, 812–13; Robert Underwood Johnson and Clarence
Clough Buel, eds., vol. 4 of *Battles and Leaders of the Civil War* (New York: The
Century Company, 1887) 426–27. Afterwards this work is cited as *Battles and Leaders*,
followed by the appropriate volume and page numbers.

camped with the rest of the army at Gadsden (21 October), Brooksville (23 October), Sommersville (25 October), and Decatur (26 October). On 29 October, Hood relocated his headquarters to Tuscumbia and moved across the Tennessee River to Florence, where they remained until 20 November. On 21 November, Hood's Tennessee campaign finally began in earnest as his invasion force left Florence heading for Nashville.[15]

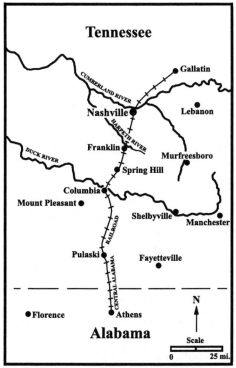

Map 12   Approach to Nashville, 1864

Nominally resupplied and reinforced, Hood crossed the Tennessee state line with around 40,000 men, including cavalry under Nathan Bedford Forrest. The Confederate infantry was organized into three corps under Major General Benjamin F. Cheatham, Lieutenant General Stephen D. Lee, and Lieutenant General Alexander P. Stewart. Hood

---

[15] McMurry, *John Bell Hood and the War for Southern Independence*, 161–65; Everette B. Long with Barbara Long, *The Civil War Day by Day: An Almanac 1861–1865* (Garden City NY: Doubleday and Company, 1971) 598–99.

would ultimately face 60,000 well-supplied Federal troops. George H. Thomas was now in command of Union forces in Tennessee and was in the process of assembling 30,000 men in Nashville. John M. Schofield was at Pulaski with around 30,000 infantry and cavalry at his disposal. It would be Schofield's job to delay Hood's advance as Federal forces organized at the state capital. During the march toward Nashville, the 15th Mississippi Infantry remained attached to Adams's brigade, Loring's division, in Stewart's corps.[16]

Hood's movements were cumbersome. He was unfamiliar with the terrain, and his reconnaissance failed to pinpoint critical Federal troop deployments. Provisions continued running low, and rain, sleet, freezing temperatures, and boggy roads hampered the entire operation. Morale in the ill-equipped Confederate ranks reached new lows. During the last week of November, Edwin Jones Boushe of the 15th Mississippi's Company G summed up the prevailing sentiment among many of the soldiers as he wrote in a letter home, " We don't have tents nor enough cover to sleep under. It looks hard that we have to keep fighting, because the northerners have all the advantages, so many more men and so much better equipped.... The war ought to be stopped."[17]

The fate of Hood's Tennessee campaign was effectively sealed on 29 November during what would become known as the Spring Hill Affair, one of the most hotly debated non-combat occurrences of the war. At Spring Hill, Hood had managed to outmaneuver Schofield somewhat, and the Confederates found themselves in position to attack with an arguable advantage. Characteristically for Hood's plans, the attack never materialized due to poor organization and conflicting orders. During the night Schofield's men retired north of Spring Hill and repositioned themselves on more favorable ground. Hood later dramatized in his memoirs that "the best move of my career as a soldier, I was thus destined to behold come to naught."[18]

Hood placed the blame squarely on the shoulders of his subordinates, primarily Cheatham. He later claimed that the corps commander failed to follow orders and that at one point he had ridden up to Cheatham and shouted, "General, why in the name of God have you

---

[16] James Lee McDonough and Thomas L. Connelly, *Five Tragic Hours: The Battle of Franklin* (Knoxville: University of Tennessee Press, 1983) 52–56.

[17] Ed Jones Boushe, letter to Grand Ma, undated.

[18] McDonough and Connelly, *Five Tragic Hours*, 52–56.

not attacked the enemy?" Cheatham, who was later cleared, countered that such a version of events "only occurred in the imagination of General Hood." The controversy was never completely resolved, and there was no guarantee that a Confederate attack would have significantly altered the dynamics of the campaign. In hindsight, however, soldiers used the event to help justify the failure of the Tennessee campaign. James Dicken of the 15th Mississippi's Company A later exaggerated that in not striking the Federals at Spring Hill, the Confederates "lost one of the golden opportunities of the war." At the time of the affair James Binford was away from the regiment on temporary assignment to Stewart's staff. On the night in question he rode with Stewart to Hood's headquarters and stayed outside while the two generals conferred. According to Binford, on the return trip, "I asked General Stewart the direct question if we were going to have a fight there. His reply was 'Not that I know of, there have been no orders for a fight.' It does seem to me that if General Hood had given such orders to General Cheatham, he would certainly have told General Stewart so he could have his own corps ready."[19]

The next day the Army of Tennessee met disaster. Believing that Schofield was falling back to Nashville, a frustrated Hood moved his troops out of Spring Hill. By the afternoon of 30 November, Stewart's corps, leading the march, passed over Winstead Hill near the town of Franklin, 16 miles south of Nashville. To the north of the hill a valley stretched to the Harpeth River. There, the Confederates found Schofield, whose orders from Thomas in Nashville were to "hold Hood at Franklin for three days or longer." Franklin was open to attack only from the south, and the Federals were in an impenetrable position.[20]

The Federals lay in wait as Hood and several other officers climbed Winstead Hill to survey the scene. After some discussion, Hood astonished his subordinates by announcing that the army would launch a headlong frontal assault. Protests only seemed to strengthen the general's resolve as he ignored suggestions that the Confederates should cross the Harpeth River and try to flank Schofield out of the town. It was as if

---

[19] McDonough and Connelly, *Five Tragic Hours*, 55; James T. Dicken, "Long Creek Rifles," *Kosciusko Star Ledger*, 1 January 1898; Binford, "Recollections," 60.

[20] Stanley F. Horn, *The Decisive Battle of Nashville* (Knoxville: University of Tennessee Press, 1956) 18; McMurry, *John Bell Hood and the War for Southern Independence*, 174.

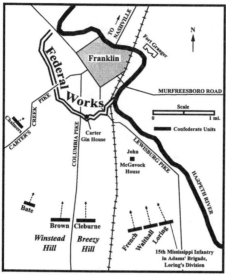

Map 13 Battle of Franklin, November 30, 1864

Hood alone was blind to the dangers that lurked behind the distant fortifications.[21] Still angry and bitter from the previous night's debacle, Hood ordered his army into position with Stewart's corps on the right and Cheatham's corps to the left. Lee's corps, still in route from Franklin, would not be in position as the assault began. Loring's division was on the right in Stewart's corps. Adams's brigade, in turn, took a position on the right in Loring's division. Thus the 15th Mississippi was on the extreme right in the line of battle, crowded near the river.

As Hood sealed the fate of his army on Winstead Hill, several officers from the 15th Mississippi consumed their last meals. Stewart's corps was in position by three o'clock, and shortly before the attack a much needed basket of provisions appeared in the regiment, courtesy of Lieutenant Charles Campbell of the 15th Mississippi's Company E, who happened to have relatives living in the area. Campbell invited several officers to join in the unexpected feast, including Michael Farrell, Captain James Smith and Lieutenant Thomas Allen of Company E, and four other officers from Mississippi and Louisiana units. During the hasty meal, "the impending battle was freely discussed by those eight officers, all of whom were in a serious, thoughtful mood." Robert W.

---

[21] McMurry, *John Bell Hood and the War for Southern Independence*, 174–75.

Banks of the 37th Mississippi, who was friendly with some of the 15th Mississippi's officers, listened to part of the discussion and later recalled that of the eight men, "two only were optimistic. The other six took a gloomy view of the situation. They had presentments that when it was over their records for time and eternity would be made up." Banks added that "prognostications more swiftly, and direfully fulfilled, it would be impossible to discover. Before the sun went down six out of the eight received mortal wounds."[22]

At four o'clock, the Confederate advance began. One Federal soldier who viewed the procession later wrote, "It was worth a year of one's lifetime to witness the marshaling and advance of the rebel line of battle.... Nothing could be more suggestive of strength and discipline, and resistless power than this long line of gray advancing over the plain." As soon as the Confederates came in range the Federals opened fire, and Hood's army responded with the last great Southern charge of the war. "They were coming on the run," another Union soldier later recalled, "emitting a shrill rebel yell, and so near that my first impulse was to throw myself on the ground and let them charge over us."[23] Despite this recollection, Schofield's men did not lay down.

A massacre followed. The Confederates blindly and repeatedly charged in the face of "one unceasing volley" of withering artillery and small arms fire. Soon, dead and dying men covered the approach to the Federal works. The Confederates occasionally breached the Federal lines before reserves rushed in to close the gaps. For several hours, well into the night, the massed Confederates loaded weapons and passed them to those in front who had enough room to aim and fire them. Blood flowed through the ditch in front of the Federal works. According to Edward C. Walthall, late of the 15th Mississippi and a division commander in Stewart's corps, the Confederate army at Franklin was exposed to "[by] far the most deadly fire of both small-arms and artillery that I have ever seen troops subjected to," and the men were "terribly torn at every step."[24]

---

[22] Robert W. Banks, *The Battle of Franklin* (New York: Walter Neal Publishing Co., 1908) 60–63.

[23] McDonough and Connelly, *Five Tragic Hours*, 109; McMurry, *John Bell Hood and the War for Southern Independence*, 175.

[24] McDonough and Connelly, *Five Tragic Hours*, 120–21; McMurry, *John Bell Hood and the War for Southern Independence*, 175.

As they charged, the soldiers on the Confederate right met a furious hail of lead from a Federal division commanded by Brigadier General Jacob D. Cox and including three brigades under the command of Brigadier General James W. Reilly and Colonels John S. Casement and Israel N. Stiles. Loring's division, including the 15th Mississippi in Adams's brigade, advanced in the face of fire from the Federal works and from a battery placed strategically at an angle on the opposite side of the Harpeth River. As they moved forward, the men of the 15th Mississippi met every conceivable obstacle. A member of Thomas' staff later recalled that "the muskets from Stiles' and Casement's brigades made fearful havoc while the batteries...plowed furrows through the ranks of the advancing foe." Lieutenant Colonel Edward Adams Baker of the 65th Indiana, in Casement's brigade, watched as "the enemy was within a few paces and received a terrific volley from our guns." According to Baker, the Confederates "fell by the thousands, and their decimated ranks fell back to reform and come again. In this way nine separate and distinct charges were made, each time men falling in every direction and each time being repulsed." Soon after the assault began, Loring's division splintered into smaller, intermingled units.[25]

With his sword drawn, Michael Farrell led the 15th Mississippi as the regiment charged headlong into explosive Federal fire near the Carter gin house. John L. Collins of Company H, who made and survived the charge, later recalled that "shot and shell poured in upon our advancing line with disastrous effect.... The cannon all along the line was in full play.... The enemy infantry in our front and near the Carter gin house, with their sixteen-shooter Henry rifles, were pouring into our ranks their deadly minnie balls.... Here the Colonel of the 15th Mississippi and many brave boys fell." According to Tom Gore of Company D, who also survived the charge, as Adams's brigade passed through the hedge in front of the Federal works, "Our lines were broken into squads, and many never got through it. I, with six others, got within about ten feet of the works and could go no farther on account of the thorn bushes.... Four of the seven, Capt. Smith, Lieut. Allen, Newt McGuire, and Frank Moore were killed and two, Evan Powell and Bud Holliday were wounded, I alone coming off unhurt." A soldier from a nearby unit who participated in the battle later recalled that the 15th Mississippi "was crushed like a

---

[25] McDonough and Connelly, *Five Tragic Hours*, 81, 143–49; *Battles and Leaders*, vol. 4:453.

dry leaf." As thousands of soldiers fell, the Confederates continued to press the Federal positions. Within an hour of the initial attack, smoke from the canon and rifle fire "settled down over the line of breastworks so thick that a man couldn't see ten feet in front of himself."[26]

The Battle of Franklin ended on the evening of 30 November as both sides disengaged. Confederate casualties were staggering. Seven thousand soldiers fell in the assault, and the officers corps was decimated. Six generals, including the 15th Mississippi's brigade commander John Adams, lay dead on the field, and five other generals were wounded. Fifty-five regimental commanders fell. The charge virtually wiped out several brigades, and one division lost all of its general officers. In parts of the ditch in front of the Union works, dead Confederate soldiers lay seven deep. Later that night, as he listened to the mumbles, moans, and screams of wounded Confederates left on the battlefield, Union colonel Israel Stiles remarked, "There is no hell left in them. Don't you hear them praying?" In contrast, the Federals reported 189 killed, 1,033 wounded, and 1,104, missing for a total of 2,326.[27]

The 15th Mississippi Infantry suffered major casualties during the assault. Michael Farrell fell mortally wounded, shot several times in the legs. The regiment lost thirteen of twenty-one officers and about half its men during a scene unmatched in their eyes since Shiloh. Four color-bearers, including Charles H. Frierson of Company F, met death before the Federals captured and trampled the 15th Mississippi's regimental banner. While official casualty counts were incomplete, the 15th Mississippi emerged from the battle with perhaps 100 effectives. As the sounds of the fight faded into the night at Franklin, Tennessee, on 30

---

[26] John L. Collins, "Gallant Mike Farrell," *Confederate Veteran* 34/10 (October 1926): 373–74;

Tom M. Gore, "Death and Identity of General Adams," *Confederate Veteran* 1/1 (January 1893): 264; David R. Logsdon, comp. and ed., *Eyewitnesses to the Battle of Franklin* (Nashville: Kettle Mills Press, 1991) 46.

[27] McDonough and Connelly, *Five Tragic Hours*, 125–28; Wiley Sword, *The Confederacy's Last Hurrah: Spring Hill, Franklin & Nashville* (Lawrence: University Press of Kansas, 1992) 254.

November 1864, A. P. Stewart lamented to James Binford of his staff, "I have never witnessed such slaughter and unnecessary waste of human life. This battle was entirely unnecessary."[28]

---

[28] Banks, *The Battle of Franklin*, 63–64; US War Department, comp., *The War of Rebellion: A Compilation of the Official Records of the Union and Confederate Armies*, 128 vols. (Washington, DC: 1880–1902) ser. 1, vol. 45(1):714; Binford, "Recollections," 60–64

CHAPTER 9

NASHVILLE, NORTH CAROLINA, AND THE WAR'S CONCLUSION, 1864–1865

> I witnessed today the saddest spectacle of my life, the review of the skeleton Army of Tennessee.[1]
>
> *Captain B. C. Ridley, A. P. Stewart's Staff, 4 April 1865*

Two hours after the Battle of Franklin ended, John Bell Hood met with his subordinate commanders. Undeterred by the events of the day, he astonished the assembly with a pledge to renew the attack at nine o'clock the next morning. An angry Hood held firm to his decision despite protests from his corps commanders that much of the army was "all cut to pieces." Fortunately for Hood's soldiers, a second attack at Franklin never took place. During the night, Schofield withdrew from the town and fell back to Nashville. There, he could report that he had successfully checked Hood's advance while dealing the Confederate army a severe blow. Hood would pursue, but for all practical purposes his great invasion of Tennessee was over. One local resident who saw the general on the streets of Franklin the day after the battle later recalled that "he looked so sad."[2] Still, Hood issued a general order to be read to each individual regiment:

---

[1] William R. Trotter, *Silk Flags and Cold Steel, the Civil War in North Carolina: The Piedmont* (Winston-Salem NC: John F. Blair, Publishers, 1988) 293.

[2] James Lee McDonough and Thomas L. Connelly, *Five Tragic Hours: The Battle of Franklin* (Knoxville: University of Tennessee Press, 1983) 157, 171; Richard McMurry, *John Bell Hood and the War for Southern Independence* (Lincoln: University of Nebraska Press, 1982) 176; Winston Groom, *Shrouds of Glory: From Atlanta to Nashville: The Last Great Campaign of the Civil War* (New York: The Atlantic Monthly Press, 1995) 209–17.

No. 38

Near Franklin, December 1, 1864

The Commanding general congratulates the army upon the success achieved yesterday over our enemy by their heroic and determined courage. The enemy have been sent in disorder and confusion to Nashville, and while we lament the fall of many gallant officers and brave men, we have shown to our countrymen that we can carry any position occupied by the enemy.

By command of General Hood:

A.P. Mason, Assistant Adjutant-General.

Hood's public assessment of the battle's outcome was at best a gross misrepresentation, and it offered little solace to his army. As the general inspected the town, his men began the grim task of gathering their fallen comrades. Every available building in Franklin became a makeshift field hospital. Many men were laid out in tents or under shade trees. Despite aid from local citizens, the sheer number of wounded quickly overwhelmed the Confederate surgeons corps. Food, medicine, and bandages were in short supply, and many men died before doctors could see them. Those who did receive medical treatment were often left crippled for life. Outside one hospital a horrified civilian observer reported seeing "several wagon loads of limbs that had been amputated." After gathering their wounded, the Confederates placed their dead in long, shallow ditches for burial, a small piece of blanket covering each man's face. Fellow soldiers placed simple wooden markers on the graves of those men who could be identified. Many graves contained only body parts.[3]

Lacking any real options other than to abandon Tennessee and admit the tragic folly of his plan, Hood remained committed to the invasion. Believing that somehow he could rally his troops or perhaps acquire reinforcements, he quickly ordered what was left of the Army of Tennessee out of Franklin, with Nashville remaining his immediate goal. On their way out of town, the surviving Confederates marched past dead and wounded men not yet removed from the field. According to one

---

[3] Ibid.

soldier, "Nothing better calculated to affright and demoralize an army could have been devised than by the exhibition of the dead, as they appeared to those who viewed them there in marching past the gin house that morning." Hood later rationalized that he ordered the further advance of his men "rather than renounce the honor of their cause, without having made a last and manful effort to lift up the sinking fortunes of the Confederacy." By early afternoon on 2 December, the army was within sight of Nashville, and that night Hood established his headquarters six miles south of the city.[4]

Since the beginning of the war, Nashville's population had more than tripled. Originally occupied by the Federal army in 1862, the city was a primary transportation and communication center and, with its vast stores of provisions, a major supply hub of the western theater. Because protecting Nashville was of vital concern to the Federals, the U.S. Army Corps of Engineers had constructed strong defensive works around the city. Consequently, in approaching Nashville the Confederates were moving on one of the most heavily fortified locations in North America. Thomas's men were well invested there, and Hood's desperate force had little chance of driving them away.[5]

By the time the Confederates arrived, their numbers had shrunk to around 25,000 men, including 18,702 infantry. Wholesale changes in the officer corps took place as a result of the disaster at Franklin. Cheatham, Stewart, and Lee retained command of their respective corps, but the Confederates significantly reshuffled subordinate command positions. The 15th Mississippi remained in Loring's division, Stewart's corps, with Colonel Robert Lowry of the 6th Mississippi replacing Adams as brigade commander. James Binford, by now a lieutenant colonel, left Stewart's staff at his own request to replace Michael Farrell at the head

---

[4] Robert Underwood Johnson and Clarence Clough Buel, eds., vol. 4 of *Battles and Leaders of the Civil War* (New York: The Century Company, 1887) 436. Afterwards this work is cited as *Battles and Leaders*, followed by the appropriate volume and page numbers; McMurry, *John Bell Hood and the War for Southern Independence*, 177; David R. Logsdon, comp. and ed., *Eyewitnesses to the Battle of Franklin* (Nashville: Kettle Mills Press, 1991) 80.

[5] Horn Stanley F. Horn, *The Decisive Battle of Nashville* (Knoxville: University of Tennessee Press, 1956) 43.

of the regiment. Other infantry regiments placed in Lowry's brigade were the 6th, 14th, 20th, 23rd, and 43rd Mississippi.[6]

Thomas had assembled more than 70,000 men at Nashville, including Schofield's command. Although there was occasional skirmishing, almost two weeks passed before a major engagement took place. In the interim, the Confederates busied themselves constructing breastworks while Thomas slowly put together a plan of action. The weather considerably hampered movements on both sides.[7]

On 8 December the weather turned bitterly cold. Unlike their well-fed, well-clothed, and well-quartered counterparts in the city, Hood's hungry men were fully exposed to "rain, sleet, and snow with scarcely no fire." By the morning of 9 December one great sheet of ice covered the landscape around Nashville. The Confederates' provisions ran frightfully low. Many of the men retired each evening to holes hacked in the frozen earth, covering themselves with a blanket as they slept three abreast. Others scoured the surrounding countryside for material to make shoes. The health of the army deteriorated, and morale remained abysmal. As the men suffered, Hood clung to his shattered plan. Apparently unaware of the strength of Thomas's force, Hood chose to dig in and wait for the Federals to attack. He surmised incorrectly that if the Confederates could lure Thomas from behind the Nashville fortifications, perhaps they could strike a decisive blow.[8]

As Hood waited, the Federal high command grew anxious. The Army of Tennessee was badly wounded but still viewed as formidable. Grant wanted immediate action and telegraphed Thomas on 6 December to attack Hood at once. Still, Thomas delayed, supposedly waiting for additional cavalry reinforcements and for the weather to break. On 15 December the Federals finally struck Hood's army with full force. Ponderously, but with massive effect, Thomas's troops lurched out of the

---

[6] McDonough and Connelly, *Five Tragic Hours*, 168; McMurry, *John Bell Hood and the War for Southern Independence*, 176; Horn, *The Decisive Battle of Nashville*, 175–81; James R. Binford, "Recollections of the Fifteenth Mississippi Infantry, CSA," Patrick Henry Papers, Mississippi Department of Archives and History Library, Jackson, Mississippi, 64.

[7] McDonough and Connelly, *Five Tragic Hours*, 169; Horn, *The Decisive Battle of Nashville*, 43.

[8] Binford, "Recollections," 64; Horn, *The Decisive Battle of Nashville*, 42–43; McDonough and Connelly, *Five Tragic Hours*, 169; McMurry, *John Bell Hood and the War for Southern Independence*, 177.

Nashville works. After a diversionary thrust to the Confederate right, 35,000 Federal soldiers swept down on the thin Confederate left. The strategy was a complete success. Although Hood's men held on for most of the day, they were finally overwhelmed and driven back about two miles. As darkness, fell the fighting ended, and both armies reformed their ranks.[9]

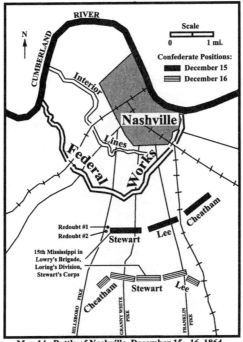

Map 14   Battle of Nashville, December 15 - 16, 1864

As part of Stewart's corps, the 15th Mississippi was positioned on the Confederate left, near a fortification designated as Redoubt Number One. The position was on the summit of a ridge overlooking a broad valley, where the soldiers "had a splendid view of the immense number of 'blue coats' forming into line." Soon the regiment felt the full effect of the Federal attack. Parts of Federal divisions under the command of Brigadier Generals Nathan Kimball, Washington Elliot, and Kenner

[9] Horn, *The Decisive Battle of Nashville*, 47–61; Everette B. Long with Barbara Long, *The Civil War Day by Day: An Almanac 1861–1865* (Garden City NY: Doubleday and Company, 1971) 610–11.

Gerrard assaulted Lowry's position. The Confederates were flanked on the left and quickly overwhelmed. The Southern lines broke in confusion, and soon the Federals found themselves "burdened with trophies and prisoners." According to one Union soldier, "It was a splendid scene to see them [the Confederates] scatter."[10] During the retreat, the men of the 15th Mississippi became separated from the rest of Lowry's brigade and intermingled at one point with troops from Edward Walthall's division. During the attack James Binford commanded both the 14th and 15th Mississippi Infantry regiments and later recalled, "I was in a quandary what to do, for really I did not know where our brigade was, whether it had been captured, or was still on the line, or possibly might have fallen back. Just at this moment, I was greatly relieved by seeing General Walthall about a hundred yards in my rear, with a flag trying to rally his division."[11]

As fighting ended for the day, the men in Lowry's brigade fell back about two miles and eventually regrouped. During the night both armies adjusted to their new positions. The Confederates significantly shortened their lines in an attempt to strengthen them. Cheatham's corps moved to the left with Lee's corps on the right and Stewart's badly damaged corps, including the 15th Mississippi in Lowry's brigade, in the center. Some of the Federal officers believed Hood would withdraw, but the Confederate commander was not yet ready to abandon the field. As a result, just after daybreak on 16 December the Federals advanced again.[12]

Using essentially the same strategy that had been successful the previous day, the Union army feinted to the right and then pressed hard on the Confederate left. Hood's men put up a fight, at times inflicting serious damage on the charging Federal troops, but Hood's men could not overcome Thomas' superior numbers, and the Federals again turned the Confederate left. According to Joel Watson of the 15th Mississippi, "Early in the morning the enemy drove in the pickets, commenced driving the left wing of our army back, and in about an hour by sun they

---

[10] Wiley Sword, *The Confederacy's Last Hurrah: Spring Hill, Franklin & Nashville* (Lawrence: University Press of Kansas, 1992) 339–42; Binford, "Recollections," 62–64.

[11] Binford, "Recollections," 62–64.

[12] Sword, *The Confederacy's Last Hurrah*, 376; Herman Hattaway, *General Stephen D. Lee* (Jackson: University Press of Mississippi, 1976) 139–44; Long and Long, *The Civil War Day by Day*, 610–12.

made a heavy assault on our works and we were being nearly surrounded." Panic spread through Hood's ranks, and the Confederate lines collapsed. One Union officer recalled, "In less time than it takes to tell it, we captured guns, caissons, colors, and prisoners galore." Stewart's and Cheatham's corps withdrew toward Franklin as Lee's corps covered the retreat.[13] The Federals took thousands of prisoners as they swept down behind the Confederate lines. Barely avoiding capture, James Binford fled the field and later described the scene: "I found retreating columns in large numbers. No, I will not use the word columns, because there was none. The proper words would be a routed and demoralized army. Hood's whole army had been outflanked and driven back in great confusion, so much I think the words routed and demoralized could alone express it correctly."[14]

For a two-day battle in which both sides were heavily engaged, the struggle at Nashville produced relatively few casualties. Thomas, who had between 50,000 and 55,000 troops in the field, suffered 387 killed, 2,562 wounded, and 112 missing, for a total of 3,061. Confederate casualties were more difficult to ascertain, but Hood probably lost around 1,500 killed and wounded and about 4,500 captured. Among the captured were a number of men from the 15th Mississippi. Two men were from Company A, Philip Dubard and Robert Meek. Dubard was sent briefly to Camp Douglas at Chicago and then on to Camp Chase at Columbus, Ohio. He died there of pneumonia in January 1865, and his captors interred his remains near the camp in "grave no. 1802." Dubard was one of eleven men from the 15th Mississippi who died during the war while imprisoned at Camp Chase. Meek was more fortunate. Though also sent to Camp Chase following the Battle of Nashville, he and several other soldiers from the regiment survived the confinement to see the war's end. Meek took an oath of allegiance to the Union on 11 June 1865 and upon his release from prison returned home to Attala County.[15]

---

[13] Sword, *The Confederacy's Last Hurrah*, 376; Herman Hattaway, *General Stephen D. Lee,* 139–44; Long and Long, *The Civil War Day by Day*, 610–12.

[14] Binford, "Recollections," 68.

[15] Compiled Service Records of Confederate Soldiers who served in Organizations from the State of Mississippi: 15th Mississippi Infantry, Mississippi Department of Archives and History Library, Jackson, Mississippi, microfilm. Cited afterwards as Compiled Service Records: 15th Mississippi Infantry; William H. Knauss, *The Story of Camp Chase: A History of the Prison and its Cemetery, Together With Other Cemeteries Where Confederate Prisoners Are Buried, Etc.* (Nashville TN: Publishing House of the

After Nashville, the hopelessly crippled Army of Tennessee fled south on a course that eventually took it to Tupelo, Mississippi. As they retraced their steps of the past few months, many of the barefoot Confederates left bloody footprints in the snow. The day after the battle ended, the men reached Franklin, where Confederate wounded still lingered in agony. As they passed through the town, several soldiers from the 15th Mississippi visited Michael Farrell, who was slowly dying in one of the upstairs rooms of a mansion owned by John McGavock. Following the battle, Farrell had been taken to the house with many other soldiers. Doctors amputated both of Farrell's legs, and since the operation the Irishman's strength had ebbed daily. Though weakened, he was still able to greet members of his old command, according to one soldier, "with a radiant and complacent smile which I hardly expected, for I had learned he would never recover." After visiting their old commander, the men continued the retreat, and a few weeks later word reached the 15th Mississippi that Farrell had died.[16]

On 17 December the Confederates camped at Spring Hill, and three days later they crossed the Duck River. The men of the 15th Mississippi passed their fourth Christmas in the army at Bainbridge, on the Tennessee River, where they helped construct a pontoon bridge. After crossing the river, the Confederates established headquarters at Tuscumbia, Alabama, from 26–28 December. The army proceeded west across the Mississippi state line to the vicinity of Corinth and then turned south. On 9 January 1865, the same day that Tennessee adopted an amendment abolishing slavery in the state, Hood's force began straggling into Tupelo, where it remained for several weeks. For the survivors in the 15th Mississippi, the winter of 1864–1865 contrasted sharply with previous winters spent in Canton and Grenada. By New Year's Day of 1865 the ranks of the 15th Mississippi had dwindled to less than 100 men.[17]

Methodist Episcopal Church, South, 1906) 328–407; James I. Robertson Jr., *Soldiers Blue and Gray* (Columbia: University of South Carolina Press, 1988) 197–98.

[16] Horn, *The Decisive Battle of Nashville*, 157–65; Binford, "Recollections," 69–70; John L. Collins, "Gallant Mike Farrell," *Confederate Veteran* 34/10 (October 1926): 374–75.

[17] US War Department, comp., *The War of Rebellion: A Compilation of the Official Records of the Union and Confederate Armies*, 128 vols. (Washington, DC: 1880–1902) ser. 1, vol. 45(1):672–74. Afterwards this work is cited as *OR*, followed by the volume number, part number (when applicable), and page numbers. Unless otherwise noted, all

On 15 January 1865 John Bell Hood succumbed to the pressure of failures that would haunt him for the rest of his life and resigned as commander of the Army of Tennessee. In less than six months he virtually destroyed the force that had sparred with Sherman during the early stages of the Atlanta Campaign. At Tupelo, the army's total strength was less than 18,000 men, many of whom were not well enough to fight. Lieutenant General Richard Taylor took command of the army on January 23 as petitions circulated among the officers and enlisted men for the reinstatement of Joseph Johnston.[18]

By early 1865 the Confederacy was on the verge of wholesale collapse. On the last day of January, in a move that came at least a year too late, Robert E. Lee was designated commander in chief of all Confederate forces. Among Lee's first official acts was the recall of his old friend Joseph Johnston to active duty. On 25 February, Johnston took command of the Confederate forces south of Virginia and east of the Mississippi River. His directive from Lee was simple: "Concentrate all

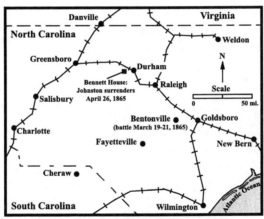

Map 15   Final Weeks in North Carolina, 1865

references are to volumes from series 1; Long and Long, *The Civil War Day by Day*, 611–21.

[18] McMurry, *John Bell Hood and the War for Southern Independence*, 182–83; Emory M. Thomas, *The Confederate Nation: 1861–1865* (New York: Harper & Row, 1979) 282.

available forces and drive back Sherman," who had followed his march to the sea with an advance into the Carolinas.[19]

Although clearly facing long odds, Johnston summoned various commands from around the South to North Carolina, including what remained of the Army of Tennessee. From Tupelo, the 15th Mississippi and the rest of the army moved sporadically by foot and over a crumbling network of rail lines to North Carolina. The final journey of the war for the men of the 15th Mississippi Infantry took them through Meridian, Montgomery, Columbus, Midgeville, Augusta, and Charlotte before they reunited with their old commander in Smithfield, North Carolina, around the first of March.[20] The reunion cheered the men somewhat, though most probably realized that their service to the Confederacy was drawing to a close.

As Johnston studied maps of the region, the Federal strategy quickly became apparent. Sherman planned to march north with 60,000 men and overwhelm whatever resistance he met in North Carolina, effectively neutralizing the state as a member of the Confederacy. He could then unite with Grant, and together they could destroy Lee in Virginia. To Johnston, who could barely muster 20,000 effectives for combat at any given time, the task of stopping Sherman seemed futile, but the general deemed it crucial to at least create the illusion that something could be done. As Sherman continued his march, the Confederate commander assembled most of his infantry, about 17,000 men, near Bentonville, North Carolina, to ambush a like number of Federals strung out in advance of Sherman's left wing.[21]

On 19 March the men of the 15th Mississippi and their fellow Confederates attacked in what would later be described as the "last rebel yell of the war." Johnston's troops initially drove the Federals back, but miscommunication among Confederate commanders and the Federals' ability to quickly mobilize reinforcements doomed the effort. The battle lasted until after dark as the Federals repulsed sporadic Confederate assaults. While there was no heavy fighting the following day, a great deal of skirmishing took place along the lines. On 21 March a serious

---

[19] Trotter, *Silk Flags and Cold Steel*, 225–26; Long and Long, *The Civil War Day by Day*, 630; Thomas, *The Confederate Nation*, 225–26.

[20] Trotter, *Silk Flags and Cold Steel*, 226–27.

[21] Trotter, *Silk Flags and Cold Steel*, 226; James M. McPherson, *Battle Cry of Freedom: The Civil War Era* (New York: Ballantine Books, 1988) 830.

struggled ensued. The Confederate battle lines eventually gave way, and Johnston's men abandoned the field.[22]

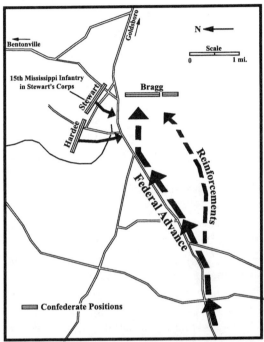

**Map 16   Battle of Bentonville, North Carolina,
March 19, 1865**

During the three-day battle the Federals lost about 1,500 men killed and wounded. Confederate losses were about 2,600 men, many of whom were captured. Among the Confederate casualties was James "Hick" Buford of the 15th Mississippi's Company F. Buford's wound led to the amputation of his leg by regimental surgeon T. R. Trotter and distinguished him as one of the last combat casualties of the war from his regiment. Years later, Trotter expressed deep regret as he told a fellow veteran "that the amputation of Hick Buford's leg gave [me] more sorrow than any [I] had ever operated on, because he had always been so

---

[22] Trotter, *Silk Flags and Cold Steel*, 255; Long and Long, *The Civil War Day by Day*, 654–56.

true and brave, then just as the war was to close, [he was] maimed for life."[23]

Following the Battle of Bentonville, the Army of Tennessee was spent. The survivors moved to Raleigh, where authorities organized an official review. The dejected men formed ranks slowly on 4 April 1865. According to one observer, "Desertion, sickness, deaths, hardships, perils and vicissitudes demonstrated themselves too plainly on that old army.... The march of the remnants was so slow—colors torn and tattered with bullets—it looked like a funeral procession." Following the review the soldiers dispersed in silence.[24]

The remainder of the 15th Mississippi's service to the Confederacy amounted to little more than a dismal, prolonged wait for the final surrender. James Binford resigned in late March, and Lieutenant Elihu Love of Company I briefly served as the regiment's last official field commander. On 9 April, Johnston partially reorganized his army, and the 15th Mississippi ceased to exist in the form that it had carried out the war. Confederate authorities consolidated the 6th, 15th, 20th, and 23rd Mississippi Infantry regiments into one unit, the 15th Mississippi Consolidated Infantry. Colonel Thomas B. Graham of the 23rd Mississippi took command of the regiment.[25] There was further skirmishing in North Carolina between various detachments, but the combat careers of the men of the 15th Mississippi were over.

The already depressed state of Johnston's army compounded on 5 April when word of the fall of Richmond reached North Carolina. More bad news arrived a few days later as the men heard of Lee's surrender at Appomattox Court House. After word of Lee's surrender circulated, many soldiers openly stated that they would refuse orders to take part in another battle. On 12 April, Johnston and Beauregard met with Jefferson Davis and his cabinet at Greensboro, where Johnston recommended negotiations with Sherman. Although Davis opposed the idea, the other participants in the discussion reached a consensus with the general. Two days later Johnston wrote Sherman, asking if he was "willing to make a

---

[23] Long and Long, *The Civil War Day by Day*, 654–56; Binford, "Recollections," 72.

[24] Trotter, *Silk Flags and Cold Steel*, 293.

[25] Dunbar Rowland, *Military History of Mississippi 1803–1898* (Spartenburg SC: The Reprint Company, 1988) 234; Compiled Service Records: 15th Mississippi Infantry; *OR*, vol. 45 (2):734; *OR*, vol. 47 (1):1055.

temporary suspension of active operations" to talk peace. Sherman accepted the proposition and on 17 April he and Johnston met at Bennett House near Durham Station. That evening the men of the 15th Mississippi and the rest of the Confederate soldiers in the field learned of the assassination of Abraham Lincoln.[26]

It took more than a week to reconcile the political and military realities of the situation, but finally, on 26 April, Johnston formally surrendered his army at Greensboro. Final terms for the surrender of the troops under Johnston's command were basically the same as those agreed upon by Grant and Lee at Appomattox: The Confederates had to deposit all public property and arms at Greensboro; troops had to pledge not to take up arms against the United States; officers could retain their side arms, private horses, and baggage; and all officers and enlisted men were allowed to return to their homes.[27] During the first week of May the Federals printed and distributed parole forms, which were simple and to the point: "[Name of soldier] has given his solemn obligation not to take up arms against the government of the United States until properly released from this obligation; and is permitted to return to his home, not to be disturbed by the United States authorities so long as he observes his obligation and obeys the laws in force where he may reside."[28]

In May of 1865 the remnants of the 15th Mississippi Infantry signed their parole forms and left North Carolina, joining the ranks of what one Northern observer described as "poor homesick boys and exhausted men wandering about in threadbare uniforms, with scanty outfit of slender haversack and blanket role hung over their shoulder, seeking the nearest route home." The surrender of the Army of Tennessee ended a four-year trek that took the regiment almost everywhere in the western theater, including Mill Springs, Shiloh, Corinth, Vicksburg, Baton Rouge, Champion Hill, Jackson, Meridian, Atlanta, Franklin, Nashville, and Bentonville. After parole, the survivors began their long trip back to Mississippi. Some hitched rides on rickety rail cars or rode horses. Others walked. According to one veteran, formerly of the regiment's

---

[26] Trotter, *Silk Flags and Cold Steel*, 301–02, 332; Long and Long, *The Civil War Day by Day*, 673–78.

[27] Long and Long, *The Civil War Day by Day*, 360.

[28] Trotter, *Silk Flags and Cold Steel*, 360.

Company F, "Bankruptcy, devastation, and ruin greeted [the men] at every turn on their long, wearisome journey."[29]

Although the survivors from the 15th Mississippi arrived home late for the spring planting season, they had successfully completed a full cycle. The men had abandoned their plows to leave home in defense of their communities and had become hardened combat soldiers during the bloodiest war in American history. After the surrender, they returned home to become farmers once again and to help their communities recover from the ordeal. Their grand Confederate adventure had evolved into a grand Confederate tragedy, and their memories of the ordeal never faded. According to James Dicken, who served four years in the regiment and suffered wounds at Mill Springs and Shiloh, the veterans of the 15th Mississippi Infantry returned home in 1865 "still believing the cause they fought for was right, and were not ashamed to be called rebels."[30] It was a sentiment that carried on for generations.

---

[29] Trotter, *Silk Flags and Cold Steel*, 360; Noah Andre Trudeau, *Out of the Storm: The End of the Civil War, April–June, 1865* (New York: Little, Brown, and Company, 1994) 382; Unknown Author, "History of the Water Valley Rifles, Company F, Fifteenth Mississippi Infantry," Supplement to the WPA Historical Research Project, Yalobusha County, 16 February 1937, Special Collections, J. D. Williams Library, University of Mississippi, Oxford, Mississippi, 63.

[30] James T. Dicken, "Long Creek Rifles," *Kosciusko Star Ledger*, 1 January 1898, 3.

CHAPTER 10

AFTER THE WAR

> We unveil to the memory of those heroes of the War of
> Right battling against Oppression, this monument as a token of
> esteem of this country for which they fought so well.[1]
> *R. C. McBee, Remarks at the dedication of the Holmes
> County Confederate monument, Lexington, Mississippi, 8
> December 1908*

The surviving veterans of the 15th Mississippi Infantry returned home in
1865 to a state immersed in economic and social chaos. More than one-
third of the 78,000 Mississippians who had participated in the
Confederate adventure were dead, representing a loss of about one-
quarter of the state's white male population age fifteen and above in
1860. Farms, large and small, had deteriorated from neglect. Debt was
rampant. Five years after the war's conclusion the state would hold more
than two million acres of land for non-payment of taxes. At the end of
the century, cotton would be selling for 4 cents per pound. Emancipation
quickly gave way to social turmoil that would not be effectively dealt
with for another century. The turbulent Reconstruction period offered
little relief, and once Democratic "Redeemers" wrestled control of the
state away from the Republicans in 1875, their conservative fiscal
policies made matters even worse. Fifteen years after Appomattox the

---

[1] *Unveiling Ceremonies of the Holmes County Confederate Monument, at
Lexington, Mississippi, 2 December 1908*, Mississippi Department of Archives and
History Library, Jackson, Mississippi, program.

per capita income in Mississippi remained one of the lowest in the country at $82.[2]

The counties that produced the 15th Mississippi Infantry suffered along with the rest of the state. Property values plummeted. Farmers worked less acreage than they had before the war, and crop yields of both food crops and cotton were tenuous. Economic hardships affected planters and small farmers alike. In 1860 the average cash value of a farm in Holmes County, one of the wealthiest of the 15th Mississippi counties, was $9,642, but by 1870 the average cash value per farm had fallen to $1,208. Similarly in Choctaw County, the poorest of the 15th Mississippi counties before the war, the average cash value per farm dropped from $1,754 in 1860 to only $320 a decade later. By 1880, with the crop lien system firmly established in Mississippi, only 55 percent of all farmers in the region that produced the regiment made a living on land that they owned. These trends, consistent with the rest of the state, would continue for decades.[3]

Of course the war exacted more than an economic toll on the veterans and their communities. In 1865 the former soldiers of the 15th Mississippi were tired, defeated, and many were crippled for life. For years the ghosts of men who should have still been living would haunt the 15th Mississippi counties. The communities that produced the regiment were closely knit—almost everyone was "some kinda kin" to everyone else—and few families escaped the loss of a friend, neighbor, or loved one during the struggle. Many of the dead lay in unmarked graves that their relatives would never visit. Shopkeeper Magnus Teague was among the soldiers of the 15th Mississippi who was never reunited with his family following the war. He joined the regiment in 1861 at the age of twenty-four, leaving behind his pregnant wife Elizabeth and a two-year-old daughter at Bluff Springs in Attala County. Teague died in 1862, probably of disease. Elizabeth Teague never learned the particulars of her husband's death. Like many Confederate soldiers, he simply did

---

[2] James W. Loewen and Charles Sallis, eds., *Mississippi: Conflict and Change* (New York: Random House, 1974) 168–74; William C. Harris, "Reconstructing the Commonwealth," vol. 1 of *A History of Mississippi*, ed. Richard A. McLemore (Hattiesburg: University and College Press of Mississippi, 1973) 542–61.

[3] United States Census, 1860, 1870 (agricultural), Mississippi; James G. Revels, "Redeemers, Rednecks, and Racial Integrity," vol. 1 of *A History of Mississippi*, ed. Richard A. McLemore (Hattiesburg: University and College Press of Mississippi, 1973) 608–09.

not return home from the war. His wife later remarried, and her two children grew to know their father in name only, illustrating the fact that Civil War casualties were not confined to the battlefield.[4]

Had Magnus Teague lived, he would have watched helplessly as the community of his childhood perished. During the 1870s a bit of progress came to Attala County in the form of a railroad line connecting the towns of Kosciusko and Durant. In addition to providing a convenient transportation link for local citizens, the line created new communities in its path. Other settlements not fortunate enough to have the railroad pass near their limits soon withered and died. One of these was Bluff Springs. Founded in the 1830s, the community produced the Long Creek Rifles, which undertook the war as Company A of the 15th Mississippi Infantry. With the railroad, however, Bluff Springs and two other nearby communities were forced to consolidate at a place that quickly grew into the town of Sallis.[5] More than 100 years later, Bluff Springs has vanished, but a common bond continues to distinguish thirteen headstones from dozens of others in the Sallis cemetery. The men who rest beneath these stones were members of the Long Creek Rifles who survived the Civil War. They were young men who, within the span of a few years, lost their town, their country, and the world in which they had grown up.

The experience was similar for veterans from Greensboro, the county seat of Choctaw County and home of the Wigfall Rifles, Company D, 15th Mississippi Infantry. In 1861 Greensboro was a bustling center of activity that included within its limits a courthouse and jail, eighteen stores, a newspaper, a livery stable, several law offices, and a brickyard. In 1864 Federal troops damaged the town, but several years later Greensboro sustained a blow from which it would never recover. In 1871 Mississippi added a new county in the 15th Mississippi region, resulting in the redrawing of several county lines and the establishment of a new county seat for Choctaw County. No longer a seat of

---

[4] Compiled Service Records of Confederate Soldiers who served in Organizations from the State of Mississippi: 15th Mississippi Infantry, Mississippi Department of Archives and History Library, Jackson, Mississippi, microfilm. Cited afterwards as Compiled Service Records: 15th Mississippi Infantry; United States Census, 1860, 1870, 1880, Mississippi.

[5] Attala County Historical Society, *Kosciusko-Attala County History* (Kosciusko MS: Privately printed, 1976) 162.

government and lacking any nearby railroad outlets, Greensboro began to decline. Many families moved to neighboring settlements and within twenty years conditions in the town had deteriorated to the point that "the saloons held full sway, and she became noted for desperate characters and crimes committed within her limits." By 1900 Greensboro was gone. All that remains of the town today is a cemetery. Several stones in the old cemetery mark the graves of 15th Mississippi veterans who went to war in 1861 to defend a community that by the turn of the twentieth century no longer existed.[6]

Despite the demise of Bluff Springs and Greensboro, most of the towns that produced the 15th Mississippi Infantry survived the war and the economic and social chaos that followed. Veterans of the regiment returned to their lives as small farmers in a region that remained dependent upon agriculture. While the war had ended, the mutual commitment between the men and their communities had not. The veterans were no longer soldiers, but they would soon be called upon again to serve in a new capacity. In 1861 the men had gone to war to protect a community ideal, but in the years following the surrender their communities would battle to protect the soldiers' legacy and the idea that their initial enthusiasm for the war was justified. As was the case in other parts of the South, it took little time for the 15th Mississippi communities to impress upon their veterans a collective identity as vanquished heroes. Regardless of their post-war activities, "the legend of the Fighting Fifteenth" would hover over the men for the rest of their lives in an ongoing war of words and rituals.

As the veterans of the 15th Mississippi and other ex-soldiers throughout the South recovered from their ordeal, the seeds of Southern mythology regarding their collective military service began to take root. Defeated militarily, the South in the decades following 1865 struggled to vindicate the ideals and decisions that had led it into conflict and cost so many men their lives. From the ashes of war and the turbulence of the Reconstruction period, a cultural identity took shape grounded in ideas and attitudes referred to collectively as the Lost Cause. Celebrations of the Lost Cause took many forms: annual civil and religious services honoring the Confederate dead, veterans' reunions, the deification of

---

[6] James P. Coleman, *Choctaw County Chronicles* (Ackerman MS: James P. Coleman, 1974) 98–99; Webster County Historical Association, *The History of Webster County* (Dallas TX: Curtis Media Corp., 1985) 59.

Confederate military leaders, the erection of Confederate monuments, and the emergence of groups such as the United Confederate Veterans (UCV), United Sons of Confederate Veterans (USCV), and United Daughters of the Confederacy (UDC). Politicians used the language of the Lost Cause—language denoting moral superiority based on abstract notions of honor and chivalry—to garner votes, and ministers espoused Lost Cause virtues from the pulpit. Textbooks "educated" generations of white Southern school children on the nature of the war as a noble struggle of principle, lost only in the face of superior Northern resources. For a century after the war the Lost Cause gave cultural authority to Confederate symbols, most prominently the "stars and bars" rebel flag. As they entered into the twentieth century, the states of the Old Confederacy did their best to maintain this cultural identity by accenting the New South with many of the cosmetic trappings of an idealized Old South. From a practical standpoint, while salving the psychological wounds of defeat, such a course also helped maintain both white supremacy and the political dominance of the Democratic Party in the region.[7]

The Lost Cause spawned a number of veterans' groups, the most prominent being the United Confederate Veterans, founded in New Orleans in 1889. With chapters in all states of the Old Confederacy, the group served as a social outlet for veterans at the local level, particularly in rural areas, and institutionalized a host of Southern myths concerning the war. The national organization allowed its membership to designate the chapters with a name of their choosing. In many cases members named their group after a Confederate general or former commanding officer that they admired. All of the counties that produced the 15th Mississippi established local UCV chapters, and veterans of the regiment were quick to enroll. Depending on their location, these groups ranged in size from about 50 to 150 men and usually included former soldiers from various commands. At Winona, home of the 15th Mississippi's Company B, the men designated their chapter as the Statham-Farrell Chapter, after the fallen commanding officers of the regiment. Another group from

---

[7] For treatments of Lost Cause ideology, see Charles Reagan Wilson, *Baptized in Blood: The Religion of the Lost Cause, 1865–1920* (Athens: The University Press of Georgia, 1980) and Gaines M. Foster, *Ghosts of the Confederacy: Defeat, the Lost Cause, and the Emergence of the New South* (New York: Oxford University Press, 1987).

Montgomery County (formerly part of Choctaw County) also named their chapter in honor of "Gallant Mike Farrell."[8]

While a national organization governed the UCV, the practical functions of the group took place on the local level. Just as the volunteer companies from the 15th Mississippi region had entered the war as community enterprises, the individual UCV chapters were sources of community pride. The community sons that had fought in the war were now community fathers and grandfathers. Through the veterans, citizens supported the Lost Cause in the post-war era in the same manner that they had supported the cause of 1861 through the efforts of the soldiers. In an article written about Robert J. Wood, formerly of the 15th Mississippi's Company A, an Attala County correspondent summed up the attachment that the communities had for their former soldiers and for what the former soldiers represented. At the time Wood was in his sixties, and he still carried an "empty sleeve," the result of the loss of an arm at Mill Springs. After documenting Wood's wartime sacrifice, the correspondent punctuated the article with a flowery tribute: "Long may Bob and all the old soldiers of the Lost Cause survive as living monuments of the valor, chivalry, and patriotic love of country, which is characteristic of the people of the South."[9]

While community support for the ex-soldiers took many forms, its most public manifestation involved annual gatherings of the surviving veterans, their families, and their friends. Reunions became a sacred ritual of a post-war South struggling to justify war and defeat. The national or state organizations of the UCV sponsored many, but most were community events. A few years after the war's conclusion, the survivors of the 15th Mississippi began holding informal regimental reunions and later more organized events after they established their local UCV chapters during the 1890s. The reunions were well attended by both the ex-soldiers and members of their communities and were usually marked by speeches from prominent veterans and local politicians. More importantly, they also served as a primary venue for the

---

[8] John L. Collins, "Gallant Mike Farrell," *Confederate Veteran* 34/10 (October 1926): 374–75; *Confederate Veteran* 9/9 (October 1901): 461; *Confederate Veteran* 21/11 (September 1909): 516.

[9] James Wallace, "History and Reminiscences of Attala County," 1916, Mississippi Department of Archives and History Library, Jackson, Mississippi, photocopy.

communal celebration of the Lost Cause and for the men to pay homage to the war itself as the central event in their lives.

In 1908 Grenada hosted the reunion of 15th Mississippi veterans, with "no efforts spared to make pleasant the stay of this rapidly vanishing body of brave and gallant followers of the Lost Cause." While the ranks had thinned, several dozen men joined more than 300 visitors for a patriotic celebration during the day and an outdoor feast during the early evening. At the dinner the veterans sat at a separate table, where "their wants were carefully looked after by the ladies," and throughout the event their deeds were celebrated with toasts and testimonials. According to one participant, the gathering "was more than a meeting of old soldiers. It was a joyous reunion with friends of long ago.... What a delight to revel in memory." In 1926 John L. Collins of Coffeeville, one of the few remaining veterans of the 15th Mississippi, attended the state UCV reunion held at Corinth. After speeches and a parade, he and his fellow veterans were taken by automobile 20 miles north to the Shiloh battlefield. Still firm in the belief that the Civil War was linked to the South's revolutionary heritage, Collins later reported that as he toured the grounds, he "saw the spot where so many of Coffeeville's distinguished citizens fell as martyrs to the cause of the South—even martyrs as our brave sires who fell in '76 for American independence." [10] Reunions sometimes served as vehicles for raising money for various UCV projects. Grenada also hosted the 1900 reunion of 15th Mississippi veterans, which was held in conjunction with a "fiddlers' contest." The event was part of a fund-raising drive "for the purpose of raising money for the erection of a monument in Grenada to the heroic members of the gallant Fifteenth Regiment of Volunteers."[11]

By the time the generation of Southern males that had fought the war began passing from the scene, their exploits as Confederate soldiers had already entered the realm of legend. In the South every veteran became a larger-than-life hero, and every battle drew comparisons with the great battles of history. As the old soldiers disappeared, the communities in which they lived made efforts to preserve their memory forever. At hundreds of sites throughout the states of the Old

---

[10] *Carrollton Conservative*, 12 September 1908; "Reunion of Mississippi Comrades," *Confederate Veteran* 34/11 (November 1926): 424–25.

[11] "A Great Day in Grenada," broadside, Special Collections, J. D. Williams Library, University of Mississippi, Oxford, Mississippi.

Confederacy, recognition of the veterans took the form of some type of statue or monument. The unveilings of these Confederate monuments were central rituals in the celebration of the Lost Cause. They were reminiscent of the flag presentation ceremonies that had sent so many young men off to war in 1861.

Unveiling ceremonies for the Holmes County Confederate monument took place on 2 December 1908 on the courthouse square in Lexington, the county seat. The Quitman Rifles, Company C, 15th Mississippi Infantry, was among a number of units from the county whose members were recognized during the celebration for "heroic service throughout the war." The ceremony was the social event of the year in Lexington and included a parade and speeches by area dignitaries. A local band performed the standards for such an occasion—"The Bonnie Blue Flag," "Tenting on the Old Campground," and "Dixie."[12] Using the high tone and vocabulary of Lost Cause rhetoric, R. C. McBee, a local politician, established the mood of the event with his opening remarks:

> The Army of the Confederate States that with noble men and brave hearts never faltered under fire is fast succumbing to the inevitable, and but a handful of the noble few now remain. We may, by our acts of kindness and appreciation, assure them of our steadfast belief in their virtue and valor; we may proclaim their deeds of matchless heroism in song and story; we may erect to the memory of them and of their sacred cause a monument that by its beauty and lastingness will for all time serve as a reminder that they hold first place in the hearts of their beloved Southland.... We unveil to the memory of those heroes of the War of Right battling against Oppression, this monument as a token of esteem of this country for which they fought so well.[13]

It was not just coincidence that the remarks at the unveiling ceremony in Holmes County echoed the sentiments of the flag presentation ceremonies. As citizens of the 15th Mississippi communities sent their sons off to war in 1861, it was important for their psychological well-being that they celebrate the war effort through

---

[12] *Unveiling Ceremonies of the Holmes County Confederate Monument.*
[13] Ibid.

rhetoric and ritual. They were sending their sons into harm's way, and they needed emotional reassurance that the mission of the men was valid. Fifty years later, residents of the communities that produced the 15th Mississippi still required the same type of reassurance. They embraced the Lost Cause to reinforce the idea that their actions were correct, that they had indeed supported a *War of Right battling against Oppression.* Otherwise, they would have had to sustain a crippling psychological blow by admitting that the entire effort had been flawed and that they had sent community sons away to be killed and maimed for no reason.

Similar rituals took place in all of the counties that produced the 15th Mississippi Infantry. In 1910 veterans of the Grenada Rifles, Company G, took part in the ceremony dedicating the Confederate monument at Grenada. Three years later survivors from the Winona Stars, Company B, and McClung Rifles, Company E, were among veterans cited for valor at a ceremony dedicating a monument at Winona. The Statham-Farrell UCV chapter sponsored the event, which ended with the assembled crowd singing "Dixie." Former members of the Long Creek Rifles, Company A, were among veterans honored at the dedication of the Attala County monument on the courthouse square in Kosciusko, the county seat. In Water Valley, a monument dedicated to the Water Valley Rifles, Company F, was placed in the local cemetery. Inscribed on the large granite marker were the names of those men from the company who died during the war.[14]

Similar to the flag presentation ceremonies, the unveiling ceremonies were class-based events. While they celebrated the exploits of all the soldiers, they were organized and carried out by only the communities' more prominent residents. Most UCV leaders had been officers in the army, and leadership positions in groups such as the UDC were usually filled by relatives of former officers or other prominent citizens. At the Holmes County ceremony, the names of all the men from the Quitman Rifles were printed in a program handed out to the crowd, but only the officers were individually recognized by name from the stage. The unveiling ceremonies were social in nature and therefore took

---

[14] "Confederate Veterans at Greenwood," *Confederate Veteran* 21/11 (September 1909): 516; Yalobusha County Historical Society, *Yalobusha County History* (Dallas TX: National Share Graphics, 1982) 19.

place under the auspices of the community's more socially prominent citizens.[15]

The Lost Cause also represented a significant political force in the post-war South. Democratic leaders were quick to realize that veterans who were perceived as heroes in their communities made good candidates for office. After Reconstruction, Lost Cause imagery and rhetoric helped elect Confederate veterans to state and local offices throughout the Old Confederacy. In post-Reconstruction Mississippi, Civil War veterans held most of the state's highest offices for years. In the 15th Mississippi region a number of the men parlayed their military service into political careers. During his successful campaign for the state legislature in 1880, 15th Mississippi veteran Frederick M. Glass solicited votes through an open letter published in an Attala County newspaper. His letter was a typical political announcement of the period, reminding voters of his primary qualification for public office: "Every interest that I have, and every tie that binds me, are in my county and state, and their interests I have defended in war and peace. I enlisted as a private soldier in Company A of the 15th Miss. Regiment, and how well I performed my duty let the record of the regiment and those who served with me tell." In addition to Glass, Marcellus H. Allen (Company B), J. W. Armstrong (Company I), James R. Binford (Company E), John L. Collins (Company H), John J. Gage (Company G), J. C. McKenzie (Company B), Lafayette Robinson (Company I), and Lampkin S. Terry (Company A) served in the state legislature at one time or another. Several former members of the regiment also served in local offices such as sheriff, chancery clerk, or mayor.[16]

Despite their status as aging symbols of an idealized Confederate heritage, most of the 15th Mississippi veterans lived quiet lives, struggling to make a living on their farms. Throughout their lifetime Mississippi remained one of the nation's poorest states, with small farmers, both white and black, occupying the lower rungs of the economic ladder. While their status as veterans established the men's reputations in their communities, their day-to-day existence remained tied to the land and to the elements. They also settled back into their communities' social hierarchies, which paralleled those of the

---

[15] *Unveiling Ceremonies of the Holmes County Confederate Monument.*

[16] *Attala Democrat*, 27 June 1880; Robert Lowry and William McCardle, *A History of Mississippi* (Jackson MS: R. H. Henry and Company, 1891) 443–611.

antebellum period. Generally, among the veterans, wartime rank translated into post-war status. Veterans who were community leaders during the post-war era in the 15th Mississippi region were usually former officers. Conversely, most of the enlisted men returned to their lives as part of their state's struggling plurality of small farmers.[17] However, the regiment did produce several notable survivors.

Augustus Mecklin received a discharge from Confederate service in June of 1862 due to illness. He returned home to Choctaw County, where he eventually regained his health and dedicated his life to religious endeavors as a Presbyterian minister. During a career that spanned fifty years, the former soldier helped found Presbyterian churches at Ackerman, Weir, and Byway, while pastoring a number of other congregations through the early twentieth century. In 1885 he was among a group that founded what became French Camp Academy, where he taught Bible classes for many years.[18] Mecklin died on 29 October 1913 at the age of seventy-eight. He is buried at Lebanon cemetery in Choctaw County. His headstone makes no reference to his service to the Confederacy. In addition to his birth and death dates, it reads simply, "Reverend Augustus H. Mecklin, Pastor of the Presbyterian Church."

James Binford served four years with the 15th Mississippi Infantry. He replaced Michael Farrell as commander of the regiment after the Battle of Franklin and left the Confederate army as a lieutenant colonel. After the war, Binford returned to his hometown of Duck Hill, won election as Duck Hill's mayor in 1872, and subsequently became involved in post-Reconstruction politics at the state level. Binford served in the state house and senate and was a member of the Constitutional Convention of 1890, which adopted Mississippi's present constitution. He named his oldest son Lloyd Tilghman Binford to honor the 15th Mississippi's brigade commander who fell at Champion Hill. In later life Binford devoted most of his idle hours to the United Confederate Veterans. He served as a department commander in the organization, traveling around the state making speeches in which he evoked the Lost

---

[17] United State Census, 1870, 1880, 1900, 1910 (population and agricultural), Mississippi; Lowry and McCardle, *A History of Mississippi*, 443–611.

[18] Augustus Hervey Mecklin Papers, Mississippi Department of Archives and History Library, Jackson, Mississippi; Coleman, *Choctaw County Chronicles*, 365–66.

Cause as he raised money for various UCV projects. Binford died at his home in Duck Hill in 1918 at the age of seventy-nine.[19]

William F. Brantley, delegate to the Mississippi Secession Convention and original captain of the Grenada Rifles, served four years in the Confederate army, achieving the rank of brigadier general. While he found success in the army, he returned home to Greensboro in 1865 to find the life he had known shattered. His wife and mother both died during the war, and he was ruined financially. Brantley eventually reestablished his legal practice. Soon Brantley was involved in local politics, but he did not live to see the end of Reconstruction. In what became one of the most legendary crimes of the region, the former general was shot and killed on 2 November 1870 as he traveled from Winona to Greensboro. Although there were a number of suspects—including political enemies and members of a family with whom the Brantleys had a long-standing feud—authorities never solved the crime.[20]

John E. Gore served three years in the 15th Mississippi's Company K and was wounded at the Battle of Franklin. He survived the war and returned home to Embry, Mississippi, where he married and raised a large family. A farmer by profession, Gore also preached and was one of his community's most prominent citizens. He served in the Mississippi legislature and along with James Binford was a member of the Mississippi Constitutional Convention of 1890. At the time of his death on 13 February 1933—the day before his ninetieth birthday—he was one of the last surviving veterans of his regiment.[21]

Charles H. Campbell was an original member of the McClung Rifles. He served until 30 November 1864, when he was seriously wounded during the Confederate charge at Franklin. Immediately following the battle Campbell was among a number of soldiers taken to the nearby home of Jacob and Susie Morton. Due to the severity of his wounds Campbell could not be moved for several months, during which time the Mortons continued to look after him. He eventually received a parole at Franklin and made his way home during the summer of 1865.

---

[19] Montgomery County Historical Society, *Montgomery County History* (Dallas TX: Curtis Media Corp., 1993) 241–42.

[20] William T. Blain, "William Felix Brantley, 1830–1870," *Journal of Mississippi History* 37/4 (November 1975): 373–80.

[21] Webster County Historical Society, *The History of Webster County*, 340.

Two years later Campbell returned to Tennessee and married the Morton's daughter, Fannie. The couple relocated temporarily to Union City, Tennessee, and then moved to Winona, where they raised five children.[22]

The veteran of the 15th Mississippi Infantry who achieved the greatest notoriety in the post-war era was Edward C. Walthall. Originally a member of the Water Valley Rifles, Walthall made a name for himself at the Battle of Mill Springs in 1862. He received a promotion to brigade commander and rose through the ranks, becoming a division commander in the Army of Tennessee with appropriate advancement to the rank of major general. After the war, Walthall returned to Mississippi a hero. An attorney by profession, he practiced law and entered politics, becoming one of the state's leading political figures during the late nineteenth century. In 1885 he followed L. Q. C. Lamar as U.S. senator from Mississippi, an office he held until his death on 21 April 1898.[23]

It was in death that the former members of the 15th Mississippi perhaps received their greatest accolades. The funeral of a Confederate veteran was one of the most hallowed Lost Cause rituals of the post-war South, providing further vindication of the lofty ideals that supposedly led the antebellum South into the war. Regardless of their status, the death of any former soldier in the 15th Mississippi region was recognized with a hero's funeral. Fellow veterans usually served as pallbearers or as honorary pallbearers and made speeches praising the service of their deceased comrade. Such tributes extended to obituaries in local newspapers or in the *Confederate Veteran*, the national organ of the UCV. Following Lampkin S. Terry's death in 1893, a friend eulogized the former captain of the 15th Mississippi's Company A by assuring listeners that "those who were with him during those four years of bloody, internecine war and strife know with what gallantry he defended the flag of his beloved Southland, and when her colors went down to rise no more, that none felt more keenly the remorse of defeat than himself."

---

[22] *Biographical and Historical Memoirs of Mississippi*, vol. 1, pt. 1 (Chicago: The Goodspeed Publishing Company, 1891) 494–95; James R. Binford, "Recollections of the Fifteenth Mississippi Infantry, CSA," Patrick Henry Papers, Mississippi Department of Archives and History Library, Jackson, Mississippi, 69.

[23] Stewart Sifakis, *Who Was Who in the Civil War* (New York: Facts on File, 1988) 689; James P. Coleman, "The Mississippi Constitution of 1890 and the Final Decade of the Nineteenth Century," vol. 2 of *A History of Mississippi*, ed. Richard A. McLemore (Hattiesburg: University and College Press of Mississippi, 1973) 22–23.

Upon the death of 15th Mississippi veteran Wiley L. Brannon in April of 1913, a fellow veteran reminded an assembly of mourners that during the Civil War Brannon and the rest of the Yalobusha Rifles "won laurels in every line that brings honor and fame as a reward for patriotic service." The remarks concerning the war records of Terry and Brannon were typical of those offered at veterans' funerals in the 15th Mississippi region, throughout Mississippi, and throughout the South as tributes to both the veterans and the Lost Cause.[24]

While the state of Mississippi celebrated the service of its veterans, it did little in terms of offering economic relief to those "faithful adherents of the Lost Cause." In 1888 the state established a pension fund to aid veterans who were "incapacitated for manual labor by a wound received in [Confederate] service" and for widows and servants who met certain qualifications. The pensions were meager, providing those who qualified with $17.85 annually. The state legislature periodically amended the pension law, and by 1920 yearly pensions had risen to a maximum of $200. While the 1920 pension law provided a stipend for all soldiers "who were honorably discharged, or paroled, or did not desert the Confederate service," only those veterans or their widows owning less than $3,000 in personal and real property qualified. For servants, the limit on personal and real property was $2,500. One hundred twenty-eight former soldiers from the 15th Mississippi Infantry received pensions from the state, along with 113 widows. Among those receiving pensions was Chatham Binford, an ex-slave who had served his owner, 15th Mississippi officer James Binford, during the war.[25]

In 1903 Varina Davis, wife of the former Confederate president, sold Beauvoir, the estate in Biloxi, Mississippi, where her late husband had spent his retirement, to the Mississippi Division of the USCV. She attached two stipulations to the sale. She insisted that the group maintain

---

[24] "Lampkin S. Terry," subject files, Mississippi Department of Archives and History Library, Jackson, Mississippi; *Confederate Veteran* 21/6 (June 1913): 307–08.

[25] Mississippi, *Laws of the State of Mississippi, Passed at a Regular Session of the Mississippi Legislature, Held in the City of Jackson, Commencing Jan'y 3, 1888, and Ending March 8, 1888* (Jackson MS: R. H. Henry State Printers, 1888) 30–31; Mississippi, *Laws of the State of Mississippi, Passed at a Regular Session of the Mississippi Legislature, Held in the City of Jackson, Commencing January 6, 1920, and Ending April 3, 1920* (Jackson MS: Tucker Printing House, 1920) 372–75; Coleman, "The Mississippi Constitution of 1890 and the Final Decade of the Nineteenth Century," 4.

the estate as a shrine to her husband's memory and as a home for Confederate veterans. The state of Mississippi eventually constructed twelve barracks there for the veterans, their wives, and their widows, with a maximum capacity of 288 residents. The Confederate veterans home operated from 1903 to 1957, caring for approximately 2,000 residents through the years. Among this number were nineteen aging veterans of the 15th Mississippi Infantry. Seven of the men died at the home and were buried in the cemetery on the grounds. Daniel S. Amyette, a former member of Company H and a Grenada resident, was the last veteran from the 15th Mississippi to reside there, passing away on 2 March 1935.[26]

More than thirty years after the men of the 15th Mississippi returned home, a relic of their military service found its way back to Mississippi, courtesy of the family of a former enemy. In 1899 relatives of the late B. M. Gregory, formerly of the 10th Indiana Infantry, returned the battle flag of the Grenada Rifles to members of the Grenada chapters of the UCV and UDC. Walter Statham originally accepted the banner on behalf of the Grenada Rifles during a ceremony in Grenada in April of 1861, just before he left with his company for Corinth. Following the 15th Mississippi's first major engagement at Mill Springs it was among several flags found by members of the 10th Indiana in the wake of the Confederates' hasty retreat. Gregory took possession of the flag and kept it as a souvenir. As an authentic Confederate artifact, the flag was received in Grenada with great reverence. A number of survivors from the company attended a ceremony, and according to a dutifully romanticized account in the *Confederate Veteran* magazine, "With tear-dimmed eyes they viewed the sacred relic, under whose folds so many gallant comrades had gone to their death, and which now recalled the hopes that had inspired them to follow where it led."[27]

Several years later the U.S. War Department returned a number of battle flags to the state of Mississippi, including two flags associated with the 15th Mississippi Infantry. One was a regimental banner, captured by Company E of the 2nd Minnesota Infantry at Mill Springs.

---

[26] "Beauvoir," Subject files, Mississippi Department of Archives and History Library, Jackson, Mississippi. The Beauvoir Museum in Biloxi, Mississippi, has numerous records concerning Confederate veterans who lived at the Confederate Soldiers Home and those veterans buried in the cemetery there.

[27] "Flag of the Grenada Rifles," *Confederate Veteran* 9/1 (January 1901): 400.

The other, also captured at Mill Springs, was the company banner of the Yalobusha Rifles. Both items were sent to the Mississippi State Historical Museum in Jackson, where they remain today. In 1920 relatives of Walter Statham contributed to the museum the gold-braided epaulets that the colonel wore at Shiloh.[28] In addition to museum pieces, other scattered relics of the 15th Mississippi survive in the form of faded photographs or family heirlooms in possession of descendants of the regiment's members.

Soon after the turn of the twentieth century, local citizens dedicated a monument specifically to the 15th Mississippi Infantry at Duck Hill, home of the McClung Rifles, the regiment's Company E. The present condition of the monument perhaps best reflects the legacy of the 15th Mississippi Infantry in the modern era. Originally erected in front of a church, it now stands alone in a vacant lot, the church building having been razed years ago. Neighboring property owners tend the grounds around the monument but view the granite shaft as little more than a curious novelty. They are unaware of its significance other than the fact that it pays tribute to a faceless group of Confederate soldiers. The lot sits beside a well-traveled avenue in Duck Hill, but few passing motorists give the monument a second glance.[29] If one takes the time to stop and inspect the marker, however, the inscription chiseled into it is clearly legible: "In memory of Col. W. S. Statham, Col. M. Farrell, Col. J. R. Binford and all the members of the 15th Miss. Regt. Infantry, CSA. Through their courage they won immortal victory and deathless fame, for to die nobly is the proudest glory of virtue. To the noble men who fought 'neath the flag of the stars and bars and who were faithful until the end.

In truth, the 15th Mississippi Infantry never took part in an *immortal victory*. All the campaigns involving the regiment ended in failure, as did the war itself. However, with the refusal of many Southerners to fully accept defeat and with their determination to render fact and myth indistinguishable through the Lost Cause, it can be said that the men of the regiment did indeed remain *faithful until the end*.

On 2 November 1937, four years before the United States entered the Second World War, John L. Collins died in Coffeeville, Mississippi. He was ninety-eight years old. An original member of the Yalobusha

---

[28] Collection Files, Mississippi State Historical Museum, Jackson, Mississippi.

[29] The author visited the site of the Duck Hill monument and spoke to neighboring property owners.

Rifles, Company H, 15th Mississippi Infantry, Collins was the last known survivor of his regiment.[30] For the young men who put down their hoes to pick up rifles in 1861, the war was finally over.

---

[30] Confederate Grave Registrations, Mississippi Department of Archives and History Library, Jackson, Mississippi, microfilm.

Appendix

The Language of the Cause, and the Lost Cause

In 1861 Althea Dawson presented the company battle flag to the Water Valley Rifles, with appropriate remarks, at a ceremony on the town square in Water Valley, Mississippi. Forty-seven years later R.C. McBee addressed an assembled crowd at Lexington, Mississippi during a ceremony unveiling a monument honoring local Confederate veterans, including members of the Quitman Rifles. The flowery language used by both speakers was similar because it sprang from the same emotional well. Both ceremonies were rituals of community vindication. Dawson's speech sought to vindicate the Cause before the Civil War actually began in earnest, while McBee's remarks were part of an ongoing effort to vindicate the Lost Cause almost a half-century after the war ended in failure. Both are reproduced here in their entirety.

Remarks of Althea Dawson at the Presentation of the Battle Flag to the Water Valley Rifles, Water Valley Mississippi, May, 1861

The Water Valley Rifles—deep and thrilling are the feelings that cling and cluster around my heart as I gaze with soul-felt pride on the noble spirits who so gallantly resolve to strike for our altars, our firesides, God, and our native South. Brothers, for may I not call you so, with bright hope and painful regrets strangely combined I yet behold you in warlike attitude. Soldiers of Mississippi, hold yourself in readiness to march at the word of command to the tomb of Washington, and swear that no northern Goth, or Vandals, shall ever desecrate its sacred precincts, that you will make of it an American Mecca to which the votaries of freedom and independence march through all time to come. March to Virginia and lay your head on the great bosom of the mother of states, hear her heart beat with new impulses for renewal of glorious independence. Surely the good and virtuous of the northern states cannot sanction the lawless and brutal despotism now inaugurated in Washington. Be ready, stand by your arms, mark time to the tap of independence and at the word, march onward to the border. Our glorious sister states are with you, their freemen are in arms; join them in their struggle for defense and let tyrants know there are men who can make them hear the ring and feel the weight of Southern steel, and wherever the Confederate flag floats there too is our country now and forever.

Lieutenant Bankhead, I, on behalf of the ladies of Water Valley, present you this proudly waving banner of noble Mississippi. Will it not return to Water Valley with a halo gleaming from every sacred fold? The proud hopes that come trembling from the very depths of my soul murmur that it will. The glory that has ever shed its luster over Mississippi volunteers, will not now be dimmed. The laurel that crowned their noble brows in other days will not now be blighted. We know that this banner is entrusted to soldiers noble and brave, that waves not over one timid heart, that if it ever goes down on the field of battle or graces the triumphal care of a conquering foe, the last of the Water Valley Rifles will rest from their fierce struggle on the bosom of our own sunny south.

You are brothers in the same glorious cause, united by memories of old family associations which will cast a hallowed light o'er the changing scenes of future days.

Now you are adrift upon the tide of life's wildest ocean wave not chartless and hopeless. But yet it is hard to nerve the soul for the last sad farewell, hard to listen to the stern mandates of duty. Fain would we linger forever, but it cannot be; we know that the Water Valley Rifles will be true to their proud name, that you go forth to meet the shadowy future with brave hearts. The cause of liberty and truth is yours. Remember then amid the tumult of strange, wild scenes there are loving friends at home offering up fervent prayers for your safety and success. May the protecting care of the God of battles be over yon nerve you gallant hearts, and crown your noble efforts with liberty and peace, while a glad and deep gratitude of happy hearts will greet your joyous return.

Address by R.C. McBee at the Dedication
Ceremony for the Holmes County Confederate Monument,
Lexington, Mississippi, December 8, 1908

Ladies and Gentleman. Time, with a relentless hand has wrought its change, and the thin gray line is fast answering the roll call to the Great Beyond. The Army of the Confederate States that with noble men and brave hearts never faltered under fire is fast succumbing to the inevitable, and but a handful of the noble few now remain. We may, by our acts of kindness and appreciation, assure them of our steadfast belief in their virtue and valor; we may proclaim their deeds of matchless heroism in song and story; we may erect to the memory of them and of their sacred cause a monument that by its beauty and lastingness will for all time serve as a reminder that they hold first place in the hearts of their beloved Southland; but never can we give them the respect and admiration that we feel for them in our hearts.

The message that we would today impart not only by this gathering, but by the erection of this monument as well, is that when the Confederate veteran passes through these streets he may behold the marble shaft, a reminder of his deeds of patriotism and valor. That the casual stranger within our midst may stop and reflect that while this lettered monument bears our silent testimonial of appreciation to the deeds of those who have honored us in the past, no monument is of sufficient size or beauty to reflect or transmit the truer and nobler monument that we have built up for themselves in our hearts forever. And that in some way the message may be caught up and wafted to those brave souls gathered around the last and brightest camp fire in the world that is 'over the river and under the shade of the tree,' saying to them as they await the final roll call, that in the name of the loved and lamented Lee, in the name of the brave and invincible Jackson, and in the name of our steadfast and unchanging belief in the right for which all the South contended, 'We love them still in Dixie.'

In the name of those in authority I bid you welcome to this day in the history of our county when we unveil to the memory of those heroes of the War of Right battling against Oppression, this monument as a token of esteem of this country for which they fought so well. 'With dim eyes, and memories fond and heart-beats like tatoo,' we commend their virtues to all the world as inspired heroes. May history deal truly with their memories, and God give peace to their souls.

BIBLIOGRAPHY

Official Documents

Compiled Service Records of Soldiers from Mississippi Serving in the Mexican War. Mississippi Department of Archives and History Library, Jackson MS. Microfilm.

Compiled Service Records of Confederate Soldiers who served in Organizations from the State of Mississippi: 15th Mississippi Infantry. Mississippi Department of Archives and History Library, Jackson MS. Microfilm.

Mississippi Commission on the War Between the States. Journal of the State Convention and Ordinances and Resolutions Adopted in 1861. Jackson MS: Mississippi Commission on the War Between the States, 1962.

Mississippi. Laws of the State of Mississippi, Passed at a Regular Session of the Mississippi Legislature, Held in the City of Jackson, Commencing Jan'y 3, 1888 and Ending March 8, 1888. Jackson MS: R. H. Henry State Printers, 1888. Mississippi Department of Archives and History Library, Jackson MS.

Mississippi. Laws of the State of Mississippi, Passed at a Regular Session of the Mississippi Legislature, Held in the City of Jackson, Commencing January 6, 1920 and Ending April 3, 1920. Jackson MS: Tucker Printing House, 1920. Mississippi Department of Archives and History Library, Jackson MS.

Official Records, 15th Mississippi Infantry, CSA. Mississippi Department of Archives and History Library, Jackson MS.

US Bureau of the Census. Census of the United States, 1820–1920. Bureau of the Census, Washington, D.C.

US War Department, comp. The War of the Rebellion: A Compilation of the Official Records of the Union and Confederate Armies. 128 volumes. Washington, DC: 1880–1902.

Personal Narratives, Diaries, Letters, or Articles

Francis Marion Aldridge. Papers. Mississippi Department of Archives and History Library, Jackson MS.

Binford, James R. "Recollections of the Fifteenth Mississippi Infantry, CSA." Patrick Henry Papers. Mississippi Department of Archives and History Library, Jackson MS.

Gladys Boyette papers. Kosciusko MS.

Brannon, John W. The John F. Johnson Journal of 1902. Eupora MS: Privately printed, 1984.

Gay Carter papers. Houston TX.

Collins, John L. "Gallant Mike Farrell." *Confederate Veteran* 34/10 (October 1926): 372–75.

———. "Mississippi and Kentucky in a Contest." *Confederate Veteran* 17/9 (September 1909): 460.

Cramer, Clayton E. *By the Dim and Flaring Lamps: The Civil War Diary of Samuel McIlvaine, February through June, 1862*. Monroe NY: Library Research Associates, 1990.

Davis, Reuben. *Recollections of Mississippi and Mississippians*. Revised edition. Hattiesburg: University and College Press of Mississippi, 1972.

Dicken, James T. "Long Creek Rifles." *Kosciusko Star Ledger*, 1 January 1898.

Dimond, E. Gray and Herman Hattaway, eds.*, Letters from Forest Place: A Plantation Family's Correspondence*. Jackson: University Press of Mississippi, 1993.

Gore, Tom M. "Death and Identity of General Adams." *Confederate Veteran* 1/1 (January 1893): 264.

Guy, Joseph S. Letter to Julia A. Berry. 30 June 1861. Grenada County Historical Society, Grenada MS.

Hamilton, W. F. Military Annals of Carroll County. Carrollton MS: W. F. Hamilton, 1906.

Hord, Henry Ewell. "Prize Drill in the Army." *Confederate Veteran* 10/1 (January 1902): 518–19.

Logsdon, David R., comp. and ed. *Eyewitnesses to the Battle of Franklin*. Nashville: Kettle Mills Press, 1991.

Augustus Hervey Mecklin. Papers. Mississippi Department of Archives and History Library, Jackson MS.

Niles, Jason. Scrapbook. Southern Historical Collection. University of North Carolina Library, Chapel Hill NC.

Taylor, John W. Letter to Parents. 11 April 1862. Southern Historical Collection. University of North Carolina Library, Chapel Hill NC.

Unknown Author. "History of the Water Valley Rifles, Company F, Fifteenth Mississippi Infantry." Supplement to the WPA Historical Research Project, Yalobusha County, 16 February 1937. Special Collections, J. D. Williams Library, University of Mississippi, Oxford MS.

Wallace, James. "History and Reminiscences of Attala County, 1916." Mississippi Department of Archives and History Library, Jackson MS. Photocopy.

Walpole, Richard. Letter to "Esteemed Friends." 4 November 1862. Special Collections, Robert W. Woodruff Library, Emory University, Atlanta GA.

Watson, Joel Calvin. Diary. Grenada Public Library, Grenada MS.
Wood, John W. Union and Secession in Mississippi. Memphis: Saunders, Farrish and Whitmore Printers, 1863.

County Histories

Attala County Historical Society. *Kosciusko-Attala County History*. Kosciusko MS: Privately printed, 1976.
Basile, Leon Edmund. "Attala County Mississippi 1850–1860, A Social History." Master's thesis, University of Massachusetts, 1977.
Coleman, James P. *Choctaw County Chronicles*. Ackerman MS: James P. Coleman, 1974.
Hathorn, J. C. *A History of Grenada County*. Grenada MS: J. C. Hathorn, 1972.
Montgomery County Historical Society. *History of Montgomery County*. Dallas TX: Curtis Media Corp., 1993.
Stokes, Rebecca Martin. "History of Grenada (1830–1880)." Master's thesis: University of Mississippi, 1929.
WPA History of Grenada County. Mississippi Department of Archives and History Library, Jackson MS. Microfilm.
WPA History of Yalobusha County. Mississippi Department of Archives and History Library, Jackson MS. Microfilm.
Webster County Historical Society. *The History of Webster County*. Dallas TX: Curtis Media Corp., 1985.
Yalobusha County Historical Society. *Yalobusha County History*. Dallas TX: National Share Graphics, 1982.

Newspapers

Attala (MS) Democrat
Canton (MS) American Citizen
Carrollton (MS) Conservative
Carrollton (MS) Democrat
Kosciusko (MS) Star Ledger
Memphis (TN) Daily Appeal
Mississippian (Jackson MS)
Natchez (MS) Daily Courier
Vicksburg (MS) Whig
Water Valley (MS) Progress
Yazoo City (MS) Democrat
Yazoo City (MS) Whig

Books

Baldwin, Joseph G. *The Flush Times of Alabama and Mississippi, A Series of Sketches*. San Francisco: Bancroft-Whitney, 1887.

Barney, William L. *The Road to Secession*. New York: Praeger Publishers, 1972.

————. *The Secessionist Impulse*. Princeton NJ: Princeton University Press, 1974.

Bearss, Edwin C. and Warren Grabau. *The Battle of Jackson, May 14, 1863; The Siege of Jackson, July 10–17, 1863; Three Other Post-Vicksburg Actions*. Baltimore: Gateway Press, 1981.

Bearss, Edwin C. *Decision in Mississippi: Mississippi's Important Role in the War Between the States*. Jackson MS: Mississippi Commission on the War Between the States, 1962.

————. *The Campaign for Vicksburg*. 3 volumes. Dayton OH: Morningside House, 1986.

Bearss, Margie Riddle. *Sherman's Forgotten Campaign: The Meridian Expedition*. Baltimore: Gateway Press, 1987.

Beringer, Richard E., Herman Hattaway, Archer Jones, and William N. Still Jr. *Why the South Lost the Civil War*. Athens: The University of Georgia Press, 1986.

Bettersworth, John K., ed. *Mississippi in the Confederacy: As They Saw It*. Baton Rouge: Louisiana State University Press, 1961.

Biographical and Historical Memoirs of Mississippi. Chicago: The Goodspeed Publishing Company, 1891.

Brown, D. Alexander. *Grierson's Raid*. Urbana: University of Illinois Press, 1954.

Brieger, James F. *Hometown, Mississippi*. Mississippi: Privately printed, 1980.

Carter III, Samuel. *The Final Fortress: The Campaign for Vicksburg, 1862–1863*. New York: St. Martin's Press, 1980.

Cashin, Joan E. *A Family Venture: Men and Women on the Southern Frontier*. New York: Oxford University Press, 1991.

Castel, Albert. *Decision in the West: The Atlanta Campaign of 1864*. Lawrence: University Press of Kansas, 1992.

Cooper Jr., William J. and Thomas E. Terrill. *The American South: A History*. New York: McGraw-Hill, 1991.

Cozzens, Peter. *The Darkest Days of the War: The Battles of Iuka & Corinth*. Chapel Hill: The University of North Carolina Press, 1997.

Cunningham, Edward. *The Port Hudson Campaign*. Baton Rouge: Louisiana State University Press, 1963.

Daniel, Larry J. *Shiloh: The Battle That Changed the Civil War*. New York: Simon and Schuster, 1997.

————. *Soldiering in the Army of Tennessee*. Chapel Hill: The University of North Carolina Press, 1991.

Degler, Carl. *The Other South: Southern Dissenters in the Nineteenth Century*. New York: Harper & Row, 1974.

Dubay, Robert W. *John Jones Pettus*. Jackson: University Press of Mississippi, 1975.

Eaton, Clement. *A History of the Old South*. Third edition. New York: Macmillan Publishing Company, 1975.

Foster, Gaines M. *Ghosts of the Confederacy: Defeat, the Lost Cause, and the Emergence of the New South*. New York: Oxford University Press, 1987.

Grant, Ulysses Simpson. *Personal Memoirs of U. S. Grant*. Mineola NY: Dover Publications, 1995.

Greenberg, Kenneth H. *Masters and Statesmen: The Political Culture of American Slavery*. Baltimore: The Johns Hopkins University Press, 1985.

Groom, Winston. *Shrouds of Glory: From Atlanta to Nashville: The Last Great Campaign of the Civil War*. New York: The Atlantic Monthly Press, 1995.

Hattaway, Herman. *General Stephen D. Lee*. Jackson: University Press of Mississippi, 1976.

Hearon, Cleo, "Nullification in Mississippi." *In Publications of the Mississippi Historical Society*, volume 12. University, Mississippi: For the Society (1912), 37–71.

Hewitt, Lawrence Lee. *Port Hudson, Confederate Bastion on the Mississippi*. Baton Rouge: Louisiana State University Press, 1987.

Horn, Stanley F. *The Army of Tennessee*. Norman: The University of Oklahoma Press, 1952.

————. The Decisive Battle of Nashville. Knoxville: University of Tennessee Press, 1956.

Johnson, Robert Underwood and Clarence Clough Buel., eds. *Battles and Leaders of the Civil War*. 4 volumes. New York: The Century Company, 1887.

Knauss, William H. *The Story of Camp Chase: A History of the Prison and its Cemetery, Together With Other Cemeteries Where Confederate Prisoners Are Buried, Etc.* Nashville: Publishing House of the Methodist Episcopal Church, South, 1906.

Livermore, Thomas L. *Numbers and Losses in the Civil War in America: 1861–1865*. Bloomington: Indiana University Press, 1957.

Loewen, James W. and Charles Sallis, eds. *Mississippi: Conflict and Change*. New York: Random House, 1974.

Long, E. B. with Barbara Long. *The Civil War Day by Day: An Almanac 1861–1865*. Garden City NY: Doubleday and Company, 1971.

Lowry, Robert and William McCardle. *A History of Mississippi*. Jackson MS: R. H. Henry and Company, 1891.

Martin, David G. *The Shiloh Campaign, March–April, 1862*. Conshohocken PA: Combined Books, 1996.

McCurry, Stephanie. *Masters of Small Worlds: Yeomen Households, Gender Relations, and Political Culture of the Antebellum South Carolina Low Country*. New York: Oxford University Press, 1995.

McDonough, James Lee and Thomas L. Connelly, *Five Tragic Hours: The Battle of Franklin*. Knoxville: University of Tennessee Press, 1983.

McLemore, Richard A., ed. *A History of Mississippi*. 2 volumes. Hattiesburg: University and College Press of Mississippi, 1973.

McMurry, Richard. *John Bell Hood and the War for Southern Independence*. Lincoln: University of Nebraska Press, 1982.

McPherson, James M. *Battle Cry of Freedom: The Civil War Era*. New York: Oxrford University Press, 1988.

Nevins, Allen. *The War for the Union, vol. 1, The Improvised War, 1861-1862*. New York: Charles Scribner's Sons, 1959.

Rainwater, Percy Lee. *Mississippi: Storm Center of Secession 1856–1861*. Baton Rouge LA: Otto Claitor, 1938.

Robertson Jr., James I. *Soldiers Blue and Gray*. Columbia: University of South Carolina Press, 1988.

Romero, Sidney J. *Religion in the Rebel Ranks*. Lanham MD: University Press of America, 1983.

Rowland, Dunbar. *Military History of Mississippi 1803–1898*. Spartenburg SC: The Reprint Company, 1988.

Scaife, William R. *The Campaign for Atlanta*. Atlanta: William R. Scaife, 1985.

Shattuck Jr., Gardiner H. *A Shield and Hiding Place: The Religious Life of the Civil War Armies*. Macon GA: Mercer University Press, 1987.

Sifakis, Stewart. *Who Was Who in the Civil War*. New York: Facts on File, 1988.

Smith, Frank E. *The Yazoo River*. Jackson: University Press of Mississippi, 1988.

Smith, Page. *Trial By Fire: A People's History of the Civil War*. New York: McGraw-Hill, 1985.

Sword, Wiley. *Shiloh: Bloody April*. New York: William Morrow and Co., 1974.

———. *The Confederacy's Last Hurrah: Spring Hill, Franklin & Nashville*. Lawrence: University Press of Kansas, 1992.

Symonds, Craig L. *Joseph Johnston: A Civil War Biography*. New York: W. W. Norton, 1992.

Thomas, Emory M. *The Confederate Nation: 1861–1865*. New York: Harper & Row, 1979.

Trotter, William R. *Silk Flags and Cold Steel, the Civil War in North Carolina: The Piedmont*. Winston-Salem NC: John F. Blair, Publishers, 1988.

Trudeau, Noah Andre. *Out of the Storm: The End of the Civil War, April–June, 1865*. New York: Little, Brown, and Company, 1994.

Wheeler, Richard. *The Siege of Vicksburg*. New York: Thomas Y. Crowell Co., 1978.

Wiley, Bell Irvin. *The Life of Johnny Reb*. Baton Rouge: Louisiana State University Press, 1978.

Wilson, Charles Reagan. *Baptized in Blood: The Religion of the Lost Cause, 1865–1920*. Athens: University of Georgia Press, 1980.

Wyatt-Brown, Bertram. *Honor and Violence in the Old South*. New York: Oxford University Press, 1986.

Periodicals

Biel, John G. "The Evacuation of Corinth." *Journal of Mississippi History* 24/24 (Spring 1962): 40–56.

Blain, William T. "William Felix Brantley, 1830-1870." *Journal of Mississippi History* 37/4 (November 1975): 359–80.

———. "Banner Unionism in Choctaw County." *Mississippi Quarterly* 29/2 (Spring 1976): 207–20.

Crowther, Edward R. "Mississippi Baptists, Slavery, and Secession, 1806–1861." *Journal of Mississippi History* 56/2 (May 1994): 139–44.

Escott, Paul D. "'The Cry of the Sufferers': The Problem of Welfare in the Confederacy." *Civil War History* (September 1977): 228–40.

Harrison, Lowell H. "Mill Springs: 'The Brilliant Victory.'" *Civil War Times Illustrated* 10/9 (January 1972): 4–9, 41–45.

Stamper, James C. "Felix K. Zollicoffer: Tennessee Editor and Politician." *Tennessee Historical Quarterly* 24/4 (Winter 1969): 356–76.

Unknown author. "Confederate Veterans at Greenwood." *Confederate Veteran* 21/11 (September 1909): 516–17.

Unknown author. "Flag of the Grenada Rifles." *Confederate Veteran* 9/1 (January 1901): 400.

Unknown author. "Gen. W. S. Statham." *Confederate Veteran* 8/1 (January 1900): 176.

Unknown Author. "Reunion of Mississippi Comrades." *Confederate Veteran* 34/11 (November 1926): 424–25.

Miscellaneous

"A Great Day in Grenada." Broadside. Special Collections, J. D. Williams Library, University of Mississippi, Oxford MS.

Collection Files. Mississippi State Historical Museum, Jackson MS.

Confederate Grave Registrations. Mississippi Department of Archives and History Library, Jackson MS. Microfilm.

Rawson, Donald. "Party Politics in Mississippi, 1850–1860." Ph.D. dissertation, Vanderbilt University, 1964.

"16th Alabama Infantry." Regimental history files. Alabama Department of Archives and History Library, Montgomery AL.

Subject Files. Mississippi Department of Archives and History Library, Jackson MS.

Unveiling Ceremonies of the Holmes County Confederate Monument, at Lexington, Mississippi, 2 December 1908. Mississippi Department of Archives and History Library, Jackson MS. Program.

INDEX